THE WILDERNESS HANDBOOK

Paul Petzoldt

DIRECTOR, NATIONAL OUTDOOR
LEADERSHIP SCHOOL

THE
WILDERNESS
HANDBOOK

W · W · NORTON & COMPANY · INC ·
NEW YORK

Photo facing title page:
Typical NOLS class session in the Wind River Range. Paul Petzoldt, left, with
Nancy Carson, instructor, and students. *Photo by Allan M. Sicks*

Library of Congress Cataloging in Publication Data
Petzoldt, Paul K
   The wilderness handbook.
   Bibliography: p.
   1. Wilderness survival.   2. Camping.   3. Mountain-
eering.   I. National Outdoor Leadership School.
II. Title.
SK606.P47   1974   796.5′2   74–2058
ISBN 0–393–08691–7
ISBN   0   393   08778   6   (pbk.)

Published simultaneously in Canada
by George J. McLeod Limited, Toronto

This book was designed by Robert Freese.
Typefaces used are Times Roman and Weiss Roman,

PRINTED IN THE UNITED STATES OF AMERICA

      7 8 9 0

To the thousands of students of NOLS
and Outward Bound who have accepted
my teaching with understanding and love

Contents

Illustrations

Introduction

The wild outdoors has been my life ever since I was a little boy. As the youngest of nine children, I was taught how to set a trap, shoot a gun, ride a horse, and catch fish. By the time I was nine years old, I had often scaled the sheer walls of Snake River Canyon near our home in Twin Falls, Idaho, to reach the river for fishing, hunting, and camping. My mother accepted such activities as a natural drive of youth.

My first experience in leading an expedition came at age twelve, when a friend and my dog, Ranger, joined me for two months of hiking in the Sawtooth Range. Perhaps it was then I realized the mountains and wilderness were indispensable to me.

The Grand Teton in Jackson Hole, Wyoming, was the first real peak I attempted. I made the summit when I was sixteen and established a mountain guide service there soon after. Running that service put me in contact with mountaineers who possessed a variety of past experience and skills, and I learned all I could from them. I started to experiment and analyze their methods.

Unindoctrinated by the standard European techniques and philosophy of that period, I developed some new skills and ideas. I invented the first voice-signal system (now universally used in America) and developed the Sliding Middleman Technique for snow climbing. Also, instead of having a party tie in all of the time for confidence, I used the rope only when belaying.

Almost from the beginning of my guiding career, I had the desire not only to guide my clients but to teach them as well. I felt that by learning techniques they would increase their enjoyment and add a new dimension to their outings.

Soon I began to train other guides to help me, and eventually I headed the Petzoldt-Exum School of American Mountaineering in the Teton Range.

Sir Alfred Bailey, Dean of St. George's Chapel and private chaplain to the King and Queen of England, invited me to be his guest at Windsor Castle for two years. Living in England enabled me to climb in Europe. There I met Dan Bryant, a young New Zealander, and we headed for the Swiss Alps. In our youthful enthusiasm, we made a double traverse of the Matterhorn in one day.

In 1938, with the financial assistance and backing of William Loomis, who had climbed some new routes with me in the Tetons, I was selected to join the first American expedition to K2 in the Himalayas, the second highest mountain in the world. There I discovered that my camping and cold-weather skills, plus methods I had used to develop and conserve energy, enabled me to reach altitudes above 26,000 feet without fatigue or breathlessness and to spend weeks above 20,000 feet without brain damage. (In those days, there were no oxygen tanks or artificial substitutes for thin air.)

I returned to the United States more convinced than ever that the failures and tragedies of former Himalayan expeditions were due to the mountaineers' lack of camping skills and knowledge of how to keep warm and strong.

At the onset of World War II, I became the U.S. representative for the Department of Agriculture in Lend-Lease. One of the products involved was sheep hide for parkas and clothing. The Russians' use of such apparel was a major factor in their ability to survive winter weather while the Germans froze.

I later taught mountain evacuation and cold-weather dress to the ski troops of the Tenth Mountain Division at Camp Hale, Colorado, and completed my wartime service as a member of the Control Council in Berlin, deducing ways to feed the defeated Germans.

A number of outdoor programs were developed after the war to combat softness and a lack of self-confidence that had been discovered in our young people. These enterprises promised challenge and raw adventure, but their success was hampered by a lack of qualified leaders. Persons skilled in mountain climbing knew little about camping and conservation; those knowledgeable about rations and equipment were ignorant of trail techniques; those who could fish were unable to motivate others, teach, or maintain discipline.

In 1963–64, I helped establish the first American Outward Bound program in Colorado and became chief instructor. My lifetime experiences in the wild outdoors proved very beneficial there, and it occurred to me that the knowledge derived from these diverse activities could benefit other outdoor leaders.

Therefore, in 1965, I started the National Outdoor Leadership School in Lander, Wyoming, to train leaders capable of conducting all-round wilderness programs in a safe and rewarding manner. We started with a handful of students and a few qualified instructors. The Wind River Range of Wyoming with its 2,000 square miles of lakes, glaciers, mountains, and forests was our classroom.

We were successful beyond our expectations. Within a few years, all of our instructors were NOLS graduates who had also received special instructor training.

NOLS is a total wilderness adventure. Most courses last five weeks. Our teaching method is demonstrated under realistic conditions followed by action. To teach mountaineering, we climb mountains; to teach fishing, we catch trout; to teach river crossing, we cross wild rivers; to teach conservation, we practice conservation.

Our courses include instruction in practical conservation, leadership, organization, supply, equipment, logistics, mountaineering, rock climbing, glacier and snow techniques, rescue, first aid, survival, accident prevention, fishing, rations, cooking, map reading, expedition behavior, and camping. We cannot make students experts in all of these fields in five weeks, but we do provide them with adequate skills, judgment, and understanding to produce capable, safe outdoor leaders with a superior standard of excellence.

Besides our Wyoming school, which we limit to about one thousand students a year, we have a high-altitude expeditionary school in Alaska, kayaking courses along the Alaskan coast, mountaineering sessions in Washington's Northern Cascades and Utah's Uintas. On the sea and wild beaches of Baja California, Mexico, we teach sailing and skin diving. In wintertime, we schedule courses in winter camping and mountaineering in the Wind Rivers and Tetons. All schools have the same purpose: to teach how to enjoy and conserve the wild outdoors.

Everything we teach is oriented toward enjoyment and conservation. Ours is not a grim exhibition of endurance, although carrying a pack over a high pass or climbing a mountain can be exhausting as well as enjoyable.

Perhaps our most important purpose is to teach practical conservation. Even after all of the wilderness laws are passed, there will still be only one way to insure preservation, and that is through the education of users in the techniques, skills, and methods that will enable them to enjoy and still conserve. A good deal of progress in this field has originated with us; much has been developed through advice and guidance of local U.S. Forest Service personnel. Although some NOLS teachings can be found scattered throughout magazines and books, most of them have never been published.

This book is intended to help all outdoorsmen. The beginner may use it as a handbook to acquaint himself with the knowledge and judgment he needs to go out into the field; veteran outdoorsmen and instructors may use it as a checklist and guide. Despite their experience, this book might open new lines of experimentation to them.

Prospective NOLS students could read the book before enrolling in our courses. NOLS graduates desiring a survey of the school's teaching will find it useful in retaining skills they have mastered.

Parents questioning the relative ability of outdoor leaders may find some answers here. A climber with a list of North Face assaults on his record is not necessarily a good leader or teacher. His motivation might be only to climb a summit and put his name on the register with no concern for safety or conservation. Important, too, is his quotient of ego. Is he out there to show off in front of an audience or to teach others how to climb and enjoy doing it?

One part of leadership is taking out groups and the other is one's own lifetime recreational needs. This is extremely important because the outdoors, if you know how to handle it, is probably one of the least expensive and most rewarding ways of achieving self-renewal.

When teaching on an expedition, as we do at NOLS, we cannot cover any one subject all at once, since, initially, we must teach the most important things necessary for that first day of walking, camping, cooking, and conservation. The next day we might cover the same subjects again and add new knowledge and techniques. We do this until the end of the course five weeks later. Then, and only then, will the student have *all* of the knowledge and skills he actually needed the first day. That is why we say to our students that when they finish our courses, they are ready to start on an expedition.

Then, too, in the field, we postpone certain teaching until we reach a place where the environment is suitable. We teach fishing where we catch trout. We teach snow techniques on snowfields. We teach fire building where we build fires.

Although we have general classes on general subjects, most of our instruction has a grasshopper approach, jumping from one subject to another as environment, time, and necessity dictate.

But remember that when the student starts on his educational expedition, we have used the sum total of all our knowledge and judgment to plan and prepare the expedition for him. During his course, he gradually learns, by the use of our planning, what we have done and how he can do it in the future by himself.

I cannot treat the reader of this book in the same way, because he may have to organize an outdoor excursion entirely on his own. In such a case, he must be aware of all considerations before he starts and visualize the complete trip from beginning to end. Therefore, here we will cover the "must-knows" of every subject in an orderly fashion, and explain why each action is necessary.

This book contains no untested theories. It is an attempt to convey, at least in part, the techniques, methods, and philosophy I have developed over fifty years so that others may discover how to comfortably, safely, and skillfully enjoy the wilderness and still conserve it for those yet to come.

I wish to thank the certified outdoor and mountaineering instructors, George Hunker, Haven Holsapple, and Mike Williams, for their photographs and critiques, Carroll Seghers II for the cover photographs, and Nancy Wise Carson for her contribution to outdoor cooking.

Only with the professional assistance, patience, and understanding of Carol Houck Smith of W. W. Norton has this book become a reality.

Special gratitude must go to Raye Carleson Price for her editorial assistance and for learning to decipher my hieroglyphics and bring order and readability to my verbosity.

September, 1973   PAUL PETZOLDT

THE WILDERNESS HANDBOOK

Survival: Avoiding Survival Situations

I stood a thousand feet below the summit of Grand Teton in Jackson Hole, Wyoming. It was New Year's Day, 1970, and the temperature on the mountain was twenty degrees below zero Fahrenheit. Ten companions watched as I scanned clouds that wound around the peak on the wings of a seventy-mile gale. Should we turn back toward the safety and shelter of our snow caves two thousand feet below, or should we rope up and go for the top? It was up to me to decide.

This was the fifth consecutive New Year's attempt on the Grand Teton by graduates of the National Outdoor Leadership School. Only once before had we come this far. Now, again, it was my decision whether to go up or down, weighing the risks of a final assault.

Our clothing was the best and we were warm, in spite of cold and wind that combined to a chilling temperature of eighty degrees below zero. The U.S. Weather Bureau, in nearby Lander, Wyoming, had assured us that the storm had reached its peak. My young companions were strong and eager. I gave the signal to rope up and climb.

Brushing snow and rime from ice-glazed handholds and footholds, we edged toward a bulbous outcrop called the Belly Roll. Hand over hand we inched around it, hanging on with our fingers, empty space beneath our feet.

We squirmed along a narrow ledge called the Crawl and looked down through swirling clouds to tops of pine trees four thousand feet below.

Then we reached an overhang, where it was necessary for the leader to stand on the shoulders and head of another climber to attain a vertical chimney leading onward toward the summit. We placed feet on one side of the wide crack, backs on the other, and wedged our way up the icy shaft.

Driving pitons into meager cracks for rope protection, we walked along an outward-sloping ledge called the Catwalk. Below us was an abyss filled with blowing snow and wind-torn clouds. There were no handholds, so we had to stand upright and lean out against the wind for balance, to keep our felt-soled shoes clinging to the icy surface.

We turned again toward the final pitch with more chimneys, more ledges, but without the frightening exposure to height. Here, if we fell and were not caught by the rope, we would only go to the next shelf and not all the way back to the valley of Jackson Hole.

Then, suddenly, we were above the clouds and in bright sunlight. We unroped and wallowed through the last snow-covered boulders.

We had made it! Clouds were flowing over the passes and milling around lesser peaks below, the wind was howling, and frost crystals were literally growing out of the rocks, but we were standing on top of the Grand Teton, warm and comfortable, victorious after five successive years of trying.

Soon I would be sixty-two years of age. Though I had made thousands of mountain ascents, never before had I viewed such beauty. Never before had I felt such exhilaration, such comradeship. It was the emotional highlight of a lifetime of mountaineering.

We had had a perfect climb. There was challenge, adventure, success after repeated failures, self-realization, and fun. Despite adverse weather conditions, proper planning of clothing, equipment, rations, timing, and trail techniques resulted in a skillful and safe expedition. It had taken me years to learn, develop, and perfect these skills, and I had come a long way from my first attempt on the "Grand" in 1924.

I was sixteen then, and full of confidence from amateur cliff scrambling I had done in the Snake River Canyon near our family farm in sourthern Idaho. I teamed up with a friend, Ralph Herron, and headed for the isolated cowtown of Jackson. Someone had told us about the impressive Teton peaks and how difficult they were to climb. Few persons had tried since 1898, when Billy Owen and his party were the first to reach the summit and chisel their names into a rock. But Ralph Herron and I were going to climb the Grand Teton!

When we arrived at Jackson, the residents could see no reason to climb mountains "if you ain't lost nothing up there," but being realists, they stopped arguing with stubborn teen-agers and provided us with a pocketknife, a couple of quilts, sandwiches, and some canned pork and beans. Billy Owen, who happened to be visiting Jackson, even sketched a little map of the route he had taken twenty-six years before.

In those days, the base of the Grand Teton could only be reached by rough wagon roads that meandered through gullies and sagebrush. You had to ford streams and cross the Snake River by ferry. Owen saved us a long hike by arranging for a car to take us there the following morning.

From its base, the Grand Teton looked easy compared to the perpendicular cliffs we had climbed in the Snake River Canyon. We decided to head straight up the east ridge to the top instead of circling the peak toward the southwest as Owen had suggested.

We carried picnic food and bedrolls and wore blue jeans, heavy cotton shirts, cowboy boots, and jackets. Although it was early July, the last snow had just left the lower slopes, and patches of white could be seen at higher altitudes.

We plunged eagerly into brush and timber and worked our way toward the lower slopes, gaining timberline by eleven. We ate our beans beside a lake and studied the terrain above us, a field of boulders topped by cliffs that stretched like a giant staircase to the summit. It was a warm day, and since the bedroll and jacket were hot and cumbersome, we stashed them with the remaining food, tied our shirts around our waists, and started to climb, expecting to return and spend that night at the lake camp.

From that point, reality took over from illusion; nothing was as it had appeared to us. The boulders were monsters, some as big as houses. A chill wind blew from a glacier that surprised us between the boulder field and cliffs and, as we started to scale the walls of the east ridge, we found the pitch much steeper than we had estimated, handholds and footholds sparse, cracks and ledges fearfully iced. Our bare hands were numb and scraped from the jagged rocks, and the cotton shirts we had put on for warmth were plastered to our backs with sweat.

We traversed ledges, climbed out on ridges, eased around bulging projections, got hung up on exposed cliffs that dropped thousands of feet into nothing. We took dangerous risks, rerouted in the opposite direction, still seeking a way to the summit, while the wind stung us and sunlight cooled and deepened into shadows. That night, we were stranded in a sheltered crack of rock, either cupped together to share body heat or flailing arms and legs to keep from freezing to death in an unseasonable storm that raged around us.

Next morning, we crawled from the crack and looked for a route back to our lake camp that was easier than our difficult ascent. All thoughts of attempting the Grand Teton summit had fled. It had stopped snowing, but wind gusted and we ached with cold. We sought the fastest escape, descended into a narrow gully, and then slid down an icy slab to a broad shelf that appeared to lead on down the mountain. We were rimrocked; twenty feet of ice sloped above us, thin air gaped below.

The pocketknife saved our lives. We had no choice but to get up that slab of ice, so I started to cut notches for handholds and footholds. The ice was difficult to chip out and, what with whipping wind and numb fingers, it took a couple of hours to make our way back to where we had bivouacked the night before.

Fortunately, then the sun came out, and we were able to endure painful thawing of our hands and climb down the original route to our timberline camp by nightfall.

Warmth of a fire, nourishment of food, and a good sleep had us discussing whether to attempt Owen's southwest route or face the mockery of Jackson residents. We rested a full day, whittled alpenstocks from trees, and resumed climbing the next morning. This time, we wore shirts, tied jackets at our waists, and traversed around the south side of the Grand Teton joining the route Owen had described.

Skirting the mountain, we dug our feet and pine alpenstocks into steep snowfields and glaciers and finally joined the Owen route high on the Lower Saddle, on the south side. We were confident now. We raced up the peak, found the Belly Roll and Crawl, and, dangerously unprotected, scaled a series of steep chimneys like a couple of monkeys. At three o'clock that afternoon, we were wahooing and slapping backs atop the Grand Teton.

Jackson natives were skeptical when we arrived back in town. Our boots had disintegrated and our swollen feet were wrapped in blanket strips, but they didn't believe our claim that we had been to the top until Billy Owen asked what we had seen. When we described the record of his climbing party—the metal pennant inscribed "Rocky Mountain Club," the autographs chiseled on a rock—and told of looking "five thousand" feet into open space as we slithered through the Crawl, Owen turned to the crowd and said, "These boys have been to the top of the Grand Teton! "

We had succeeded through sheer guts and luck. We were improperly dressed, had insufficient food and inadequate equipment, knew nothing of snow and ice techniques and very little about rock climbing. We had neglected to ask for a weather report that might have saved us from the unseasonable storm, and foolishly ignored directions furnished by the only available man who had actually made the climb. Worse yet, there were only two of us, both novices.

Perhaps it was that experience that motivated a lifetime of study concerning mountaineering skills, psychology, and judgment, and inspired my sympathy and understanding of today's youth who make the same dangerous mistakes. The NOLS curriculum disseminates what it took me half a century to develop.

Condensing these years of knowledge into five-week courses or a few hundred pages poses obvious problems. We must be selective. While there are many factors of outdoor living that are interesting or enjoyable to know, our primary concern must be immediate protection of the individual, the environment, and the equipment. Thus, time and space limit us to the teaching of those things which *must* be known.

As an example, let us take the novice camper tackling his first fire.

For his own protection, he must learn how to stack a small pile of twigs and light them with a minimum number of matches so that he may produce heat enough for warmth and cooking.

To protect the environment, he must gather wood from the ground, construct his fire in such a way as to prevent permanent scars, and avoid danger of forest fire.

For protection of equipment, he must build his fire away from tents, sleeping bags, or any other items not being used which might be damaged by sparks or extreme heat.

These are the points with first priority: "*must*-knows." When they are mastered, he may progress to those things which are interesting or enjoyable to know, but again in terms of protecting the individual, the environment, and the equipment.

Now, he could make things more convenient for himself by learning to gather enough wood to fuel an entire cooking session and leave some extra for morning. He could be cautious about placing his fire too close to rocks that might become blackened or exfoliated. He could prevent burning of utensils and foods by digging one end of his pit deeper to allow a heat choice of coals or active flames. None of these have the immediacy of the "*must*-knows," but all contribute to camping enjoyment and protection.

The "*must*-knows," alone, comprise an impressive number of skills. One must learn to build a simple fire, but it is necessary to know how to gather wood and where to lay it before striking the match. Of course, one might have to set up a tent before that, yet this requires knowledge of how to get to where one wants to pitch it, how to pack, read a map—ad infinitum.

Unfortunately, one is not likely to master all of the techniques he needs to get to his camping spot without ever having had to set up a tent or build a fire, and one would probably starve to death if he tried to learn all about building fires before cooking his first pot of macaroni. So we must start somewhere.

One must develop the judgment to make his own workable and practical decisions about many related factors. As he learns to perform elementary tasks and understand the reasoning behind them, he will be better prepared to master techniques which are interesting and enjoyable to know, through personal experimentation in the field.

This is the real core of everything I have to teach, be it in the wilderness or in a book. Judgment. I define judgment as the ability to relate a total experience to a specific activity. Learning judgment, assessing priorities, is as important as perfecting techniques; in fact, the teaching of techniques without judgment can be dangerous.

I could teach how to camp in one specific location, but camp a lifetime and you'll never find another area exactly the same, where the fire, tents, latrines, and so on will be in an identical pattern.

In mountaineering, I can show how to drive pitons into special cracks and set up a rope rappel to slide down a particular cliff. Climb a lifetime and you'll never find piton cracks or a cliff exactly like those on which you learned.

The human mind must be programmed to bring forth answers for similar situations, not just situations identical with those already encountered. This, of course, is judgment.

Experience may not always make for better judgment or technical ability. A person can be in the outdoors for years and repeat the same mistakes time after time.

Consider the cowboy hunting guide. He rides into camp in the fall, temperature near zero, wind bellowing, and he wears a Stetson hat with his ears out in the wind, tight cowboy boots that keep his feet cold through lack of circulation, and jeans that have him wet and shivering most of the trip. He's been making these same mistakes for thirty years and never thought about changing them. Yet if he would adapt to change, analyze and experiment with ideas (such as ours), and apply them to his own situation, his excursions would be more comfortable and successful.

Judgment is being able to relate one thing to all the other things you know. Judgment is being able to change plans when conditions suggest that necessity. Judgment is qualifying the importance of preconceived rules. And using good judgment in pre-planning an expedition can make the difference between the safe, enjoyable and the dangerous, uncomfortable way of carrying out the mountain or wilderness experience.

There are many questions one should ask oneself before taking off for the wilds. What area will be traveled, how much time is planned for the trip, what is the purpose, how much will it cost, and what is the strength and experience of the leadership? What equipment, clothing, food, and other supplies will be needed? How much weight must be carried and how? How dangerous is the trip and, in case of accidents, are first aid, evacuation facilities, and emergency retreat organized? What skills and abilities must the members have?

Political and social structures of the region must also be taken into consideration. Most wilderness areas are administered by the U.S. Forest Service, U.S. National Park Service, Fish and Game departments, and other such organizations. Some areas are on private property or Indian reservations. What permits are necessary and what rules and limitations of law must be observed?

Getting to the take-off point is another problem. Must one have a four-wheel-drive vehicle to negotiate access roads? Is there a safe place to leave a car without danger of theft or damage? Have the best available maps (topographical, if possible) been secured?

All of these matters will be discussed in detail throughout the book, but one vital question concerns us here. How can individuals participating in the expedition be protected?

There are three primary factors to consider: control of the climate, wise use of time, and development of energy. In order to impress upon our students the importance of taking these things into consideration before and during an expedition, we have coined the terms Climate Control Plan, Time Control Plan, and Energy Control Plan. While these plans cannot eliminate all dangers during outdoor excursions, they do reduce them.

Climate Control Plan

When we talk about climate control, we realize that we can't actually control the weather, but we can do our best to control its effects by being prepared for most eventualities. This involves interrelationship of the many facets of outdoorsmanship. Knowledge that the temperature is likely to drop to twenty below at night isn't necessarily useful until it is translated into terms of what type of sleeping bag is needed, what clothes, what kind of shelter. Predicting the temperature is only one of several factors bearing upon comfort and safety. Other considerations are the moisture content of air, wind velocity, exposure to wind, and dampness of clothing. Judgment in interpreting all available information and relating it to every aspect of the trip—clothing, equipment, rations, environment, personnel—is imperative.

Unbelievable as it may seem, some persons start trips ranging from a few hours to several weeks without taking into consideration the weather they are likely to encounter. Assuming they have no subconscious death wish or intentional malice toward themselves, I have concluded that they don't check into the weather because they don't think of it. It doesn't occur to them that a balmy morning might precede a stormy afternoon.

Some time ago near my home, a game biologist drove into the back country on a warm, sunny day, parked his pickup truck, and walked into the timber to observe an elk herd. A mild storm came up, and two days later he was found sitting under a tree, dead from exposure.

Three boys from Cheyenne, Wyoming, left their car by the highway and walked to some big rocks to practice climbing. The cotton T shirts and blue jeans they were wearing were fine when they started, but a storm surprised them, too. Within a few hours, one of them, lost in a mad dash for the car, was chilled beyond recovery.

What weather information does one need? This depends upon the type of trip planned. If it is just an afternoon hike, probably radio or newspaper forecasts would suffice. All one needs to know is if the weather is going to change and the probable amount of cold, wind, rain, or snow.

An unfortunate tendency is to underestimate the weather's ability to get nasty in a short time, especially in the mountains. "Eyeballing" the sky won't do, because a perfectly clear sky can change unexpectedly. Arthritis, corns, bunions, and sore thumbs may be claimed as impressive weather prognosticators by mountaineers and old-timers, but the most dependable source of information is the U.S. Weather Bureau, as close as a telephone call.

Modern satellite forecasting has made great strides in determining probable conditions for five-day periods, but what of extended expeditions? There have been booklets published about reading the clouds and deciphering other weather signs but, while it is interesting to know that a streak of late-afternoon sunshine on the mountain after an extended period of heavy clouds means that the western storm center is breaking up, reliance upon this type of knowledge is undependable. Instead, there are certain questions one can ask the Weather Bureau in order to make judgments about longer periods of time beyond the reliable five-day forecast.

For the season of the proposed trip, find out what the average day and night temperatures are, the *probable* weather, the coldest and warmest temperatures ever recorded. Then judge the *possible* consequences of an unusual storm.

Remember that temperatures can vary considerably with altitude. When seeking information from the U.S. Weather Bureau, be specific about what elevations will be reached, especially if any climbing is intended above timberline, and be definite about the area to be used and the dates.

Ask about the average wind velocity and the maximum velocity in a storm. The wind-chill factor can affect cold temperatures dramatically. For instance, if the temperature reads zero and there is a fifty-mile-per-hour wind, a person may feel a chilling intensity equal to fifty below zero on a calm day.

Obtain data on precipitation patterns, rain or snow, cloudbursts, drizzles, the percentage of stormy days. And don't forget that at higher elevations, the mountains can make their own local weather.

To sum up, reasonable certainty of what the weather *will* be for the first few days combined with past records of what it *has* been will help one estimate what it *might* be for the duration of a trip.

How much should one prepare for the freak storm that hits an area every so often? Should one have tents that will withstand winds that come every twenty years or so? Should one be equipped with snowshoes in case of that once-in-ten-years unseasonable snowstorm?

Obviously, preparation for the worst possible weather will result in excess clothing and equipment and add weight to packs. On the other hand, if only average weather is planned for, a worse than usual storm might be dangerous. Once again, judgment must be used.

It is rarely practical to prepare for extremes. We have found that preparing for *slightly more weather* than that predicted by the Weather Bureau or the historical average enabled us to safely wait out the extreme storms.

Time Control Plan

For every outing, whether it be a one-day trip, one day of an expedition, or the entire expedition, a Time Control Plan is necessary to correlate the factors of terrain, distance, altitude, trail condition, group strength, and purpose into a realistic schedule. Outdoorsmen have the responsibility of letting family, friends, and the administrative agency know this plan. With no idea of itinerary, when does the worry start for relatives and friends waiting in the valley, when do would-be rescuers implement action, when does a party risk embarrassment from a premature rescue or tragedy from one too long delayed?

An eastern mountain club in the early 1960s undertook what was to have been a thirteen-hour round trip on the Grand Teton, but encountered a seventy-two-hour ordeal involving injury, death, and a hazardous rescue.

Without registering at the National Park Service ranger station, they set out in Levi's and summer gear, provisioned with a lunch of sandwiches, a few raisins, crackers, and jam. They selected an unknown and intricate route up the southeast face, despite partly cloudy weather that morning. When the usual Teton afternoon storm riddled them with hail and strong winds, they continued up the mountain, rather than retreating. Even had the weather been perfect, their progress precluded the possibility of meeting the proposed schedule. This one realization could have saved a life and much suffering.

The party, whose members came primarily from sea level, allowed no time to become acclimated to the higher altitude of the Jackson Hole area, and the varied ages, physical condition, and climbing experience of the group necessitated a slow pace.

Yet their time schedule called for eight hours to reach the summit and five hours for return to base camp—thirteen hours in all. In later calculations, I figured that with the progress they were making, even if they could have maintained the pace, it would have taken them thirty-six hours to travel from base camp to the top of the "Grand."

Judgment to accept the necessity of retreat or, better still, to formulate a Time Control Plan for the specific group and situation, would have told a different story.

Perhaps the strongest consideration is flexibility. Progress should be checked frequently, and if it is found that estimated goals are not being reached, the trip should be revamped. Reevaluate each succeeding day's plans according to the previous day's learning. It is better to err on the side of allowing too much time than to risk allowing too little.

Knowledge of terrain is essential in formulating a Time Control Plan. If one has been to the area before, one has the advantage of relating all other factors to the previous trip. If one has never traveled there, one must familiarize oneself with it through artificial means. An excellent source of information is the topographical map, which details distances, trails, and elevations so that one can visualize the trip from start to finish and estimate how long it should take. (Use of topographical maps will be treated in Chapter 5, pages 101–5.)

Energy Control Plan

Many tragedies and accidents are caused by fatigue. Outdoorsmen often become overtired because they do not know how to develop and conserve body energy. They push beyond their capacity, eat improperly, consume liquids infrequently, over- or underdress, or exhaust themselves with anxiety and nervousness. The Energy Control Plan is designed to combat these conditions by considering trail techniques, nutrition, control of body heat, and other contributors to physical stamina.

On Switzerland's Matterhorn, I encountered a survival situation that involved ignorance of energy conservation. In the first light of dawn as I was ascending, I saw a party racing up the mountain using the "run and stop" method. They would go as fast as possible, then stop to rest, and then plunge on again.

Later in the day, on my descent, I met them again part way down the mountain. I could see that they were exhausted, and it was apparent that by themselves they would never reach the halfway hut before darkness. A storm was developing, and in their exhausted condition it was questionable whether they could survive the night.

Without being able to converse, owing to the language barrier, they let me take charge and protect them by rope as they climbed downward. They had not eaten, and the little energy remaining was rapidly being depleted. I could not get them off the mountain before dark, and the storm brought on a survival situation, but thanks to a tentlike bivouac sack and extra food and clothing I carried, we managed to live through the night and retreat the next day.

On an expedition, especially at high altitude, a person can *never* afford to become overtired. Even if the purpose of a particular trip is training to get into shape for more difficult climbs later on, stamina will build naturally and more safely if energy is rationed through adopting judicious standards of behavior, using proper trail techniques, and practicing techniques that develop or conserve strength.

In 1938, I climbed on K2 in the Himalayas, the second highest peak in the world. On that expedition, I used the techniques of energy control, since I carried no artificial oxygen, but I did not know if these techniques would safely take me to extreme altitude and back without death or injury.

I suppose that although Columbus was convinced the world was round, he wasn't absolutely sure that he wouldn't drop off the edge and be gobbled by the giant turtles. This was my sensation when climbing to the vicinity of 27,000 feet on K2. Climbers had written about hideous high-altitude sickness. Sometimes climbers had hallucinations, gasped for breath, were unable to eat or sleep. I felt great. I wasn't exhausted or short of breath. But still I was frightened; I thought I might suddenly pass out for lack of oxygen on the next step. After all, the great English mountaineers, Mallory and Irvine, had disappeared at this altitude on Everest and never returned. Their fate was still a mystery; perhaps they had fallen unconscious. This was the unknown. I concentrated on my breathing and paced myself as a precaution.

Our party did not conquer the entire 28,250 feet, but we went high enough to prove that K2, then reputed unclimbable, was climbable indeed. I made the final retreat at about 27,000 feet. I am convinced that my theories on conserving energy not only saved me from the crippling effects of altitude but made it possible for me to go higher than any American had then climbed. In addition, I was comfortable, maintained a reserve of energy, and had a good appetite. (For energy control techniques, see Chapter 5, pages 92–98.)

It is a good idea to prepare oneself physically for the wilderness outing. One of the best practices is climbing stairs up and down—one to three steps at a time—but take it easy! Don't run upstairs. A normal pace will get muscles in shape without straining the heart.

Isometric exercises can be done while driving a car or sitting at a desk. Deep-breathing exercises prepare the lungs for adjustment to high altitude. Starting an expedition with a few pounds of fat is an asset. It will be consumed gradually as food, and it is a safety factor of reserve energy.

Climate, Time, and Energy Controls are planned at home before an expedition; they are implemented in the field. The balance of this book will detail the selection of clothing, equipment, rations, and the trail techniques which will enable one to survive by avoiding survival situations.

2

Dressing for the Wild Outdoors

High fashion is of little concern in the wild outdoors. The important rule governing dress for any hike in the mountains or wilderness regions is that a party be able to survive one night of bivouac in case of injury, becoming lost, or other emergency.

While this chapter will cover the type of clothing needed under our circumstances at NOLS, the reader can adapt these suggestions to meet slightly different climatic conditions in other regions. Our discussion will primarily involve summer weather in the Rocky Mountains. The temperatures and weather anticipated will be those of Colorado, Wyoming, Montana, northern California, Washington, and Oregon in altitudes from eight to fourteen thousand feet. Here we dress for sudden rainstorms, hail, even snow at timberline and above. High winds of sixty to seventy miles per hour are common. (Clothing for winter conditions will be discussed in Chapter 11, pages 204–6.)

Although there may be long periods of good weather with sunny days, comfortable shirt-sleeve temperatures, and nights well above freezing, a person who knows about the Climate Control Plan will not gamble the success and comfort of his outing—even his life—that he will have such weather for the entire expedition.

There are many things to consider in selecting clothing for an expedition. Naturally, protection of the wearer is foremost. There should be nothing to restrict vision, such as wide, flopping hatbrims, tight hoods that make it difficult to turn the head, or voluminous jackets that block the view of one's feet. Avoid long belts, dangling tie cords, tabs, or anything that might snag or catch on vegetation or rocks. Non-slipping shoe soles and clothes allowing free movement are other considerations.

Clothes should suit the types of activities planned. One wouldn't wear the same items for climbing as for horseback riding, for instance. Also, adequate changes should be geared to length of trip, possible weather fluctuations, personal cleanliness, and comfort. Weight and packability are other important factors, especially for the backpacker. Apparel must be easy to care for, non-shrinking, reasonably neat, and should conform to that worn by companions.

There are three important qualities to consider when purchasing outdoor wear: insulation, ventilation, and protection against the elements.

Insulation consists of dead air space which imposes a barrier between the heat-producing body (the wearer) and the cold outdoors. The deader this air—i.e., the less convection and heat transferal there is and the thicker the barrier—the more effective will be its insulating powers. The idea is to create the most dead air possible in the form of air trapped within the body of the garment. One might think that one could wear a pumped-up suit like an air mattress, but the air inside would be too free to move around and would transfer heat outside. The best insulation traps air in smaller compartments with less opportunity to circulate. However, there must be enough ventilation to carry away body moisture.

Ventilation is a way of rotating air inside-outside in order to keep the person dry and warm. Even when one is sitting still, the body generates heat and produces water as a by-product. This problem is compounded when one is moving or working. If clothing does not provide adequate ventilation, the body moisture will build up on the surface of the skin and in the air pockets of the clothing. Perspiration is harmless as long as exercise continues—the simple fact that one is wet does not make one cold—but difficulty arises when one slows down and perspiration starts to evaporate. Then the moment of truth has arrived; the wetter one is, the more chilled one becomes because evaporation and dampness drain heat from the body, which is producing less heat as activity decreases.

Protection against the elements is also important in selecting clothing, but too often it is the primary point of consideration by purchasers. Coated nylon parkas, silicone-treated boots, and other such waterproof articles are frequently selected as if surface protection were the only requirement. Simple protection against the elements is not enough in the wild outdoors. To be completely successful, outfits must also provide insulation and ventilation.

A rain slicker might be fine for a dash across a city street, but in the mountains a waterproof garment must be used with discretion. Body moisture which is unable to escape increases humidity inside of a waterproof garment, making the wearer feel colder with it than without. Humid cold is more intense than dry cold; when the temperature is zero in Chicago, it feels colder than when it is zero in Denver. It follows that when one is standing around camp and puts on a rain parka, he will be creating his own damp Chicago air underneath that parka. He may feel colder with the parka on.

There are many sporting-goods stores or mail-order houses where outdoor wear may be secured. For those on a limited budget, inexpensive clothing can be found in Good Will, Salvation Army, or Army-Navy surplus outlets for a fraction of the original cost. One's attic or basement may produce usable items.

Nearly all outdoor clothing and equipment is designed for short backpacking or weekend expeditions or camping near roadheads. Many items have not been constructed or tested for longer or cold-weather expeditions or those based upon the expertise of this book. We have generally found such products inadequate for the specialized conditions of extended NOLS courses. The Paul Petzoldt Wilderness Equipment factory manufactures many products to our own design. As demands for changes and improvements increase with more experienced and informed expeditioners, we experiment and modify our designs. Paul Petzoldt products may be purchased by mail order from: Paul Petzoldt Wilderness Equipment, Lander, Wyoming, 82520.

NOLS Standards for Outdoor Wear

Years of experimenting with outdoor wear with thousands of people and under varying conditions have led us to develop certain standards for clothing designed for wilderness areas of the western Rocky Mountains during June, July, and August. A quick checklist of the NOLS Minimum Clothing allowance appears in Appendix 1. (Winter clothing will be treated separately.)

Head Gear

If your feet are cold, put on a hat.

The body produces a great amount of heat but has a kind of built-in thermostat which attempts to maintain a steady temperature within a few degrees of 98.6 degrees Fahrenheit. It is the job of the bloodstream to distribute this heat throughout the individual.

When heat is lost for any reason, such as underdressing, being bareheaded in the cold, and so on, blood is rushed to the critical internal organs and brain. Therefore, the extremities—i.e., the hands and feet—receive less circulation. This is one cause of frostbite. Prevention of heat loss anywhere in the body will directly benefit the extremities by allowing a greater flow of blood to them.

One might argue that the head is also an extremity. But proximity of blood vessels to the surface radiates tremendous amounts of heat. The blood in this area cannot be decreased, as in the other extremities, or shared with them to reduce heat loss. Serious complications to the brain could result. Thus, while the head might not feel cold, heat being lost from its uncovered surface could be used to warm hands and feet.

For sheer warmth and protection, nothing surpasses an old-fashioned wool stocking cap that can be pulled down over the ears. Many persons wear wool hats while sleeping in their bags, as well as when hiking above timberline.

We talk so much about cold in the mountains that it is easy to forget that high-altitude sun is more severe than that at the seaside because its rays travel through thinner, clearer air. A brimmed felt hat is recommended for sun protection. It also has the advantage of shedding rain and dripping water away from the face, as well as affording protection from wind, snow, and bruising hailstones. When possible, select hats made of fur felt, which last longer than those of wool. The latter tend to lose their shape when wet. Add a chin strap as insurance against loss on windy passes or when climbing. Brimmed cloth hats shed less water but may be substituted if felt is not available.

Parka

A combination wind and rain parka is necessary in the mountains. Best for backpacking and mountaineering purposes are those made of light waterproof coated nylon. Ordinary knee-length raincoats or ponchos used for walking on level ground are unsatisfactory as they are likely to hang so as to block the wearer's view of his feet when he is stepping across boulder fields, crossing logs, or climbing on snow or rock. A preferable length is about six inches below the crotch.

As mentioned earlier, any waterproof material covering the body will prevent moisture from evaporating and cause damp air to gather underneath the rain gear. Advertisements for garments which release body moisture and at the same time repel moisture from precipitation are completely misleading. No fabric to this date has realized this claim. Garments that keep water out must be waterproof, and therefore they will keep body moisture in.

There is no perfect solution to this problem, but a partially satisfactory answer is to have the parka loosely fitted, with slits under the armpits, so that air may circulate inside. The neck should also be loose enough to allow air to escape. Air space between the parka and other clothing affords additional pumping action during body motion or in wind. Body moisture will be forced out with this exchange.

A loose nylon coated rain parka is a good windbreaker in summer weather. When wind is blowing sufficiently to warrant the parka, fluttering will cause enough movement to allow exchange of outside and inside air. (Inadvisability of its winter use will be explained in Chapter 11, pages 204–5.)

Parkas with hoods are not recommended for summer use. Maximum circulation of air in and around the neck is prevented and, more important, ears are covered in such a way as to interfere with hearing and body balance. Restriction of body movement, the inability to make quick head movements, and hindrance of vision are other drawbacks to be considered. A hoodless parka and felt hat are the best solution.

One must take certain precautions with nylon garments. Wearing them near fire is unwise; sparks can destroy the fabric, and nylon has a tendency to melt when subjected to high heat. Avoid sitting on sharp rocks or on the ground, where ragged debris might puncture the light cloth. Store parkas in small nylon stuff sacks rather than poking them into backpacks, where they may be damaged by contact with other gear.

The greatest drawback to using nylon parkas in mountaineering is that they may be ruined by a single rappel. Heat friction from ropes passing around the shoulders can melt the material. Except in an emergency, it is advisable to remove such a garment before rappelling and place it where it will not come in contact with rope (not tied around the waist).

Wool Shirt

A tightly woven wool shirt can act as a windbreaker against a mild breeze. Wool also sheds a certain amount of water and possesses insulating properties to keep one warm even when wet. If one wears the proper wool shirt, a rain parka may not be necessary, even on a long, wet hike.

Shirts must be large enough to allow freedom of movement, even with two sweaters worn underneath. Zippered or buttoned fronts that make temperature adjustments possible are desirable.

Most wool shirts on the market have drawbacks for use in wet or cold weather. A cotton lining around the inside collar will absorb moisture like a dishrag, making it almost impossible to keep the neck warm. Standard collars provide little warnth and are bulky and inconvenient when worn under outer garments.

Whether the hem is even or the shirt has tails, normal-length shirts are too short for strenuous outdoor activities and tend to expose one's middle when leaning over or reaching up. Shirts hanging well below the crotch are preferable. In case of wet weather, if they are left hanging outside the trousers, water will be conducted quickly downward through the wool and drip off the bottom rather than running over the body.

One solution to the shirt question is that which has a Nehru-type collar with no cotton lining and is manufactured extra long. The collar is warm and does not interfere with outer sweaters or parkas. Such styles are rather difficult to find in stores. If they are unavailable to the reader at local outlets, they may be ordered through Paul Petzoldt Wilderness Equipment.

Wool shirts will shrink somewhat in wet weather. Care must be exercised in laundering them, as boiling them or drying them at high heat not only shrinks them but causes them to lose some beneficial properties of wool. Wash water should be cool or slightly warm.

Brightly colored outdoor clothes have been popular in the past and may be necessary during hunting season to protect the wearers from being shot by hunters, but it is our growing conviction that outdoorsmen should wear greens, browns, and other colors that blend into the environment. Since much of the joy of a wilderness experience lies in not seeing other groups—even at a distance—we feel that inconspicuous tones are to be encouraged.

Sweater

When one needs more than a wool shirt on the upper body, a loosely knit sweater of exceptional length is advised. Tight weaves prevent elimination of moisture, especially when one undertakes heat-producing activities such as backpacking or climbing. A loosely knit garment contains less wool than a tighter knit of the same thickness and, consequently, weighs less. Loose knits also stretch more easily and do not restrict body movement, an important factor in energy conservation.

When wool is to be worn next to the skin, it is best to choose lamb's wool, cashmere, or virgin wool, rather than coarser fibers, goat hair, or reprocessed wool, which may scratch or irritate the skin.

Many persons claim to be allergic to wool and therefore insist upon wearing cotton next to the skin. I doubt if anyone is truly allergic to wool. However, irritation to the skin may develop for several reasons.

Some breeds of sheep produce coarse wool. The fibers are heavy and may scratch the skin. Wool garments that have been boiled or shrunk in very hot moisture or overheated dryers lose their texture and tend to scratch the wearer. Wool washed with soap in cold water to prevent shrinking may retain some soap residue if inadequately rinsed. This residue might transfer to the skin by perspiration and redden the skin or cause a rash or infection at the base of hairs.

In the ski troops during World War II, I had the opportunity to observe thousands of men living outdoors in Colorado winters at Camp Hale. They were all issued woolen underwear and socks, but many of them swore they were allergic and so wore cotton next to their skin. They were the ones who ended in the hospital with frostbite and other ailments.

I was asked to investigate these complaints of wool allergy, and was given the assignment of teaching the men how to dress for comfort and survival. At the beginning of class, I would select several GIs to put on various combinations of socks. A sergeant would then double-time the men for about half an hour to work up a sweat and, when they returned, I would have them remove the socks. The results were usually dramatic. All of the stockings were somewhat damp, but the GIs wearing two or more pairs of wool socks had fairly dry feet with the outermost sock containing most of the moisture. The men who wore cotton under wool had pink, clammy feet and the cotton socks were quite wet. Sometimes I could actually wring water from them! It can easily be imagined whose feet got cold first when the men were standing around after such vigorous exercise.

The consistent use of wool socks after these demonstrations decreased the number of frostbite cases considerably. Persons with sensitive skin discovered finer wool non-irritating, and there were no further allergy complaints after a few days' trial.

The wool-sock theory can be applied to all woolen garments; dampness in wool moves through progressive layers *away* from the body. While the outer layer might be moist, the body remains fairly dry and warm.

The sweater we have developed for NOLS use is actually a combination of two garments. An old sweater is cut off below the armholes and sewn to the bottom of another sweater so that it extends at least six inches below the crotch. This extra length prevents the sweater from riding up above the belt when one is climbing or hiking.

Open necklines or those with buttons are preferable to turtleneck sweaters. They are easier to take off and on and not as restricting.

There are many uses for any sweater. It is most often worn under a wool shirt as underwear, can be used alone on warm days, and is excellent for lounging around camp or as sleepwear. Girls sometimes wear our combination sweater as a short dress.

At the top of the mountain or in freezing temperatures, a second sweater may be necessary. This need not be the extended type described above, but should be loosely knitted and large enough to allow ventilation and ease of movement.

Cotton Shirt and Pants

On hot days, when one is carrying a pack, a lightweight cotton shirt might be more comfortable than wool. In most cases, long sleeves are preferable, to guard against sunburn and afford protection from insects. But one warning: if the weather turns cold, don't put a wool sweater or shirt on top of the cotton. Only wool worn next to the skin will give the warmth and ventilation needed.

A light pair of cotton pants may be used as extras for hot weather, but again are no substitute for wool pants in cold weather. If your tan and the mosquitoes permit, a sleeveless cotton top and cotton shorts may be in order when wool clothing is relegated to the pack.

Gloves or Mittens

Only in extreme situations are wool gloves worn during actual climbing, but mountaineers are sometimes subject to forced bivouac, sudden storms, accidents, and the like, so I always recommend that wool gloves or mittens be carried when traveling above timberline. Inexpensive gloves can be purchased at Army-Navy surplus outlets.

It is a good idea to store wool gloves in a plastic bag and use them only during emergencies, because they wear out very easily. Never use them around campfires or when you're handling hot cooking utensils.

Although synthetics are less absorbent than cotton, and preferable to cotton, they do not have the warmth of 100 percent wool, especially when wet. Knitted gloves or mittens with leather palms are not practical.

Cotton becomes very cold when wet, but a pair of cotton gloves is convenient for preventing abrasion to hands when gathering wood, sliding down snowfields, handling campfire cookware, or as protection from wind. Another advantage is that they are inexpensive.

Wind or Rain Pants

Non-waterproof nylon wind pants are useful to wear over other trousers in windy, frigid areas and when climbing extensively above timberline, because wool does not have the windbreaking power necessary under such circumstances. Wind pants should be loose-fitting and have a drawstring around the ankles to prevent wind from blowing up the legs.

Rain pants, of similar design but in waterproof fabric, might be of some value in wet, brushy areas or for riding horses or motorcycles, but in general the lack of ventilation makes these pants unsatisfactory when hiking. In very wet weather, a rain parka will provide adequate protection for the upper body without lessening ventilation, and wool trousers, even when damp, will protect the legs.

Wool Trousers

Wool is the best answer for outdoor wear for trousers. Tough, tightly woven materials are preferable to soft weaves which tear easily on rocks and brush.

Be sure the trousers are roomy. They must be ample around the waist in order to accommodate a heavy sweater, shirt, and extra layer of wool, and still allow unrestricted movement. Tight trousers and those with narrow legs which pull at the knees each time the leg is bent drain body energy. They are uncomfortable and hinder balance.

A combination of wool and synthetics is fine when the warmth of pure wool may be sacrificed. Cotton pants or shorts may be worn on hot days, but to rely on them completely in high mountain country is dangerous. There is little place for cotton when warmth is a consideration. Even cotton pocket and waist linings on wool trousers tend to be cold and uncomfortable when wet.

Trousers should reach to shoe tops for maximum warmth and protection and to keep debris from getting into the top of boots. At NOLS, we run nylon strings through hems in the legs so that trousers may be tied at the ankle, knickered with enough looseness around the knees to prevent "drag" (restriction of knee movement), or allowed to hang naturally when traveling in rough, cold country.

Surplus military trousers cost less than new wool pants. A wool patch sewn on the seat insures extra wear. Care should be exercised in laundering or dry-cleaning woolen fabrics to avoid damage.

Wool knickers, as a substitute for wool pants, have disadvantages. Knicker styles often conform to the tight-pants vogue and are much too restrictive for strenuous outdoor activity. In addition, the knicker-and-knicker-socks combination lacks warmth. Socks are easily torn by brush and afford little protection from water, damp grasses, and brush.

Wool Underwear

Long, soft, loosely knit wool sweaters can double as underwear for the upper body. Wool underpants might also be necessary in early or late summer.

Wool "longjohns" are difficult to find in most retail stores. Ski underwear, which is tight and form-fitting, causes too great an expenditure of energy when muscles must fight resistance of the fabric. Thermal underwear, when made of cotton, is subject to dampness and will cause chilling. Even if thermal underwear were made of wool, its close, tight weave would stifle aeration.

Since the perfect underwear pant is not readily available, one must use judgment in choosing among imperfect garments. Avoid those containing a large percentage of cotton. Try to select styles with the least restriction to movement.

We have made loose-fitting underwear pants from old, lightweight wool suits by removing cotton pockets and lining, cutting off cuffs, and inserting a drawstring in the waist. Instead of being skintight, the legs drop comfortably inside the outer wool trousers.

Cotton Undershorts

Barring extremely cold weather, cotton undershorts are permissible next to the skin. Here cotton is recommended for the sake of cleanliness for both men and women.

Ease of laundering is an important advantage, as the shorts can be rinsed out and dried quickly during extended trips. Another feature is protection of the inner thighs from rubbing on rougher wool trousers.

Shorts should hang below the crotch for comfort. Jockey shorts, which tend to be tight and binding, cause raw places on the skin and may create "galls." This could be serious enough to incapacitate a hiker, or at least afford him discomfort; therefore boxer style shorts are recommended.

Belt or Suspenders

Leather, webbing, almost any type of belt is suitable, as long as it is adjustable enough to hold up pants, with or without extra sweaters and shirts.

Suspenders are comfortable but rather impractical, especially in cold or stormy weather. When one puts on extra clothing with suspenders, it is a struggle to take down one's trousers, and another struggle or puzzle to refasten suspenders. Humorous to viewers, perhaps, but a nuisance to wearers.

Gaiters

Gaiters are sleevelike coverings made of cloth that fit over the tops of boots and calves of the legs. They may be ankle height for trail walking or knee height for deep snow. Their main purpose is to keep snow or debris from getting into the boot, and to protect wool socks from sharp objects. Gaiters are optional for summer use, but essential on glaciers or deep snow.

Gaiters made of waterproof material prevent circulation of air around the foot, and those with tight elastic around the leg will prevent proper blood circulation to the foot. Even the slightest restriction will make the foot cold, since blood carries heat to the extremities. In cold weather, such restriction could trigger frostbite.

Wool gaiters are comfortable but tend to rip easily. Canvas will withstand abrasion, but gaiters made of canvas are bulky and when frozen are stiff and hard to manage. The best solution is nylon gaiters.

Wool Socks

For the climate we are anticipating, there is no substitute for heavy woolen socks. Since other materials wear longer than wool, it is difficult nowadays to find pure wool socks on the market. In summer, 75 percent wool is acceptable, in combination with fibers such as nylon. Socks made of pure cotton tend to "grab" the skin with each movement of the foot inside the boot. This encourages blisters, and in very cold weather there is the danger of frostbite because cotton holds moisture.

Tightly woven socks prevent moisture from escaping, so loose knits are best. When wearing two pairs of socks, if there is any difference in their weave, the looser sock should be worn next to the foot, to encourage ventilation.

There are several good reasons for wearing two pairs of wool socks. A double layer provides warmth, and allows movement between the foot and shoe to take place with less chance of blisters. Wool's ability to conduct moisture away from the skin is another factor.

However, two pairs of socks are not practical in boots that have been fitted for one layer. A tight boot is less warm and will cause more blisters than a loose boot over a single pair of socks.

Boots

Proper footgear on an outdoor expedition is all-important. Tennis shoes, or leather soles so thin that sharp objects or rocks can be felt while walking, are hard on the feet in mountainous country. Persons accustomed to street shoes and sidewalks find that the bones and ligaments of their feet are not used to this type of bending and stretching.

I witnessed a classic example of this in 1938 when I participated in the K2 expedition in the Himalayas. We walked a long distance through foothills and rugged country en route to base camp, and some of our party started the trip in light tennis shoes. After two days of hiking, their feet became so sore (not because of blisters or abrasions but because of the movements of ligaments holding the foot bones) that they couldn't walk without severe pain for several days. It was interesting to note that our porters, who had gone barefoot all their lives, suffered no problems because their feet were used to bending.

For a weekend climb of cliffs near the roadhead, a climber needs tightly fitting, stiff-soled boots. One will not suffer ill effects in making the short approach to the base in these boots. Generally, too, on such climbs, warmth is not a vital consideration and the varied conditions of an extended expedition are not present.

This stiff-soled boot, on the other hand, would cause misery on a hiking expedition. Persons taking an occasional hike with light pack, or none at all, probably require nothing more than an inexpensive, lightweight pair of hiking boots. The boot selected for most outdoorsmen will be a compromise between these two extremes.

There are certain points to look for when choosing the boot for a backpacking trip lasting a week or longer. The same boot should be acceptable for moderately difficult climbing. Many styles and brands are available, both American and European made. Each has good and bad features.

Many boots have scree collars, tight padded rings at the top intended to prevent stones ("scree") or debris from entering the boot. Most scree collars cause "squeak heel," or tendonitis, which is an inflammation of the sheath of the Achilles' tendon, or soreness above the heel, caused by continuous slight pressure over long periods of time.

"Squeak heel" is seldom a worry on a short trip. One might return home with a sore tendon, but when hiking boots are replaced by regular shoes, discomfort disappears within a few days. Serious "squeak heel" afflictions normally take a few days to develop. The condition is very painful, and the cause must be removed even if one must slit open the back of the boot.

The best way to avoid this malady is to be cautious when buying boots. Besides those with scree collars, boots whose backs slope forward above the heel are offenders.

As a rule, inner padding built into boots is a handicap. It is a place for water to collect and keep the inside continuously wet.

For traveling in mountain country on rocky trails or trailless terrain, one needs a sole that will bend for comfortable walking yet be thick enough to withstand sharp, pointed rocks. Many brands of boots are constructed with soles of the same thickness for size 6 and size 12. When I carry a heavy pack, my combined pack and body weight is around 300 pounds. With a size 14 boot, I need the heaviest sole on the market. However, a young person or a woman weighing 120 pounds with a 40-pound pack will be more comfortable in a lighter shoe with a much thinner sole. There is no reason for the smaller person to carry the extra weight of a thick sole such as I need.

Some climbing boots have soles which have been artificially stiffened with steel or Fiberglas. These rigid soles are designed to make it possible to put a small part of the toe or side of foot on narrow ledges. Although they are often sold as hiking shoes, these boots are unsatisfactory for backpacking; they are almost as stiff as ski boots.

Vibram lugged soles prevent slipping. Soles of sponge rubber or without lugs are only usable on smooth, near-level trails.

Toes should be solid enough to afford protection against rocks and stones on boulder fields or talus slopes and to avoid discomfort to toes when the wearer is step-kicking up a snowfield. If one carries an axe on an expedition, hard-toed boots are an extra safeguard against inexpert woodsmanship.

Unless one has some special reason (snakes, thorns, personal preference), boots that reach higher than the ankle should be avoided. Ventilation to the feet is hindered, as is full freedom of the ankle, necessary in climbing and crossing rough terrain. The addition of a good pair of gaiters is preferable to high boots.

It is best to have a boot tongue that is sewn all the way to the top of the lacing to keep out water when walking in damp areas, fording streams, crossing snowfields, or traveling on rainy days. The upper part of the boot should be pliable and the lacings easily adjustable.

Boots must fit properly. We know that a boot which fits loosely is better ventilated, will keep the foot drier and warmer, and will cause fewer blisters than a snug-fitting boot. However, the conviction that a snug fit is necessary is so prevalent that it is difficult to overcome. In fact, nearly all our students who bring their own boots (which have been fitted in stores) have foot problems on an expedition because the boots fit too snugly.

To insure proper fit, take off all socks, place bare foot in the boot without lacing it, and push the foot as far forward as possible. Stand with full weight on the feet, with toes touching the end of the boot, and bend knees forward. There should be enough room between the heel and back of the boot to insert a finger without pressure. This is the minimum space for preventing toes from hitting the boot when one is descending slopes. People who wear larger sizes should allow slightly more space. Starting with size 7, the space should be gradually increased up to one and one-half finger widths for size 12; that is, from ⅝ inch for size 7 to one inch for size 12.

Next, try on the boots with the socks which will be worn in the field. If climate and foot care demand two pairs of heavy or medium-heavy wool socks, fit with two pairs.

Stand in unlaced boot with full weight on the feet. The sides of the toes or ball of the foot may lightly touch the inside boot, but if there is pressure that tends to stretch the boot outward, it is too tight.

Lace the boot comfortably, not too tightly. (When hiking, even well-fitted boots can cause foot problems if laced too tightly.) Kick the toe of the boot against a solid surface. If this causes the toes to touch the end, a larger-size boot is required.

Persons with one foot longer than the other have special problems. There is little choice but to fit the larger foot, or purchase two pairs of boots.

Boots must be broken in for maximum comfort. It is important that the inside sole adjust to the curvature of the sole of the foot. The boot will then adjust to other parts of the foot.

However, leather will not adjust unless it is damp. Normal perspiration will dampen it, but a faster method is to fill the boot with water. Leave water for several minutes and then wear the wet boot to allow it to conform to the foot. Hikers hesitate to fill a new pair of boots with water, but why not? It does not hurt boots to stay damp. If a hiker is concerned about keeping his feet dry, wearing two pairs of dry wool socks will accomplish this even if the shoe leather is wet.

Many people feel that they must dry out boots when not wearing them. Care must be exercised in doing this. Direct sunlight will shrink leather and curl the soles; heat of fires will build boot temperatures to around 170 degrees and harden the leather permanently so that the boots will crack and fall apart. The only satisfactory way to dry boots is to wipe the insides with a cloth and place them in the shade to dry naturally.

Each outdoorsman must make his own additons or omissions to our recommended clothing allowance after considering relevant factors of climate, length and purpose of trip, and activities anticipated. But one should always bear this in mind: *Clothing must enable a person to survive one night's bivouac in case of emergency.*

3

Equipping for the Wild Outdoors

On a camping expedition, we discover that we can do with very little. Necessities are those items which contribute to our safety and comfort without posing a burden in transporting them. When one must carry a supply of food, clothing, shelter, and equipment on one's own back, selectivity and careful planning are critical.

Before starting an outing, I ask beginners to divide the gear they have brought into two piles: items they consider absolutely necessary and those things which might be needed. I reject the second stack completely and then check the first one and discard about half of its contents. The remainder is generally about right.

It is a tendency of everyone to overequip or add inessential items to the pack. There is always a temptation to take another small item that "won't weigh anything." Is a flashlight really necessary? If so, is one for the entire group adequate? Will just a penlight do? Shouldn't the big hunting knife with scabbard be left behind? What about the heavy Swiss knife with leather punch, screwdriver, bottle opener and so on? Isn't a small knife with two blades sufficient? Unless the expedition includes bird watching, is the weight of binoculars worth while? Since a good 35 mm. camera and film will weigh several pounds, must everyone carry one? Cannot picture taking be pooled? Every item must be questioned even though "it doesn't weigh anything."

A student who drilled holes in his toothbrush handle to save weight may have gone to extremes, but it is good judgment to split a towel and take the smaller part, if one insists on having a towel. Perhaps a large handkerchief would suffice.

If one purchased everything one "could use" or that "would be handy to have along," one could have a truckload. Overstocking food is especially tempting. Few outdoorsmen know how to select and package food for backpacking trips or realize that two pounds per person per day (including packaging) is enough. (See Chapter 4, pages 67–71.)

Conversely, it is dangerous to underequip on essentials. If it is necessary to take a mountain tent for shelter from possible storms, then one must take that tent and possibly leave camera, film, and other extras behind.

A small shovel is essential for "practical conservation," and no one has the right to go into the wild outdoors without this means of eliminating fire scars and disposing of human waste in a non-polluting manner.

Provision must be made for activities anticipated. If snowfields will be traversed, an ice axe will be included; if fishing is planned, rod and tackle will be carried. There is nothing more disappointing than attempting an activity without the proper tools.

Backpacking equipment may be purchased in mountaineering stores and some general sporting-goods stores. There are also many excellent mail-order sources. Some items may be rented.

Numerous brands and styles of tents, sleeping bags, expedition packs, and clothing are on the market and most of these are fine products, but we have found them generally inadequate for the specialized conditions of an extended NOLS course. The Paul Petzoldt Wilderness Equipment factory manufactures these items to our own design. They may be purchased at the store or by mail order.

NOLS Standards for Equipment

Because it is necessary for the backpacker to travel light, it is vital that his equipment be functional and carefully selected. As in the case of clothing, the following NOLS Minimum Equipment List has been developed from our experience. A checklist is included in Appendix 3.

Sleeping Bag

Protecting the individual from cold is the primary function of a sleeping bag. Temperatures in mountainous regions drop considerably during the night, and the body produces less heat at rest than when active, so the amount of insulation sufficient to keep one warm when moving is not enough for times of sleep.

Wool would be an ideal material for sleeping bags. Just as it is recommended for outdoor clothing because of its ability to provide warmth even when wet, wool would keep the sleeper cozy. But the extra amount of thickness necessary would make this type of bedroll too heavy and bulky for backpacking.

In backpacking, one wants the lightest bag possible with maximum warmth. Prime goose down meets these qualifications when fluffy and dry, and such bags are satisfactory for infrequent weekend outings. But for continuous use and extended backpacking expedition, I consider down dangerous.

The fluffed thickness, or "loft," of a new, dry down bag provides a great deal of warmth and comfort. But let that down become wet, and there is little or no insulation. Instead of loft, the down is matted into clumps, leaving empty spots where there is no insulation at all. In cold weather, this could present a survival situation.

I remember one occasion when a NOLS course was struck by an unseasonable mid-August blizzard in the Wind River mountains. On that trip, I had a beautiful new sleeping bag filled with five pounds of prime northern goose down. After heavy rains, snow, and temperatures hovering at the fifteen-degree mark, the bag was impossible to keep dry. I was sleeping between two thicknesses of soggy nylon with a few hard balls of prime northern goose down here and there, and it took several days for the bag to dry out. Needless to say, I got little sleep during that stormy ten days and have never relied on a down bag again.

In another instance, during the fall of 1970, some of our instructors took a reconnaissance trip to Alaska's Prince William Sound in small kayak-type Folbots. They experienced rain, wet snow, heavy seas, and breakers on the beaches. With such extreme exposure to the elements, it became impractical to attempt to keep anything dry. At night, temperatures dropped near zero. Luckily, the men were well equipped with both down and Dacron sleeping bags. It didn't take them long to discover that the down bags were useless. There was no way to dry them. But the Dacron bags could be wrung out and used regularly for comfortable, warm sleep.

Shortly before the trip ended, skies cleared but winds gusted and temperatures dropped to a survival situation. Even under these conditions, the Dacron dried out in an hour or two, but the down merely froze into lumps.

Therefore, the main criticism of down is that, no matter how excellent the original quality, it is useless for warmth when wet, and almost impossible to dry under expedition conditions. Down bags are also very expensive.

Dry-cleaning is another problem. Only a specialist with knowledge of proper cleaning solutions should be allowed to care for a down bag. Careless washing is also harmful. A down bag should be laundered in warm water with a mild detergent and an extra rinse in clear water. Hang it for a few days to dry. This method, however, will not eradicate all of the spots and stains on outer coverings.

For many years, I considered Dacron the only suitable filling for sleeping bags. Unfortunately, most bags of this material were big, rectangular "station wagon" models which were unsuitable for backpacking.

Recently we discovered an even better Dacron. For two years, NOLS field-tested Dacron Fiberfill II as an insulation for sleeping bags. The Du Pont company has since put it on the market.

Fiberfill II requires about 25 percent more space in a stuff bag than goose down of the same weight. Even so, if the bag is strapped on the bottom of a pack frame, the larger stuff bag makes little difference.

Under field conditions, Fiberfill II retains its loft even when wet or damp. The fibers themselves absorb practically no moisture. Because of this, the bag will dry after a few hours' exposure to wind or sun.

Fiberfill II is also relatively inexpensive. A bag may be purchased for about half the price of a down bag of comparable quality and construction. Laundering does not seem to have adverse effects on this material, but some cleaning fluids might be harmful. One should follow manufacturer's directions.

A waterproof covering on a sleeping bag is not advisable. There is enough moisture leaving the body in one night's sleep to make a bag very wet if it has such a covering.

A hunting companion brought a big "space blanket" to camp one year. This was supposed to be the ultimate in warmth and render a sleeping bag unnecessary. One side of the blanket had a silvery finish to reflect heat back toward the body. The material was airproof and waterproof, so that neither air nor water could introduce cold from the outside. The blanket had all of the principles of a thermos except dead air space. Therefore, it didn't allow for ventilation.

The hunter decided to go one better and wrap the space blanket around his down sleeping bag. He woke up soaking wet and couldn't get his sleeping bag dry for several days.

Insulating material in a sleeping bag must trap air yet allow it to move enough to carry away moisture from the body to the outside. Any vapor barrier between the body and outside of the bag will prevent this escape of moisture. Thus, in order to keep the bag, its occupant, and his clothing dry, there cannot be a waterproof covering, be it coated nylon, plastic, a space blanket, or foam rubber.

Even if waterproof material is not actually touching the bag, a few inches of air space will not carry away the moisture. When a hiker is sleeping in a tent made of waterproof material, the air will become so humid that condensation may occur inside the bag.

The cloth exterior of a sleeping bag should be light and strong. Non-waterproof nylon is such a material. It allows air to pass through but does not absorb moisture. The inside of the bag should be made of a lighter-weight permeable nylon, so that when the bag is turned inside out, the insulation will dry faster.

It is important to realize that a sleeping bag is really another article of clothing and must fit the individual. If one can't wear one's brother's boots, chances are his sleeping bag couldn't be used either. Too large a bag will result in excess space around the body and more air to keep heated. Too small a bag will be uncomfortable; the body will press against the insulation and decrease its warming powers.

The ideal bag should be comfortably snug, with room for the feet to be free of restriction. The hood must be large enough to allow head movement, but tie so that only a small breathing space is left and cold air does not reach head and shoulders. The breathing hole should fit naturally over the mouth. Over-all length should be several inches longer than the occupant to permit changes of position during the night.

In fitting a sleeping bag, be sure to wear the maximum clothes that might be worn during sleep. One might select a bag that is fine for summer mountain use and still be large enough for use with insulated parka, pants, mittens, and other apparel in winter.

A larger, heavier bag than necessary is a waste of energy. A five-foot girl weighing 100 pounds need not carry a sleeping bag large enough for a 170-pound man. Certainly a man six foot three does not want a bag made for someone who is five foot ten. The sleeping bag must be made to fit the individual user.

Certain measurements are needed for accurate fitting of tailor-made bags: the individual's height, weight, foot size, circumference around the body below the shoulders with arms at sides, and hips. Information about clothing that will be worn inside the bag is also important.

Where and how the bag is zippered or closed is a matter of personal choice. Various models zip on the side, down the front, all or part way, with double zippers which open at either end, and so on. Whatever style is chosen, the edges of the insulating fabric underneath must meet at the zipper closing so that excess heat cannot escape or uncomfortable cold spots form.

Sleeping Pad

On chilly nights, when it might be a problem to keep warm and comfortable, extra padding between the ground and sleeping bag is essential. In my youth, when camping out in sub-zero winter weather, I carried pieces of elk or deer hide with the hair still on them for insulation at my hips and shoulders. In the Himalayas, I took pieces of beaver hide for the same purpose. Another solution was a layering of boughs.

Now, however, because of our concern for the environment, we can no longer tolerate the practice of breaking pine boughs from trees for insulation. An alternative is necessary.

One might hear that a certain sleeping bag is adequate for temperatures of ten degrees below zero, but such information is not dependable unless one knows what material was placed underneath the bag when a test was made. A ten-below-zero bag might be cold at thirty degrees above zero without adequate insulation underneath.

Down compresses so much with body weight that its usefulness for underneath insulation is negligible. Fiberfill II and other synthetics will maintain more loft under body pressure than down, but generally not enough to be completely satisfactory.

Recent technology has developed a wide variety of synthetic paddings that are lightweight yet furnish excellent insulation under a sleeping bag. The best of them is Ensolite, a closed-cell foam material. It resists compression and has very little sponging effect. Miniature air pockets surrounded by waterproof material furnish secure protection for the individual on lengthy trips and under adverse weather conditions.

An Ensolite pad of one-fourth to one-half inch thickness is adequate. This will not provide a mattress protection against rough ground surfaces, but it will offer insulation against the cold ground.

A softer effect can be had with an air mattress. However, a mattress that will withstand a long trip without puncturing or tearing must be strong and therefore possibly heavy. Air mattresses also provide less insulation than Ensolite pads because the larger air compartments of the air mattress have little insulation power and allow body heat to be drained quickly.

The same theory applies to canvas cots. Free movement of air underneath the cot allows body heat to escape—fast.

Tents

When purchasing tents, remember one simple axiom: any material that will keep water out will also keep it in. I once had a nice tent with a waterproof floor that extended several inches up the sides for added protection. It was fine until the night I got water inside on the floor, and then it was just like sleeping in a bathtub.

Before World War II, we had light tents made of long-fiber cotton (Egyptian type). Like all cotton, or canvas, tents, they would absorb outside moisture, the fibers would swell as a result, and the cloth would shed the rain. However, when the fabric was touched on the inside, it had a tendency to leak. The tents were also heavy to transport when wet, and in colder weather they froze and became difficult to handle. At the same time, on winter expeditions or at altitudes above 18,000 feet where melting snow was not a problem, these tents broke the wind, allowed moisture to escape, and shed snow.

Waterproof nylon provides a strong material with less weight, but the condensation always associated with waterproof material is a problem. Attempts to solve this difficulty have not been completely successful; however, improved designs have evolved from experimentation. The following can be recommended:

First, a waterproof bottom to protect against ground moisture. (Pinpoint holes caused by rocks, twigs, and rough surfaces will eventually modify efficiency.)

Second, a non-waterproof top that will allow inside moisture to escape. Obviously, under storm conditions, this does not suffice.

Third, a fly (sheet of fabric having no sides or floor) of waterproof material pitched over an entire non-waterproof tent. The fly is pitched to provide a few inches of free air space between it and the tent. Theoretically, this free air space will carry away moisture before it condenses on the waterproof fly. Unfortunately, some condensation does take place on the fly and may drip through the tent below. In winter, special problems of frost condensation may occur.

We have designed a tent for our courses in Baja California, Mexico, which solves condensation problems. It can also be used successfully under all except winter conditions in the Rocky Mountains and similar regions. (At present, Paul Petzoldt Wilderness Equipment is the only manufacturer of the Baja-style tent.)

The Baja tent has a waterproof floor as a moisture barrier. The sides and top are made of reinforced nylon mosquito netting which zips into a mosquitoproof, bugproof shelter. The net top allows ventilation and eliminates all interior moisture. It also allows one to go to sleep looking at the stars, feeling the softness of summer breezes, and savoring the outdoor fragrances.

In foul weather, the tent is covered with a tailor-made fly of waterproof nylon. The occupant will remain dry, and there will be ample ventilation.

Another advantage of the Baja tent is that it weighs less than shelters that are necessary for freezing conditions. (See Chapter 11, pages 207–8, for winter tentage.)

The perfect tent for all conditions is still a dream.

A good, and less expensive, tent substitute, which can be used for summer outings, is the waterproof nylon fly used alone. It can be strung over sleeping bags to deflect rain or snow, yet leaves ample ventilation space. Disadvantages are that it gives no protection against bugs and crawling things or heavy wind and blowing snow.

If one anticipates high-altitude expeditioning or serious winter camping, one should get a tent for that purpose and use it for summer also. Never attempt to adapt a summer tent to extreme conditions. All tents or flies, summer or winter design, must be strong enough to withstand greater than average winds and storms, or survival situations may result.

Shelters made of plastic, so-called survival sheets, can only be used where one may risk their failure. If, under emergency situations, one can rush to nearby buildings or automobiles, these tents may be tolerated because of their small cost. However, on more remote trips, their use should be discouraged.

Backpackers may save a few ounces by selecting a very small mountain tent; however, if the occupant is cramped or uncomfortable, such a saving is not an asset. A large person will need a larger shelter; if two persons are to share a tent, sleeping quarters should be ample enough for undisturbed sleep and for storage of clothes and other equipment.

The Pack and Frame

During my youth, the "Trapper Nelson" pack board was essential for trappers and other outdoorsmen carrying heavy loads. This board was constructed of wood with a canvas covering and fitted snugly against the back. It was strong and durable, but heavy and rigid.

The later development of an aluminum pack frame made it possible to curve the metal to fit back and hips. More balance was possible for the load, and the frame itself was much lighter than the old-style board.

Most pack bags and frames on the market today are adequate for weekend trips in warm weather and with light loads up to thirty pounds. On longer trips, when one must have clothing and camping equipment for varied weather conditions, or one is carrying climbing gear, fishing equipment, and a fourteen-pound week's food supply, packs weighing fifty or sixty pounds are common. Most pack frames, their carrying straps, stitching, buckles, and other parts are designed for lighter loads and are apt to fail under expedition conditions.

When beginners carry heavy loads, it is often difficult for them to avoid half dropping the packs when taking them off their shoulders. If the corner of a welded aluminum frame sustains a blow, great strain is placed on the welding and it tends to crack. Once a hairlike split develops, the frame has a tendency to crack in the other welds within days.

Manufacturers have tried replacing welds with plastic connections or unwelded metal, but these have also failed under heavy loads and expedition experience. There are bound to be some equipment failures on extended trips with persons carrying fifty or more pounds. About the only thing a person can do is purchase frames that a manufacturer recommends for heavy duty. Special bracing and extension bars to accommodate extra bags give some additional support.

The old "Trapper Nelson" pack board did not have a special sack of its own. A number of stuff bags were lashed to the back with string. Actually, this was a great system for winter, as one sack could hold sleeping gear, another food, a third clothing, and so on. Thus, individual sacks need only be opened when contents were to be used.

The modern aluminum pack frame with an attached sack has some disadvantages. If the pack contains only one compartment, everything inside is exposed when opened in rain or snow, and it is difficult to plan in order to have everything needed during the day readily available. If the sack contains several zippered compartments, these spaces are difficult to stuff full and zip shut, and therefore hold less than is necessary for a long trip.

The most satisfactory design is the pack with one large compartment and pockets on the outside. A large stuff bag generally carrying the sleeping bag can be strapped to the frame underneath. However, most such packs are designed for short trips and do not have the volume necessary for equipment on long outings, for additional activities such as climbing or fishing, or for cold weather when bulkier clothing and extra sleeping and tenting gear are needed. Consequently, when people use these weekend packs for such trips, they generally tie items onto the outside, giving a sloppy appearance, exposing equipment to the elements or possible loss, and hindering proper balance of the pack.

In order to eliminate these problems, the Paul Petzoldt Wilderness Equipment factory manufactures extra-large pack sacks with big outside pockets so that everything for a lengthy trip can be put inside with good balance. A roomy stuff sack strapped underneath will hold the sleeping bag and other materials. These special bags are made to fit most brands of strong pack frames. The expeditioner may remove his regular small sack from the frame and replace it with the larger expedition pack. The packs can be purchased individually or with a frame.

Group Equipment

Axe

Many outdoorsmen carry an axe in order to collect firewood. In the Rocky Mountain wilderness, where chopping marks would be noticeable, one should not fell trees, and it is rarely necessary to chop wood that lies on the ground; therefore an axe is not essential. In areas such as Tennessee or New England, where timber has been felled many times and regrowth is rapid and thick, an axe may be used with discretion.

A short "Hudson Bay" variety is generally sufficient. While this axe is lighter than other styles, it is more dangerous, so should be handled cautiously. With a long-handled axe, when a blow is missed the blade will usually hit the ground away from the foot. With the short-handled type, it may end up in the vicinity of the foot.

Use of the axe is one of the most dangerous aspects of an outing for beginners. A good leader will insist upon lessons in axemanship and safety before allowing anyone to handle the tool. (Axemanship will be detailed in Chapter 6, pages 122–23.)

Shovel

A shovel is mandatory in the outdoors, for digging latrines and firepits and burying ashes or decomposable debris. Small, lightweight shovels are sufficient if one is careful not to force them beyond their strength.

First-Aid Materials

While every group should carry first-aid supplies, most outdoorsmen take more than is practical. Only a few items are truly necessary on a backpacking trip.

1. Moleskin for blister prevention and treatment.
2. Band-Aids.
3. Tape.
4. Small roll of gauze.
5. Medicated foot powder for treatment and prevention of athlete's foot.
6. Salt pills or rock salt to prevent dehydration.
7. Pain pills (by doctor's prescription). One must have exact information concerning their use and the dangers of overuse. These are only for severe pain, such as associated with broken bones.
8. Sleeping pills (by doctor's prescription). Leader must have knowledge of use and dangers. These may be used as painkillers for less serious injuries and may be helpful to beginners who are restless during the first night or two in a strange environment.

I do not advocate inclusion of antibiotics for treating sore throats or virus infections. Their use, even if a physician is a group member, should be banned since an adverse reaction in the wilds could be very serious.

Iodine, salves, and other medication to kill germs are also of questionable value in high mountain country, as they might injure healthy tissue and slow down healing.

Splints, bandages, litters, and other items for extreme emergencies can be improvised from tree limbs, ice axes, clothing, pack frames, and similar available gear. (See Chapter 12.)

Miscellaneous

Extra string is always useful for extending tent-flap ties, repairing broken pack-frame straps, tying off tears in tents, and so forth.

Flashlight. One large flashlight is usually adequate for the group; however, individuals may wish to carry small penlights.

Topographical maps.

Compass. The type inserted in a rectangle of plastic to be used with topographical maps is recommended. One compass in the group is sufficient.

Supplies for equipment repairs (tape, horseshoe nails, needle and thread).

Small notebook and pencil.

Book on flora and fauna.

Cooking Utensils

Aluminum cooking utensils which stack inside one another make good use of space and are excellent for backpacking. Such camp gear is rather expensive, however, and should be treated carefully. Cook sets are sold in most camping and sporting-goods stores.

A Teflon treated frying pan is recommended for its non-stick qualities. One should avoid excessive abrasion in cleaning as the surface is easily scratched.

No. 10 (gallon) cans, nicknamed "billy cans," and those of smaller size adapt well to cooking, eating, and drinking. The emptied cans must be checked for smooth openings to avoid sharp edges. If a group needs a large number of billy cans, they are available free from restaurants or institutions. After the outing, cans may be discarded upon returning to civilization.

All cooking utensils should be carried in a cloth bag to prevent soot from rubbing against other items in the pack. Cans in graduated sizes may be stacked like the aluminum cook sets.

On extended trips, one has little use for plastic plates; they are hard to pack without bending and food tends to cool quickly on the flat surface. We have found that a bowl, cup, and spoon are the only eating utensils needed. Meals are usually eaten one course at a time, so the same bowl may be used for an entire meal. Metal bowls and cups are easier to clean and sterilize than plastic.

A collapsible plastic water jug is handy for carrying water to the cooking area.

Metal pot grips for handling hot cooking utensils are recommended.

Food

The logistics of an outing are greatly affected by the amount of food carried. On a trip where one is carrying the minimum clothing, camping gear, equipment for planned activities, and personal items, one will be carrying at least twenty-five pounds. Adding food soon increases the load to its maximum.

Packaging in plastic bags or light plastic containers is helpful for limiting weight and practicing conservation. Two pounds of food per person per day is an approximate average. Consequently, a ten-day trip requires twenty pounds of food. This will decrease about two pounds each day, but one must still start out with the maximum load when he is least in shape.

Careful planning in food selection will contribute to a more enjoyable trip. This subject will be covered in detail in the following chapter.

Personal Equipment

Toilet paper. Store in two plastic bags, tied at the top.
Toothbrush.

Toothpaste or powder. Only a very small amount is needed. Salt may be used as a substitute.

Biodegradable soap.

Comb. Small and unbreakable.

Large handkerchief or small towel.

Small knife. Can be used as nail file.

Lip protection. May also be used on nose.

Insect repellent.

Suntan lotion.

Glacier cream. To block sun's rays when traveling on reflecting snow.

Hand lotion. Carry in plastic bottle.

Face cream. Cleansing or moisturizing creams are optional. They must be carried in lightweight plastic containers.

Cosmetics. Makeup or other skin-care items are optional but should be kept to a minimum and carried in plastic containers.

Shaving equipment. Razor, blades, small mirror. One can shave with warm water and a little biodegradable soap. Foam lather is too heavy to carry.

Sanitary napkins or tampons (with paper, not plastic, inserters).

Wooden matches. Carry in small plastic bag.

4

Rations for the Wild Outdoors

No canned goods, foil-wrapped food, pre-packaged dinners, fresh meat or produce should be taken on extended expeditions in the wilderness. Glass, tin, and foil are heavy, and good conservation practices demand that they be carried out of the wilds for disposal. Perishable items are impractical for lengthy outings.

Pre-packaged meals or freeze-dried steaks are fine for brief trips if one can afford them, but for a backpacking expedition of a week or more such meals are expensive and cumbersome and do not allow for the variety and fun of self-planned menus. I believe that one can really have more satisfying meals, a better-balanced diet, and more enjoyment with personally selected foods.

Cooking in the outdoors is one of the most pleasurable aspects of an outing. It is very rewarding to see the glow of achievement on a beginner's face when he displays his first loaf of yeast bread baked over a campfire. Even the failures have their compensations. One of our students burned the crust of his bread so thoroughly that after eating the center part, he used the hard outside shell as a water container, with humor and pride.

There are hundreds of different powdered, freeze-dried, or dehydrated foods. These include cereal products, self-rising mixes such as Bisquick and gingerbread, fruits, vegetables, dairy products, seasonings, powdered desserts and beverages, and many other lightweight preparations available at supermarkets or specialty shops. Obviously, when one is planning a trip, one cannot select every variety of suitable food. Yet upon encountering shelves lined with tempting goodies, how does one choose?

Should the person planning the rations work out a menu for each day so that the correct amounts and variations will be considered for every meal? The answer is an emphatic no!

NOLS has developed a system that has proved very successful. We select a variety of food that makes a balanced diet possible, and consider caloric requirements for the trip and limitations of carrying weight. Then we instruct expedition members to eat as much of anything they want as frequently as they wish. No one should ever feel hungry.

We allow two pounds of food, averaging at least 3,700 calories, per person per day. These figures multiplied by the number of days involved determine individual ration supplies; a seven-day trip would thus require 14 pounds of food and 25,900 calories for each person. We then multiply this total by the number of people in the expedition to arrive at the required amount of rations. To meet these specifications, we learn each ingredient's weight and the number of calories per unit of weight and then select a variety of well-balanced foods.

Students are on their own as to what they eat and when. We impose no daily rationing system.

With minimal planning in the field, one can save enough margarine to fry fish the last day of the trip. However, if that last day is spent eating "what's left," so what? Some discretion should be exercised, of course, but a detailed, planned menu is not practical from a purchasing, packaging, logistical, psychological, or enjoyment standpoint. Obviously, for a shorter outing, more attention must be given to menu planning, since the variety and amounts of food are more limited.

A shopper should consider basic ingredients for meals. Quick-cooking hot cereals or pancake mix are staples for breakfast; pastas and soup bases may be combined with vegetables, cheese, fresh mountain trout, or a number of other foods for dinners. Usually, time is not taken for an actual lunch, so nuts, dried fruits, and similar between-meal snacks for trail food are necessary. Coffee, tea, cocoa, fruit crystals, and other drinks are essential.

Under the healthy conditions of a backpacking trip, one need not worry about getting too much sugar, fats, or starch. Strenuous activity and higher altitudes demand extra amounts in order to manufacture needed energy. Preference should be given high energy-producing protein foods such as cheese, powdered milk, nuts, ham- and bacon-flavored bits, and wheat products.

Daily requirements of vitamins, minerals, proteins, fats, and carbohydrates are present in carefully selected rations. Recent government reports indicate that vitamin tablets are unnecessary under most conditions. Inclusion of these supplements on an expedition is a matter of personal preference. Persons such as diabetics with special dietary problems probably should not go into the hills except with explicit permission of a physician. In the summer, vitamin C is supplied by edible green plants, which are found everywhere.

All foods must be dry, non-perishable, and easily transported. Regardless of original packaging—glass, cans, foil, cardboard, and so on—supplies should be repackaged in small, strong plastic bags or lightweight plastic containers. Plastic bags weigh little, are reusable, and can be burned with inconsequential pollution effect. When one bag is empty, it may be placed over another to reinforce its contents.

It is preferable to close bags with a simple, loose knot rather than metal ties, which might cause holes and must be carried out of the mountains for proper disposal. Bagged food may be placed in a light nylon bag for extra protection in the backpack.

Beginners sometimes have trouble identifying contents of the unlabeled bags owing to similarities in appearance and color. One student mistook butterscotch pudding for cornmeal when breading his trout; another ''sweetened'' her coffee with salty beef base instead of brown sugar. Experience usually solves the problem, however, and cooks learn to identify rations by odor and texture as well as appearance. (Bisquick holds its shape like a snowball when squeezed; dried milk is granular.) Bags can be marked for identification if desired.

Cooking with dehydrated apples. Note that rations have been repackaged in plastic bags.

The NOLS Field Ration Form included in Appendix 5 lists suggested foods and their approximate calories per pound, but some discussion of the various categories and possible uses might be helpful. Naturally, an imaginative cook will provide his or her own ideas.

If one doesn't know the calorie count of these foods, figure about 1,700 calories per pound for starches, milk, sugars, or their combinations (puddings, cake mixes, etc.). Generally, foods containing fats and oils (nuts, bacon bits, etc.) exceed 1,700 calories per pound. Pure fat will contain over 3,000 calories per pound. Knowing these estimates will give one a practical guess at the caloric measurements. Specific information can be obtained from Agricultural Handbook No. 8, *Composition of Foods,* which can be obtained from: Superintendent of Documents, U.S. Government Printing Office, Washington, D.C. 20402.

Dairy Products

Milk

Dry milk does not spoil and is easy to carry. It is high in protein and contains many other nutrition essentials.

Uses of powdered milk are almost unlimited. It may be added to coffee, cocoa, or tea, used to enrich soups, baked goods, or cereals, and added to sauces for spaghetti and macaroni. This wonderful food should be a main part of the diet for any backpacking trip.

Cheese

An excellent source of protein, cheese may be purchased in approximate pound quantities. Often it has already been wrapped in plastic, but it is a good idea to put it in an additional plastic bag for traveling so that it will not damage other items if it melts.

Cheese is a favorite trail snack and has many uses in cooking. It may be added to breads and pastries, used to top pizzas and flavor soups, or be melted for sauces on pasta or vegetables. Cheddar cheese is recommended because of its popularity and versatility, but other kinds are good for variety.

Try to keep cheese out of the sun so that it will remain firm. If it does soften or even form a little mold, it will still be edible and should last the duration of a trip.

Fats

Margarine

Margarine is one of the least expensive foods, yet provides fats which are vital in the wild outdoors for heat and energy. It can be spread on breads and biscuits and added to sauces, soups, and vegetables. In frying, it prevents fish, pancakes, or other foods from sticking to the pan. Margarine will blacken if melted over a direct flame.

Carrying margarine is somewhat of a problem, as it will melt easily or cling to the sides of plastic bags when it becomes soft. While this does not harm the product, it is messy and unappetizing. We have found that a lightweight plastic jar with screw lid is a convenient container. These reusable jars are available at outdoor stores.

Grains and Starches

Biscuit Mix

Biscuits, pancakes, dumplings, and fried bread can be made with this ready-mix product. No yeast is needed in quick batter because baking powder is included. One can mix ingredients and bake without allowing time for the dough to rise.

At high altitudes, it is a good idea to add some flour or other grain to pre-leavened mixes, as they tend to overrise and fall. Also, adding a small amount of mix to plain flour will produce a slight rising effect in pizzas, cobblers, and crusts.

A cake is basically a thin, "runny" mixture of Bisquick, water, and sugar. A biscuit is a stiff dough of Bisquick and water.

Flour

Both white and whole-wheat flour have their uses on an expedition. Fresh baked bread is extremely popular in the wilds, and the longer one is on an outing, the better it tastes. If the bread isn't totally devoured while piping hot, it is excellent to carry for snacks or on extended trips above timberline.

Many outdoorsmen prefer whole-wheat flour for bread because of its nutritional value. White flour is often used for pizzas and pastries and in thickening sauces.

Cornmeal

Biscuits, bread, muffins, and crusts of cornmeal make a pleasant change. This versatile product can also be used for breading trout and as a hot morning cereal. Leftover cornmeal mush is delicious when cut into strips and fried in margarine.

Pasta

Macaroni, noodles, and spaghetti are staples for outdoor meals. Generally made of hard wheat, they are relatively high in protein and are not "pure starch" as many people think. They may be combined with numerous foods, and many campers even fry the evening's leftovers for a quick, hot breakfast.

Rice

White rice requires more preparation time than pasta, but it is equally versatile for use in casseroles, soups, fish patties, and so forth. Boiled rice is always good alone or when combined with dried fruit for pudding.

Brown rice takes even longer to cook; therefore, it is advisable to pre-soak it. The rice may be placed in water upon leaving camp for the day, and on one's return late in the afternoon, it will be ready to cook. It will cook a little more quickly if covered and not stirred. Because of the cooking time required, the use of brown rice is not recommended where wood is scarce or when stove fuel must be carried.

Pearl Barley

For a different flavor and texture, pearl barley is a nice substitute for pasta, rice, or potatoes and may be boiled plain for hot cereal. Like brown rice, the necessity of pre-soaking and lengthy cooking time make its inclusion in the ration supply questionable; however, a quick-cooking variety is available. Barley is an excellent addition to soups.

Cereals

Ready-to-eat cereals such as corn flakes are too bulky to carry on a backpacking trip. Cooked cereals are compact, appetizing, nutritious, and filling.

One should take a variety of these cereals to suit one's moods and avoid monotony. A small amount added to boiling water will cook quickly and may be flavored with brown sugar, margarine, milk, dried fruit, cinnamon, and so forth.

Many cooks like to add these raw cereals to flour when baking bread, cakes, and biscuits for additional protein and flavor.

Wheat Germ

This effective source of protein and other nutrients may be added to almost any dish as a food supplement. Wheat germ will not keep indefinitely like flour, but will remain stable for the length of most outings.

Popcorn

The social aspect of popping corn around a campfire makes popcorn a good item for lengthy trips. Popped corn can be carried as a snack by itself or mixed with dried fruits and nuts for trail food.

Dried Vegetables and Meat Substitutes

Freeze-dried peas, green and red peppers, mixed vegetables, chop suey, and so on lend color, taste, and eye appeal to the predominantly bland dishes made of pasta, rice, and other staples. Freeze-dried vegetables reconstitute quickly and require approximately the same cooking time as fresh produce. They are not too expensive if bought in bulk and used sparingly.

Dried onions lend zest to just about everything, from soups and casseroles to bread and potato patties. Because so much of the outdoor food is rather bland, onions are a great addition.

Dehydrated potatoes may be reconstituted in boiling water without cooking and are good alone or combined with onions, vegetables, or cheese. Mixed with flaked cooked fish, mashed potatoes may be fried as patties, or they can be added to chowder as a thickening. The short preparation time makes potatoes especially welcome in the wild outdoors.

Split peas are nutritious and flavorful but require pre-soaking and extensive cooking, so are not too practical for mountain trips unless ample rest days or semi-permanent camps are planned. Lentils require less cooking, especially if pre-soaked.

Fresh meats are inconvenient and too perishable to carry on extended trips. Ideally, the outdoorsman will have opportunities to supply protein needs with game and fish caught in the field.

Soybean products which have the texture and taste of ham and bacon are easily packed and add meat flavor to soups and many other dishes. They will usually satisfy the craving for meat that one may experience after a time. Dried meats or freeze-dried meat products are for those with unlimited budgets. In winter, fresh and pre-cooked meats will last several days without spoiling.

Fruits and Nuts

Dried fruits are especially tasty in the field and have the added advantage of being easily carried and non-perishable. They are excellent between-meal snacks and can be used in cereals, baked goods, salads, puddings, sauces, and candies.

Raisins, dried apples, peaches, pears, prunes, apricots, figs, and dates may be eaten dry or soaked before use in cooking or baking. These fruits provide an abundance of vitamins and other body builders.

Peanuts are a fine source of protein and are also popular snacks or additions to salads, cereals, and desserts. Peanut brittle is easy to make in the field for a treat. Walnuts, cashews, almonds, hazel nuts,

Brazil nuts, and sunflower seeds are other possibilities, although they are frequently more expensive than peanuts.

Shredded coconut makes an energy-giving snack, and its distinctive flavor and texture enhance curries, puddings, and other desserts.

Sweetenings and Sweets

Sugar

Many campers learn to prefer brown sugar as sweetening for cereals and beverages and even eat it plain as a between-meal snack. It is very easy to make into candy such as peanut brittle.

In the mountains, a normal person need not worry about eating too much sugar, as the natural appetite usually controls cravings to balance food intake.

Honey

There are many uses for honey. It can be spread on baked goods and cereals or used in recipes as a sugar substitute. To avoid messy accidents, carry honey in a lightweight screw-top plastic container and place that container in a plastic bag.

Puddings

Instant puddings are in abundance on grocery-store shelves, and many require only cold water for preparation. These desserts are delicious plain or with dried fruits, nuts, and coconut.

Cake Mixes

Cake mixes are available in a number of flavors and brands. Chocolate and gingerbread have been the most popular with our students. These mixes may also be used for cookies.

Beverages

Coffee

It is a good idea to include both regular and instant coffee. Besides furnishing a morning "eye opener," coffee may be used as flavoring in desserts.

Tea

Carry tea bags and instant tea crystals in a small plastic bag.

Cocoa

Cocoa is available ready-mixed, needing only the addition of hot water, or in pure form, requiring sugar and powdered milk to taste. For extra food value, margarine may be added to the hot cocoa drink. Cocoa may also be used in pastries, frostings, and candies.

Fruit Crystals

Unmixed, pure fruit crystals can be purchased from specialty stores. We add sugar to the mixture before packaging the crystals.

Other types of fruit bases for drinks are available at grocery stores. I have a personal prejudice against artificial sweeteners, so prefer those sweetened with sugar. If these are not available, flavored gelatin (Jell-O) may be substituted. It can also be used for hot beverages, salads, and desserts.

Fruit bases come in a variety of flavors and are equally refreshing served hot or cold. One can mix them with snow for "snow cones" on warm days in the snowfields or glaciers. Adults sometimes used the mixes as a base for alcoholic cocktails in the evenings.

Alcoholic Beverages

Some outdoorsmen welcome an evening drink. Liquors should be regarded as food and their calories included in the suggested allowance per day.

Glass bottles are too heavy to carry and are against the principles of conservation. Alcoholic beverages should be transferred into screw-top lightweight plastic containers.

Beer can only be taken in cans or bottles, and the empty containers must be carried out. Beer cans littered by the "green pigs" outdoorsmen will last till eternity.

Condiments and Miscellaneous

Beef and Chicken Base

Beef- and chicken-flavored bases are essential for making hot soups and flavoring main-course dishes. They are extremely salty, however, and must be used sparingly. It is wise to taste while adding the bases in small quantities.

Tomato Base

Tomato base can be reconstituted into a good tomato-juice drink and is a versatile addition to pasta, soups, and chowders. As with meat bases, it is quite salty.

Spices

Small plastic bottles with screw tops can be used for carrying spices. Selection of seasonings is an individual matter, but too often campers overlook the benefits of varied flavorings. There are certain spices that I consider essential.

Regular salt and *black pepper* are very important when so much of the outdoor diet is built around pastas, rice, and potatoes.

Rock salt is also necessary, not for flavoring but to take with drinking water to avoid dehydration and maintain the body's salt content for strength and the prevention of mountain sickness. Rock-salt crystals are less expensive than commercial salt tablets and if necessary can be used in cooking.

Garlic powder, used sparingly, adds zest to soups, pasta dishes, and potatoes.

Curry powder gives an exotic taste to rice, spaghetti, soups, and fish entrees.

Chili powder puts a little bite in soups, sauces, and pizzas.

Parsley flakes can be sprinkled in soups, casseroles, and fried dishes, and are delicious on mountain trout.

Dry mustard may be added to sauces when a delicious "hot" flavor is desired.

Oregano lends a special flavor to soups and pasta.

Cinnamon is added to baked goods, desserts, hot beverages, and cooked cereals.

Nutmeg is delicious on dried fruits, rice, in desserts, and in hot alcoholic drinks.

MPF (multi-purpose food) is a product with a soybean base. Added to cereals, breads, and pasta dishes, it provides extra protein and other nutrients. MPF is available in supermarkets.

Dry yeast must not be forgotten if the camper wishes to make bread, rolls, and such.

Vinegar and *oil* may be carried in plastic containers for salad dressing with natural greens and roots.

Natural Foods

Expeditioners should take advantage of natural foods along the way, as long as their use does not disturb the ecosystem in the specific territory. There are many publications today which provide the basic knowledge whereby one can make such judgments. Every group should carry a small handbook describing flowers and plants indigenous to the region traveled. (See Bibliography for suggested reading.)

Wild plants are not as dangerous or poisonous as is generally supposed. For instance, the death camass, a lily found commonly in the western mountains, could be easily confused with the wild onion. But should a beginner eat one by mistake, it is unlikely to be serious. One would have to eat at least a couple of pounds of death camass to be severely threatened.

Green plants can be carefully tasted with safety. If a small bite is bitter or unpalatable, it can be spit out without harmful effects. If the plant is tasty, it can be eaten in small amounts for experimental purposes.

This does not hold true in the case of mushrooms or non-green plants. Leave them alone unless you are absolutely certain that they are safe to eat.

Diet experts tell us that one needs vitamin C every day. Practical experience has shown us that persons short of this vitamin react unfavorably. The symptoms vary with the individual, but many persons lose the feeling of companionship or enjoyment of the environment. Energy is depleted. People become more self-centered and selfish, find fault with others, feel abused, or become argumentative, critical, and intolerant. More dangerous, they may become careless about their safety, sloppy in their habits.

While one might wish to carry vitamin C tablets in winter, this is not necessary in summer. Natural greens or roots are high in vitamin C. We teach our students that they must form the habit of eating some greens every day in the wild outdoors. As vitamins are more effective in uncooked plants, most of the edible varieties are sampled raw.

Some Edible Plants

Grass leaves are usually not especially palatable but may be eaten safely.

Sedge, a plant with a triangular or three-cornered stem, is found everywhere. Both the top and roots are palatable.

Bistort grows profusely in the mountain meadows. The flower, stem, and white roots below the ground are good to eat and make fine salads.

Spring beauty is one of the best foods found in the outdoors. It grows in abundance just as the spring season comes to the hills. The two-leaved plant stem and flower are not only edible, they are delicious. A bulb about the size of a fingertip grows from one to four inches underground. This crisp bulb is very tasty, somewhat similar to a new potato. All parts of the spring beauty may be eaten raw, as trail food or as a source of vitamin C. Bulbs make good additions to soups and other cooked dishes.

In the West, where sheep have grazed, the spring beauty grows large and beautiful. One can dig bucketfuls of bulbs and find on returning the next year that the supply has not been diminished. After blooming and seeding, the plants wither away, and by mid- or late summer they are no longer visible. Sometimes they are available in late summer adjacent to snowfields, however.

Elk thistle is another great plant to eat plain or as a salad ingredient. The stem, when carefully peeled, has a sweet stalk, similar to celery. The root is also edible.

Brook saxifrage grows along streams and springs. Although old leaves taste somewhat bitter, the young ones are as delicious as any lettuce. Leaves may also be cooked, but boiling destroys the vitamin C. White roots just below the surface are also palatable.

Shooting star. This beautiful flower can be eaten along with the leaves, stem, and root. Here, again, old plants are less palatable than young. When first starting to bloom, they have a pleasant, individual flavor. They may be eaten plain or in salads.

Wild onions give wonderful fresh flavoring to cooked dishes and soups and are also good in salads. There are many different varieties. Some carry quite a punch, so it is wise to taste before eating them too freely.

Mountain sorrel is a delightfully pleasing, slightly sour-tasting plant. It can be eaten as trail food in quantity and is an excellent source of vitamin C. Mountain sorrel is good raw or cooked and adds color to many dishes. This plant is found below and far above timberline, and it sometimes seeks the protection of overhanging boulders.

Bitterroot. The root of this plant is bitter when raw but is palatable when cooked. The modern outdoorsman might not want to take the trouble to collect, peel, and dry or cook the root as did the Indians and explorers on the Lewis and Clark Expedition; however, the elongated leaves are plump and delicious when young. Bitterroot has flowers similar to the spring beauty and is one of the more palatable plants.

Stonecrop is a succulent plant that grows profusely in the mountains. When young and moist, it is one of the most common and popular salad greens and is high in vitamin C content.

Dandelions grow everywhere from timberline on down into the valley. The young leaves are edible and are an easily recognizable source of vitamin C. If one can identify no other edible plant, dandelion leaves should be eaten every day.

If one plans to make salads from local greens, small screw-top plastic bottles of vinegar and oil should be carried. If an adequate supply of oil is taken, it may also be used for frying as a substitute for margarine. Dehydrated salad dressings are also available in grocery stores and make a nice change.

Wild berries can be gathered at certain times of the year. Strawberry, grouse whortleberry, thimbleberry, and raspberry are a few.

As to mushrooms, only persons who are 100 percent sure of their ability to identify the safe varieties should harvest and eat them. Although one might use some boletus and other edible mushrooms in soups, chowders, pastas, and cooked or raw by themselves, one must remember that the same region produces the destroying angel and fly agaric and other extremely dangerous varieties. One taste could be fatal.

Campfire Cookery

Chapter 6 will deal with the physical aspects of cooking, such as building the fire, organizing the fire area, care of utensils, and personal safety precautions. NOLS recipes are included in Appendix 6. Meanwhile, here are some cooking tips to keep the novice camper from starving to death.

There are three methods of cooking in the wild outdoors: boiling, frying, and baking. Boiling and frying are most common if the expedition is constantly on the move and involved in much activity. Rest days allow time for baking.

The boiling point of water drops at higher elevations. Water boils at 212 degrees Fahrenheit at sea level but falls one degree every five hundred feet above that level. Thus, in the mountains, boiling action might occur when the water is not really cooking as fast as one would expect. Therefore, preparation of coffee, cooked cereals, soups, and pastas might take a few extra minutes.

Food prepared when the water is merely simmering requires no longer cooking time. It is best to avoid cooking with vigorously boiling water, as one is apt to scorch pans and many nutrients may be boiled out of the food.

Frying should be done slowly over hot coals rather than on a blazing fire, to avoid burning. Ample margarine or oil should be used in the pan so that the contents do not stick. Teflon frying pans are recommended.

Baking on the campfire is much easier than one might think. The secret is in the coals. Have a good supply of coals, spread them evenly, and test the heat by holding the hand five to eight inches above the coals. One should feel heat but not burning, and be able to keep the hand there comfortably for several seconds.

Make an "oven" by placing a covered frying pan on the coals. Place hot coals on the lid so that heat comes from both top and bottom; add coals on top as necessary. One set of coals is usually sufficient underneath the frying pan. The lid may be inverted when baking a dish such as pizza, which will not rise a great deal.

Always grease the baking pan well before adding the dough or batter. Avoid hitting or jarring the "oven" during baking, as the cake or bread might fall.

To test if baked goods are done, push *lightly* on the top. If cake or bread springs back, poke a thin, barkless twig into the center. If it comes out clean, the baked food is done. Turn it out of the pan and place on a trivet (three small rocks) so air can circulate around it and it will not be doughy.

Altitude affects baked goods. Yeast-bread dough rises more rapidly in the mountains and should be watched carefully. Also, flour dries out faster at high elevations, so extra liquid may be needed for breads, cakes, and so on.

Once the variety of rations and simple cooking methods are understood, camp cooks should be innovative. Boiled oatmeal, boiled macaroni and cheese, boiled chicken base with vegetables for soup will provide nutrition and calories without too much trouble, but could become quite monotonous as a steady diet on an extended expedition. Don't be afraid to take chances. You might create something delicious.

5

Trail Techniques

Many outdoorsmen think that the acquisition of proper clothing, equipment, and rations is all that is needed to guarantee a perfect trip. They pay little heed to matters of the actual hike. Yet good trail techniques can make the difference between a disagreeable, dangerous outing and an enjoyable, safe wilderness experience.

Trail techniques are the means by which one prevents fatigue and avoids mistakes which might lead to survival situations. These skills involve efficient use of backpacks, group organization along the trail, conservation of energy, safe maneuvering over varied terrain, and knowing one's location and destination at all times.

Using the Backpack

Before one can intelligently organize a backpack for the day's movement, a topographical map should be consulted. (See pages 101–5 for use of these maps.) Interpretation of the selected route will give an idea of the ground to be encountered. The rougher and more varied the terrain, the more a backpacker must know about organizing packs and how to carry them with the greatest conservation of energy.

A well-organized backpack lessens the drain on one's physical resources. Hikers are able to carry extremely heavy burdens fairly comfortably if they follow certain procedures.

On a smooth trail, heavy items are kept high in the pack so that much of the weight comes straight down and is balanced over the hips. This prevents the pack from pulling back on the shoulders.

If the trail is rough or if one is going cross-country where stepping over logs or traversing steep inclines is necessary, heavier gear is lowered to the center of the pack. A high load would tend to pull the body sideways when leaning or making sudden movements.

When one is jumping from boulder to boulder or crossing steep snow slopes, weight should be at the bottom of the pack to lower the center of gravity and ease balancing and maneuvering.

No matter where the weight is placed, put heavier items as close to your back as possible. This conserves energy and aids balance.

Pack frames come in a number of sizes, generally small, medium, large, and extra large. Selecting the proper frame is vital to one's comfort and efficiency. The lower back band of the frame should rest on the upper portion of the buttocks, just below the small of the back. Higher placement results in discomfort and energy loss because the shelf of the buttocks is not taking part of the load from the shoulders. A lower position allows the band to slip downward over the buttocks and increases strain on the shoulders.

The pack should be fitted so that the shoulder straps curve over the shoulders and are fastened to the frame approximately two inches below them. A well-fitted pack enables a hiker to distribute any percentage of weight to hips and shoulders by tightening or loosening the waistband. The pack itself does not rest directly on the back, causing unnecessary strain.

The sleeping bag is generally carried in a waterproof stuff sack strapped to the lower end of the pack frame.

Sleeping bags should be unzipped and stuffed (never rolled) foot end first into the stuff sack. This allows air to escape during compression. Firmly push the sleeping bag down to the bottom and around the edges on all sides of the stuff bag. In this way, space might remain for an insulation pad, a mountain tent, a rain fly, or even extra clothing to be stuffed in the same random manner. When the sack is full, close it by pushing contents down with one fist and pull strings tight with the other hand. Tie strings and push loose ends into the bag.

An ample stuff sack is useful for longer trips because items other than the sleeping bag can be accommodated. Normally, carrying the stuff sack at the bottom of the pack frame presents no problem of balance, and if it is strapped solidly, the pack may be set down in an upright position, as well as laid down flat. This is an advantage when one lifts the load again.

To strap the stuff sack to the lower crossbars of the pack frame, lay the frame on the ground and position the sack on it. Wrap two straps around the sack and around both crossbars at the back of the frame, pull straps and buckle them on top. If necessary, apply pressure with your knee to compress the bag and pull the straps tighter. Strap ends may be tucked under the tightened strap so that they will not dangle.

Deciding where individual items go in the pack is a matter of personal preference, convenience, and weight distribution. If some things, such as maps, are put in the same place each day, one can remember their exact location for easy reference along the trail. However, a total plan whereby every item is packed in the identical place every day is not workable. This method does not allow for weight distribution, availability of gear, and other considerations.

Each day before packing, consider all equipment that might be needed en route and place it in pack pockets. For instance, rain parka, gloves, sunglasses, drinking cup, lunch snacks, and maps could go into side pockets that can be reached without opening the main section of the pack. Extra sweaters or hats might fit on top of the main section. It is always annoying to wait while someone rummages through a whole pack to retrieve something at the bottom.

Don't fill the main pack with myriad loose items. Use several nylon stuff bags and put clothes in one, toilet articles in another, food in another, cooking utensils, toilet paper, and so on in others. Smaller plastic bags with various items can be placed inside of these.

The small stuff bags can be waterproof. Some items must be protected from dampness at all costs. Food and maps should have such protection. Toilet paper can be carried in double plastic bags.

For a long expedition, the ordinary pack bag made for the "week-

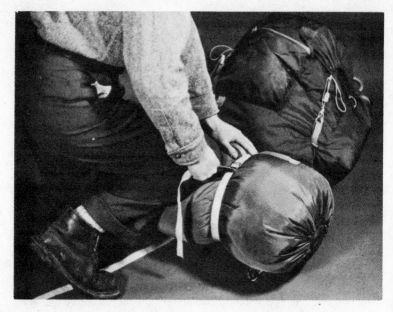

Attaching sleeping bag to pack. Knee pressure should be exerted
on the stuff bag in order to secure the straps tightly.

ender'' or overnight hiker can be grossly inadequate. There just isn't
room for everything. As a result, the expeditioner is tempted to tie
pots and pans, climbing rope, shoes, and other bulky materials to the
outside. Such practices are sloppy and time-consuming. Articles are
apt to be lost or damaged. Proper balance and weight distribution of
the pack are hard to maintain. Extra-large expedition packs made to fit
most frames are available. A hiker may remove his original bag and
replace it with the larger one for lengthy outings.

A beginner should experiment with various methods of putting on a
pack to determine which is best for his individual needs. Often the
technique will be predicated on the weight involved.

There is no set way to put on a pack. Once in South America where
we had no native help to establish base camps, I found that there was

only one way I could put on a pack weighing 150 pounds. I still use the method for heavy loads.

Place pack upright on the ground and sit down with your back to the pack and arms through shoulder straps. Adjust straps, move forward onto hands and knees with the pack on your back, and stand.

A more common way of putting on average-weight packs is to lift the pack up onto the extended right knee, place the right arm through the appropriate shoulder strap, and swing the pack around the right shoulder. The left arm is inserted in its strap after pack is in place on the back.

Packs under fifty pounds may be swung in an arc up to right shoulder where right arm is placed through its strap. The left arm is then put through its strap when pack is on the back.

Pack frames are fragile, so there is always a chance of damaging them while unloading. If the frame's corner strikes a rock or hard surface, a terrific strain is exerted on the equipment. A minute crack might develop in a welded frame and worsen with additional usage. Frames joined by plastic couplings and other methods may also be broken if heavy loads are dropped. To take off a pack, remove it from one shoulder, balance it on a bent leg, then gently swing it to the ground.

Upon arriving at a campsite, remove only items that will be needed. Lean the frame against a tree or place it carefully on the ground out of the way of fire-building or tent-pitching activities. Items to be used in camp are placed close to their area of use and other articles are stored neatly in the tent or left inside the pack. Neatness and organization are essential.

Organization of Trail Movement

Every hiking group should travel as a unit. Large parties might wish to split into individual patrols, but no one should ever hike alone. On trails where there is little chance of mishap and other people are within a reasonable distance, travel in pairs may be permissible; however, threesomes or foursomes are the recommended minimums. In the event of emergency, one person can remain with an injured companion while the others go for help.

A small party of experienced persons may be loosely structured, although every group must have a leader. A larger expedition which includes beginners must be well organized and appoint a guide, "smoother-upper," logger, and "end man," as well.

The *leader* has total responsibility and may travel anywhere he desires among the line of hikers. His main job is over-all supervision and judgment.

The *guide* sets the pace, stopping and starting the group for any purpose. He carries the map and selects trails or routes to reach a particular destination, with the assistance and supervision of the leader. The guide always travels in front.

The *"smoother-upper"* travels ten to fifteen feet behind the guide in order to observe how the guide circumvents obstacles such as boulders, fallen logs, and bushes. By such observation, he can make small improvements on the guide's route that will save energy for himself and others. In a day's time, these minor trail adjustments can add up to an important factor in energy conservation.

The *logger* keeps a record of the day's trip, including the starting hour, location and time of each major stop, lunch breaks, and so forth. The leader and guide might want to check with him to determine how closely the Time Control Plan is being followed. The logger's records become the basis for debriefing and discussion at the end of the hike. In this way, accuracy and good judgment of various plans may be assessed and the information used for planning subsequent trips.

The *"end man"* must keep in communication with the group at all times in order to provide information to leader and guide on needed stops. If someone is lagging, he must suggest slowing the pace. Under no circumstances can he allow the group to proceed and leave one person behind. There are numerous examples of persons who have been lost because the party didn't notice their absence or were too selfish to wait.

In the Smokies of Tennessee, a group of youths under adult leadership let a boy drop behind unnoticed. He was found dead two weeks later after hundreds of people had searched for him. In Colorado, a boy attending a camp separated from his patrol. He was found drowned in a stream. Even in cases not ending in tragedy, the effort and expense of massive searches are exorbitant.

The trail organization described here promotes learning and judgment. By assigning new people to the responsibilities from time to time, leadership experience and decision-making are spread among the group. Such methods also alternate the pace so that a weaker member can enjoy the expedition and stronger ones will learn consideration of others.

As mentioned before, the "smoother-upper" stays from ten to fifteen feet behind the guide, who is leading the column. This distance is necessary to provide the option of improving upon the route.

Six feet, or roughly the length of one's body, is enough space between the remaining hikers under normal conditions. Less distance will cause a follower to stop suddenly or break his pace when the person in front of him hesitates to step over logs, slows up on steep slopes, and so forth. Under such circumstances, hikers may even collide.

If an interval of six feet is standard, then one is not affected by slight speed deviations of the person in front. At times, one may fall behind as much as ten feet. Thus the line moves smoothly in a slight accordion motion and everyone is able to maintain an even pace.

Beginners have a tendency to travel too close together. Following too closely can be annoying psychologically as well as physically. The threat of being knocked down by a falling companion is almost as irritating as the reality.

If one suspects the beginning of foot trouble, it is selfish to push on without asking the group to stop so the problem may be treated. The backpacker must travel on his feet, blisters or not. An individual's discomfort could slow progress of the entire party or, in extreme cases, necessitate his evacuation.

If shoes are new or improperly broken in, they should be dipped in or filled with water and wiped out immediately before the outing. Thus, the hiker is wearing damp boots the first day, allowing them to conform to his feet. The same should be done for boots which haven't been used for a long time.

One should start a trip with wool socks that have been thoroughly rinsed of soap. Fold down the socks or wear gaiters to prevent pine needles, gravel, or other debris from entering shoes. Anyone with the slightest trace of athlete's foot must treat feet with medicated powder and be sure an adequate supply is taken on the outing.

At the first indication of a hot spot or sore on the foot, an inspection must be made. Perhaps all that is necessary is to loosen overtight laces or smooth a seam or wrinkle in the sock or boot. A blister should be covered with moleskin or similar adhesive tape.

Sometimes a person has to change his natural way of walking. Keeping feet flat will prevent the heel from rising and rubbing on the boot. One frequent cause of blisters is tensing the ankle while hiking. The shoe will generally hold in place better while traversing a hill if the ankle is relaxed and the full sole has purchase against the slope. Edging the boot will put pressure on the side and twist the foot inside the boot. Walking "duck-footed" also tends to twist the foot. Such friction under pressure causes blisters.

During the hike, special care must be taken to prevent pollution from human elimination. One must refrain from relieving oneself near rivers and lakes or in a low place where water might run after a rain and carry pullutants into the watershed. On high ground near the base of a tree or rock, urine will filter into the earth rather than flow into natural waters.

If the area has heavy use, dig a small hole and replace removed soil before leaving so that odors will not remain on the surface.

Human excrement should be buried on high ground about eight inches deep. Burn toilet paper in the hole before covering it and relandscaping with vegetation and debris. Under no circumstances may excrement be left in the open where it can attract flies and animals or wash into streams.

Conservation of Energy

There are ways to minimize the effects of unusual physical demands. One way is to keep the body's energy output as even as possible so as not to use up reserves. Most hikers breathe faster as they climb a hill, slower when they descend, harder when they carry a heavy pack, and so forth. The speed and depth of their breathing depends upon the pace and rate of energy expenditure. This becomes exhausting.

A technique to combat this problem is rhythmic breathing, in which the rate of breathing controls the speed of movement rather than the reverse. Conscious rhythmic breathing coordinated with body movements conserves much energy. The technique is easy to learn. In fact, some persons even practice it automatically, without realizing that they are doing so.

I once went hiking with a man much older than myself who set a perfect pace. I studied his breathing as we walked along the trail. He breathed evenly at all times. I asked who had taught him rhythmic breathing.

"What's that?" he replied.

I explained that I had noticed him taking two steps each time he inhaled or exhaled when on level ground.

"Well, maybe I do breathe like that," he said, "but I've never thought of it that way. I just try to set an even pace, put out about the same effort all the time, and keep my old ticker going at about the same speed. No need to race the motor at my age!"

Since then, in teaching rhythmic breathing, I've always compared the heartbeat to the rpm of a motor. If one decided in the morning what rpm to use during the day and adjusted movements within those limits, one's heart would beat at about the same rate, whether going up- or downhill. This is only possible if the breathing rhythm coincides with movements.

For example, when walking on level ground, one might take three steps with an in breath and three with an out breath. If the grade steepens a little, this does not mean that one starts puffing or that the heart begins to thump. Just shift gears. Breathing remains the same, but now two steps are taken with an in breath and two with an out breath. If the trail steepens even more, shift to one step with each inhale and one with each exhale. In this way, the heartbeat remains almost constant but the hiker slows down or speeds up according to the number of steps taken with each breath. The output of energy remains about the same.

For extremely steep terrain, high altitude, or when one is carrying a heavy pack uphill, shift to "compound low," an in-and-out breath with each step.

Rhythmic breathing conserves energy, increases endurance, sets a good pace, and discourages the run-and-stop method practiced by beginners. It also prevents fluctuation of body temperatures and heart-beat by eliminating fast starts and prolonged rests. We know that if two people of equal strength walk the same trail carrying identical packs, the one practicing rhythmic breathing will arrive at the destination less tired and in better spirits than his companion, who might even experience headache, nausea, lack of appetite, or bad disposition. The difference will be more pronounced on longer trips. Rhythmic breathing is an absolute necessity in high altitudes when one does not carry auxiliary oxygen and might risk loss of judgment, have hallucinations, or even suffer brain damage.

Pace—or the speed at which one walks—is controlled with rhythmic breathing patterns according to the rpm at which a hiker wishes to operate. Judgment as to the speed of travel and amount of energy output should be related to one's physical condition and the needs of the day. How tired can one afford to be when arriving at the campsite? Is there need to set up camp? Will climbing or prolonged hiking be scheduled for the next day or will it be a rest cycle? What are the capacities of the party's weakest member?

The slowest member of the group must be given every consideration. It is important that everyone in the party agree to this principle before undertaking the trip. If anyone *needs* to stop for rest, the group's pace is too fast. Rest stops should be necessary only to relax one's back from heavy packs, eat, drink, make clothing adjustments, or enjoy the experience by taking pictures or studying flora and fauna.

Stops should be brief. It takes more energy to get going again once one has cooled, so if longer periods are required for photography or other activities it is wise to add clothing and avoid chilling.

A large group will travel more slowly because of more frequent stops, foot checks, and clothing adjustments. The larger the party, the greater the chance will be that someone must slow up or stop temporarily. Persons from sea level or low altitudes should maintain a comfortable pace for a couple of days to allow adequate time for some acclimatization.

Expedition motives also figure in pace setting. If the purpose is a one-day hike without packs, travel could be faster because there is little weight to carry, no camp to set up, and no need to conserve strength for a hike the next day.

If there is need to become acclimated to altitudes of 14,000 feet or more, it is preferable to take it easy at the start to avoid fatigue. Perhaps members will not sleep well the first few nights away from civilization; blisters, squeak heel, or other foot problems might arise. Pushing too hard at the outset could ruin the entire outing.

People go to the outdoors for many reasons. Each purpose has its own time and energy limitations. Climbers must acclimate slowly to higher altitudes and they must save strength for the actual assault. Vacationers may desire a leisurely pace with plenty of time for fishing, flower gazing, conversation, and frequent rest stops. Photographic expeditions involve heavier packs and more stops at scenic spots along the trail, so the pace must be set with this in mind.

Assuming that adequate climatic information has already been gathered, the weather predictions must be assimilated into the Time and Energy Control Plans. If adverse weather is expected, a slower pace should be set so there is no overfatigue when the storm arrives. If temperatures are hot, danger of excessive fatigue increases and stops for water and salt tablets must be anticipated.

A reserve time margin should always be figured for the unexpected; obstacles such as boulder fields or fallen timber, or personal problems. A novice leader should be particularly cautious in allowing for all contingencies in making his first Control Plans. Only after a leader has considered all of the above information is he ready to formulate his schedule.

Eating and drinking properly are vitally related to energy conservation. One should never allow himself to get hungry or thirsty in the wild outdoors. A constant intake of food and liquids to keep the stomach working continuously and maintain energy reserves is extremely important. Several small meals are preferable to large, regular ones.

Generally in the mountains, it is best to eat and drink as often as one wants. Carry trail food and a canteen of water when hiking, and have a snack ready in case you wake up hungry in the night. This will prevent morning chill and store energy.

Many people fear that this unstructured eating program will cause them to gain weight. Hikers often maintain their normal or reducing diets on the trip, only to find themselves weakened with increased activity. There is little chance of gaining weight on a backpacking trip. In fact, it is the best and safest way I know to lose pounds. At NOLS, we have had persons experiencing beneficial weight losses of thirty or forty pounds in thirty-five days while eating all they wanted of any food, day or night. One very overweight boy lost seventy-five pounds on a five-week course. At our graduation banquet, he demonstrated this loss by tightening his belt and throwing the excess end over his shoulder.

Dehydration is a danger at high altitude. Lack of body moisture can cause weakness, frostbite, or mountain sickness with its symptomatic dizziness, blurred vision, lack of equilibrium, headache, nausea, and stomach pains.

The body must be well supplied with liquids, salt, and solid food, but no ordinary diet provides enough salt to supply the needs of a hiker or backpacker. Even though one may not be perspiring profusely, moisture is lost when hiking, and in high altitudes, where one breathes faster in the thin, dry air, more moisture is lost with every exhalation.

Also, evaporation is faster at high altitudes because there is less air pressure. One might be conscious of losing moisture through perspiration at low elevations, but evaporation is so fast at greater heights that it is less easily detected and the drain on body fluids might go unnoticed until it is too late to avoid dehydration.

When it is cold or windy, the body utilizes extra energy. Heat is transferred to the extremities through the bloodstream, but if the system becomes dehydrated, the volume of blood and heat is diverted to the vital, internal organs and as a result it is decreased in hands and feet which become candidates for frostbite. In the Himalayas, climbers developed frostbitten feet even in their sleeping bags, probably because of dehydration.

We were the first to develop a "salt cure" for mountaineers as a means of preventing dehydration and maintaining a normal saline solution in the blood. Our system involves using extra salt in food, drinking liquids frequently, and taking salt tablets or rock-salt crystals with approximately each pint of water consumed. This helps prevent fatigue, sore muscles, cramps, frostbite, and mountain sickness.

Avoid becoming too hot or cold in the wild outdoors. Sweating or chilling drains energy. Proper use of clothing can prevent either extreme. We tell our students, "If you're not comfortable, you're not dressed right."

Assuming that one has packed the required apparel, judgment must dictate the efficient use of it. Clothing should be adjusted as often as necessary to keep comfortably warm.

Sometimes hikes are started in cool morning hours when it is obvious that temperatures will rise shortly. It is better to begin with an extra sweater and stop to remove it a few minutes later than to set out feeling chilled.

On the other hand, it is unwise to overdress. Excessive perspiration may dampen clothes as much as actual precipitation. Waterproof parkas may cause the body and clothing to become damp and chilled by condensation.

Often in the mountains a cloud moving in front of the sun can mean a terrific drop in temperature. A hiker suddenly coming up over the top of a ridge from the calm lee side and facing a stiff gale can be chilled in a few minutes. One must keep taking off and putting on clothing as one is subjected to these sudden changes. In some cases, buttoning or zipping of clothing might suffice. Adjustments should be made before chilling or overheating take place; there is a tendency for the unschooled outdoorsman to wait until he is forced to do so by discomfort.

In camp, when activities are less demanding, more clothes are needed. But remember, wearing a waterproof parka in these conditions will only result in lack of ventilation and chilling.

Tight clothing prevents air circulation necessary to allow body moisture to escape and uses up valuable energy because muscles are forced to work against restrictions. If trousers bind around legs and knees, exertion will be expended with each step. A day of hiking under such conditions could be equivalent to an extra mile of travel.

Clothing with elasticized bands that restrict the flow of blood can trigger frostbite in cold weather.

Maneuvering over Varied Terrain

There is more to mountain walking than putting one foot in front of the other. One moves differently on the trail than in the city, where one springs up on the foot and calf muscles are brought into play. The slower hiking pace does not require this. Using the calf muscles is fatiguing. One should walk flat-footed and employ the large thigh muscle for propulsion instead.

Avoid long steps when going uphill. It takes far less energy to gain one foot of elevation with two steps than with a single stride. Take an ordinary staircase, for example. It is quite easy to ascend one step at a time, but if two steps are spanned, the forward knee is so far advanced that the lower foot must exert greater energy to combat the lack of leverage.

One can waste energy by stepping up and down on logs, rocks, or slight rises in the trail instead of stepping over or around them. To step up, then down, could add several hundred feet of elevation to a day's hike.

Violent movements to regain balance also waste energy. To maintain balance when going down a steep hill or slippery surface, lean forward. Do not stand up straight. If one slips when erect, the body is thrown back beyond the center of gravity and recovery is impossible. By leaning forward, one is thrown into an upright position and is able to avoid falling.

Stand erect when going uphill. If balance is lost, the body will be thrown forward but not so far as to cause a fall.

When traversing a slope, drop the downhill shoulder and lean slightly out and downhill. A slip will throw the body uphill into an upright position. Standing straight in this case will force the body beyond the center of gravity and necessitate violent balancing movements. Naturally, leaning toward the slope will compound the problem and the feet will be pushed down and out from under the hiker.

At the base of steep pitches or on the approach to the moraines of glaciers, one often encounters boulder fields. If one cannot jump from boulder to boulder and still maintain balance, the time it takes to cross the area could be doubled.

In walking over boulders, use eye judgment in planning the route two or three steps ahead. Ride the boulders high; that is, choose the highest boulder and the highest part of each boulder. In this way, feet move freely from high point to high point rather than circumventing them to reach lower spots.

The larger the rock, the heavier it will be and the less one's weight will affect it. Small boulders tend to overturn if you step on the downhill side. Step on the uphill side for safety.

When fording rivers and streams, the pack should be in its normal position, but with the waistband unfastened. The fairly heavy pack will help keep feet firmly planted on the river bottom. In case of a fall, the pack can easily be removed so that its weight will not hold the bearer under water.

A balancing stick several feet long is sometimes handy for river crossings. Face upstream, placing the pole into the river bottom while moving sideways. The current will move against the pole and keep it firmly anchored. This poling technique is useful in strong currents, but not advisable in potentially dangerous situations, i.e., where rapids are involved. River crossings requiring mountaineering equipment and techniques will be treated in Chapter 9, pages 190–92.

Except in instances where soft, sandy bottoms are assured, boots should be worn when crossing rivers. Even smooth or dull-edged rocks can cut when bare feet slide over them. It is easy to bruise ankles, pull ligaments on toes, or tear off toenails. Icy mountain water can deaden feeling in feet and one might not be aware of an injury until reaching the opposite bank.

Mountain boots are best to wear during river crossings. Sneakers are preferable to bare feet but do not prevent bruises. Remove socks before crossing and lace boots firmly. I have seen waders step completely out of loosely laced boots and lose them. In one case, the expedition had to wait while runners went for replacements.

As boots are already wet after a crossing, it is a good opportunity to wash óut the insides and free them from grime. One might want to wipe the insides dry with a handkerchief or sock top. Getting boots

River crossing using ice axe as a "third leg." Backpackers are facing into the current, and have detached waist belts from their packs, so that they can be abandoned quickly in the event of a fall.

wet does not hurt them if they are dried properly. (See Chapter 2, pages 48–49.)

In glacial streams or extremely cold waters, I prefer to wear wool socks while wading and change to dry stockings afterward. In water only a few degrees above freezing, feet will numb quickly and a strong current is apt to fill the shoe with gravel. Wool socks will protect against excessive cold and sharp debris.

Most river rocks are worn smooth and are extremely slippery, especially if covered with slime or moss. Rubber-cleated mountain boots do not cling well to such rocks. One must be careful to place a foot securely on the rock before shifting one's weight to it.

Crossing a stream by jumping from rock to rock above the water can be treacherous, since these rocks may be waterworn to the smoothness of glass and be coated with slime. Long, uncontrolled jumps must be avoided.

Fallen trees often serve as bridges. Whenever possible, select a dry log; rubber-cleated boots will not give purchase on a wet surface, and it is virtually impossible to cross water-splashed logs without falling. Keep eyes steadily on the log. Allowing eyes to focus temporarily on moving water underneath will hinder balance. It might seem that the water is still and the log itself is moving.

The Topographical Map

Topographical maps graphically represent the exact configurations of an area. By studying a "topo" map, hikers can determine if a proposed route is up- or downhill and identify any trails, roads, streams, glaciers, or other natural features that will be encountered.

I advise beginners to learn to interpret a topographical map before actually going into the hills. Maps are available from several sources. National Park Service, Forest Service, or Bureau of Land Management headquarters usually carry them for regions within their jurisdiction, and sometimes maps are available from such outlets as sporting-goods stores or bookstores. The best source is the U.S. Geological Survey. Maps can be ordered by mail from the U.S. Geological Survey at the following addresses:

1028 G.S.A. Building
18th and F Streets, N.W.
Washington, D.C. 20242

345 Middlefield Road
Menlo Park, California 91025

Denver Federal Center, Building 41
Denver, Colorado 80225

8102 Federal Office Building
125 South State
Salt Lake City, Utah 84111

On request, the Geological Survey will send an index map of the state in question which will identify regions covered by individual maps and facilitate ordering them. A guide to topographical map symbols is also available, and is essential for beginners.

Post–World War II topographical maps issued by the U.S. Department of the Interior Geological Survey are extremely accurate, since they are based upon aerial photographs and show every stream, ridge, and lake in exact position. Older maps are also usable because natural features remain unchanged, but new roads, trails, dams, and so on might not be included.

There are only a few things one needs to know about a map to keep from getting lost. The following is a simplified teaching procedure we have developed for the "must-knows" of interpreting a topo map—understanding the symbols and having the ability to measure horizontal distances by the scale on the map and vertical elevations by the contours.

Orient the map so that the top points toward the actual north of your present location.

Consult the mileage scale at the bottom of the map. Mark the distance of one mile on a piece of paper or break a matchstick to the exact length. This measuring device can then be used to determine linear miles of an imagined route. Measure one mile at a time, turning the measurer to conform to the general direction of the trail. This will give the approximate mileage.

To measure vertical elevation on a topo map, study the brown wavy lines called contour lines, which connect points on the land surface

Map reading. Rocks have been used as anchors, to prevent movement when maps are oriented toward the north.

that have the same elevation. The footage between contour lines is called the contour interval. A scale at the bottom of the map will indicate the number of vertical feet between contours.

This information gives a basis for judgment in many ways. If you are hiking upriver one mile, an additional five hundred feet in elevation requires extra energy comparable to that used in climbing a fifty-story building or walking two level miles. Walking downhill is no less tiring. It takes energy to hold the body back, too, so the elevation lost should not be regarded as a gain. The distance, with regard to expenditure of energy, remains a full mile.

The amount of time one needs to traverse a certain area can also be estimated through interpretation of a topo map. Without stopping, a fast walker can travel three horizontal miles an hour on smooth, level road, but in the hills on good trails, one should not expect to make more than two miles an hour. When carrying heavy packs, stopping for blister control, clothing adjustments, and short rests, a mile an hour is a reasonable pace. Trailless cross-country travel can take from two miles an hour to ten hours for the first mile. When contour lines on a topo map are very close together, the terrain is extremely steep. Generally speaking, anything approaching equal distance vertically for equal distance horizontally takes mountain-climbing technique to negotiate.

I know of one trail sign that used to read, "Surprise Lake, 6 miles." Many an unsuspecting tourist thought he could reach the lake in two hours, but was not halfway there three hours later because the sign failed to say, "Surprise Lake, 6 miles horizontal distance and 3,000 feet straight up." This hike is equal to twelve miles on the level.

Notice that all contour lines crossing a stream form a V. The point of the V always points upstream. Because of this, we can look at any stream and know which way it is flowing. In studying a lake, we can tell where the stream enters and leaves since the V points upstream.

There is an easy way of demonstrating this principle. Open up a book part way, set it on a table, and slant it so that water would run down the middle and toward you. The crease represents a stream bed, the side of the book the valley walls.

Draw a line from the stream to each side, making the lines an equal elevation above the table. You can see why these lines of the same elevation make a V pointing uphill.

Then can we assume that all V-shaped contour lines indicate upstream and uphill? No. This is one of the points of confusion for novice map readers, but the explanation is simple.

Open the book part way, turn it upside down so that the spine is on top, and slant it toward you. The book could then represent the ridge of a hill or mountain.

Draw a line from the top of the ridge toward the book's edge, again keeping it at the same elevation above the table. Do the same on the opposite side. We have another V-shaped contour line, but this one points downhill. Thus, contours on ridges point downhill and those in valleys or along streams point uphill.

Even when streams are not present, it is easy to tell in which direction a contour points. On the map, find a mountain or hilltop. Notice that the summit will be shown by a contour line making a complete circle. You are looking at the map in the same way you would see a peak from an airplane 30,000 feet high. Notice that the sides of the peak contain contour lines with slight Vs pointing away from the top. These are ridges of the mountain. Between these ridges, there are Vs pointing toward the top of the peak. These indicate the valleys.

When one has learned to recognize natural features on a topographical map, it is possible to orient oneself without a compass. In the field, if one matches an actual mountain peak or lake to its configuration on the map, all one has to do is place the map in the same position and the top will point north automatically.

However, if one is unskilled in map reading or forgets to keep track of where he is on the map, a compass is useful. A compass can be indispensable when the terrain is obliterated by fog, snowstorms, or in flat, timbered country where no hills or landmarks are visible.

The needle of a compass does not point toward the true north but rather is drawn toward the magnetic field located near, not at, the North Pole. At the bottom of a topo map, two lines point toward true north and magnetic north, which is at an angle. The latter matches with the compass needle. The variation between true and magnetic north differs from region to region, so the map shows the angle in the location involved. This angle is measured by degrees; thus, if the scale is marked 17 degrees, you know that your compass needle would point 17 degrees from true north.

It should be mentioned that the proximity of metal objects can interfere with the accuracy of a compass needle. One must be careful to avoid having a knife, ice axe, or other metal equipment nearby.

Because continual use of topographical maps minimizes the necessity of a compass, I do not consider further information on compass reading among the "must-knows" included in this book. More detailed reference works are listed in the Bibliography.

6

Camping for Conservation

Camping is an art. When practiced correctly, it provides pleasure and comfort in the most primitive surroundings. Over the years, good campers have concentrated on devising short cuts and labor-saving methods to increase personal enjoyment and insure greater protection of themselves and their equipment. Manufacturers have developed sophisticated, lightweight gear. But only recently has emphasis been placed on ways to protect the environment, an increasingly vital issue which is inseparable from the art of camping.

Our wilderness needs protection from lovers of the outdoors. Wild areas are being destroyed by the very persons who use them and have fought for their preservation—nature lovers, hunters, fishermen, mountaineers, bird watchers, outfitters, horsemen, dude ranchers, church groups, youth organizations, and all others who venture in the wild outdoors but have not yet learned how to conserve.

Imagine a lake in the heart of a mountain range. This lake is primitive, unspoiled, untouched. No man has camped on its shores. The water is rimmed by pines. Mountains and glaciers are reflected in its depths. There are fields of flowers and tall grass waving in the breeze. Here is an outstanding beauty spot. The wilderness.

Now comes the nature lover, the hunter, fisherman, mountaineer, or hiker. He does the natural thing—the thing that most everybody does—he camps on the shores of this untouched lake, where breathtaking scenery can be viewed from his very own campfire. Here is water handy for cooking, bathing, washing, and watering pack animals. Here is fishing, ten steps from the frying pan. Here are dead, silhouetted trees ready to be chopped down for firewood, meadows of grass and flowers which will make good feed for horses.

After a few days' vacation, our sojourner returns to civilization. What has he left? Fire scars along the lake shore, grasses trampled by horse hoofs, a campsite worked into dust, depleted vegetation with permanently injured roots. Trenches that he has dug around his tent leave ugly scars. Trees whose roots are exposed by the restless pawing of horses face a slow death. In the shallows along the lake shore are bits of food from dishwashing, where not only grease and leftovers but soap and detergent pollute pure mountain water. Flies swarm over a deserted garbage dump and piles of human excrement can be found behind bushes and rocks, ready to be washed into lake and streams at the first heavy rain.

And this was a good camper. Magnify this by ten camping parties, a hundred, a thousand. What do you have? A beautiful lake ruined.

The wilderness can be traveled without harm. There are ways to camp without destroying natural beauty. We now have proved methods of taking groups through the wild outdoors without harm to the ecosystem. Camping with techniques of practical conservation is the answer.

There is no excuse for a camper to litter. Regulations of most regions request that non-disposable containers be carried out, but, unfortunately, this is like ordering the waves to stop. While most commercial packers, dude ranchers, and outfitters do bring out their debris, too many outdoorsmen do not. More often, they bury cans and glass to be dug up later by wild animals: they throw aluminum foil into fires, where it is invisible under coals until exposed by wind or rain and blown around the abandoned camp like confetti. Even foil wrappers on gum, candy, and cigarettes remain after being burned.

One should avoid buying brands of outdoor food wrapped in foil that cannot be repackaged in plastic bags before the outing. The best solution is to leave non-disposable materials at home.

Cigarette filters will last years, so they should be broken open and thrown into a hot fire where most of them will disintegrate. It is a good idea to check the brand before the trip to be sure this is possible. Plastic cigar butts are virtually indestructible in the outdoor environment and should be carried out.

Pull tops from beer and soft-drink containers are often found in streams and along trails. If you feel these drinks are necessary, an easy way to dispose of such tabs is to drop them into the can after opening. The small pieces of metal will not fall out while one is drinking, and they can be carried out of the hills with the container.

Increased use of the wild outdoors also threatens serious damage to ground cover, especially in those areas most frequently visited. When one walks on a meadow, grass and wild flowers are crushed. Horses trample foliage, and eat it as well. This is a natural use of the environment, but a good camper will take care not to inflict damage that will take more than a year to recover. Thus, if we let our horse eat the vegetation, we should be sure that he grazes lightly in several areas so that when we return next year, after winter snows and spring showers, the grass will be replaced.

If we temporarily crush plants under our sleeping bags or step on them as we walk, we should be certain that the injury is not irreparable and that by the same time next year there will be no sign of our passing.

There are ways to lessen the destructive power of horses in the wilderness. Horse travel might eventually have to be drastically regulated. Even now, their numbers and the weight they carry should be limited. Skillful camping procedures and use of lightweight, modern equipment enable one horse to carry all gear and food for two persons on a two-week vacation, instead of the two or three horses per person formerly used by old-fashioned outfitters. (Horse packing will be discussed later in this chapter.)

When and Where to Camp

Beginners often wait too long to make camp. Perhaps their final destination is at a great distance and they want to travel as far as possible each day. Nevertheless, selecting a campsite and attempting to pitch tents or cook by campfire when one is overtired and pressed for time usually results in a sloppy, unsatisfactory performance. It might save time in the long run to extend the trip an extra day.

Few persons can make camp after dark without danger of fatigue, irritability, accidents, or environmental damage. A leader must assess his party's energy ratio and ability when he makes a Time Control Plan. Whenever possible, it is preferable to camp early, before exhaustion sets in and while there is still daylight.

This advice is increasingly important when traveling in crowded areas or where good camping spots are hard to come by, in rocky terrain or areas distant from water. Then it is wise to be an opportunist. Stop traveling even if a few hours of hiking time remain; a good site is half the battle.

To most campers, a wilderness experience includes being alone with one's group and away from hordes of other people. Therefore, the educated outdoorsman will plan his trip accordingly.

This means that camp is off the trail, far enough away so as not to be seen or heard by others. It is human nature to choose a campground for its aesthetic qualities. This is fine so long as conservation is kept in mind, but beauty is everywhere in the wilds, not just on lake shores or riverbanks, along trails, and in other scenic spots. One comes to a lake to fish, stroll, or silently commune with nature. One does not wish to hear the noise of a camp there or see the scars of one abandoned. Camp away from the lakes so they can be visited in their natural beauty.

If the campsite must be off trails and away from lake shores, where might one camp? Between the trails, off the beaten track, there are great expanses of forest, small streams, springs, and meadows where one can have a secluded wilderness experience without causing damage. Is it not better to walk half a mile to fish where flowers perfume the air, trees grow undamaged, and natural debris rustles underfoot?

Another important consideration in selecting a campsite is safety. Never camp at the foot of a cliff or other sheer escarpment where falling rocks might be a hazard. Look to the treetops to be sure that a dead tree could not be dislodged and tumble in heavy wind. Check the ground for unexpected roots that could be tripped over, and see that no eye-level twigs spear into areas of activity.

Seek shelter from the elements. Try to determine the direction of prevailing winds and avoid them. Don't camp in dry washes or barren riverbeds. Stories are legion about sudden mountain storms that turn channels into flash floods in a matter of minutes.

Although the campsite should be away from lakes and rivers, it is well to have a water supply within reasonable walking distance. One can conveniently pack a light, collapsible plastic container which can be filled with several gallons of water and carried back to camp.

Proximity to firewood is essential. Tinder may generally be obtained from dead twigs and limbs lying on the ground. It is destructive to break off branches of trees or scar the forest with unnecessary axe marks. If gasoline stoves are used, settling near a supply of firewood is not essential. (Camp stoves will be discussed in Chapter 11, page 211.)

The Latrine

A camper has no more right to pollute mountain waters with bacteria from his own elimination than a factory has to dump deadly mercury into the rivers. No one should venture into the wild outdoors without a means of burying human waste and the knowledge of how and where to bury it.

Digging a latrine is one of the first orders of making camp. Latrines are situated on high ground where rain water soaking down will be filtered before joining a spring or stream below. This means that no slit trenches or individual holes should be dug in low places or near swamps, rivers, lakes, or other bodies of water.

The hole must be eight to fourteen inches deep, so that bacteria may convert the feces into soil. If buried too deep, bacterial action will be retarded, and if too shallow, excrement might be dug up by small animals.

Care must be taken with toilet tissue, as well. If there is no danger of fire, the paper should be burned in the latrine before being covered with soil.

The shovel used for digging latrines should be placed nearby, and dirt sprinkled into the hole after each use, to avoid attracting flies and insects. Upon breaking camp, the area must be completely filled with soil and turf; litter, rocks, and other natural features should be replaced. In emergency, a makeshift latrine may be improvised by overturning a large rock and using the depression, but this should be done only in the absence of a latrine. Be sure to replace the rock in its natural setting.

The Camping Fire

Before starting on an expedition, check local rules and regulations concerning fire building. This information may be obtained through the U.S. Forest Service, U.S. National Park Service, or other administrative body. If a fire permit is necessary, carry it at all times. The U.S. Forest Service now charges a person the expense of putting out a blaze he has started. Proven guilt could cost an offender his life savings.

If it has not rained for some time, is dry, hot, or the air has little moisture, be especially careful in selecting sites for fires. Damp ground and high humidity provide less threat.

Recognizing the difference between litter, duff, and mineral soil is an absolute must for all campers.

Litter is material such as pine needles, pine cones, leaves, dead grass, small twigs, and burnable, visible debris found on the ground.

Duff lies under the litter and to a "greenhorn" might look like good, rich soil. A closer inspection will generally show that it is composed of minute particles of decayed or partially decayed organic matter; i.e., litter that has turned to duff. Duff burns like a cube of incense—slow but sure—and many a forest fire has been triggered by a smoldering bit of duff days after the fire maker has left.

Mineral soil is the real soil of sand, gravel, and dirt. It will not burn and therefore is the only place to build a fire. However, make sure there are no dead roots running underneath or near the firesite. These, too, may smolder underground like duff and start a forest fire later.

Do not dig firepits on slick, sloping ground where someone might slip and fall into the fire. Pick up large pieces of debris and clear a ring at least seven feet around the location selected. Extra wood may be dumped several feet fron the firesite, and cooking and eating utensils stacked in another place. Keep the mixing and food-preparation area approximately six feet away from the flames. A large rock used as a counter top here minimizes stooping. If possible, select a site with boulders or fallen logs to sit on during meals and while socializing. If logs and stumps must be carried to the area, return them to their natural setting before leaving.

Nearly everyone who backpacks carries lightweight nylon tents or shelters. Sparks landing on nylon burn very small holes, unnoticeable, perhaps, until the next rain, when one finds the coated nylon is leaking. Therefore, fires must be built at least thirty or forty feet from the tents to be comparatively safe. If the tent is down-wind or if too much wood is put on the fire, the nylon will be in additional danger. Sudden, shifting gusts of wind must also be anticipated.

In digging a firepit, use a small shovel to prepare a hole in the mineral soil about eighteen inches wide and twenty-four inches long. If there is grass or vegetation, carefully remove it in small clumps, trying to leave soil in the roots, so that all vegetation can be replanted in its original position upon breaking camp. Dirt, sod, gravel, and rocks to be replaced may be piled several feet away from the firepit.

The pit need only be eight to twelve inches deep. Dig one end a few inches deeper for disposal of excess food and dirty water.

Make a little cushion of sticks and/or litter on the bottom of the pit. This slight insulation under the starting fire will keep cold ground or rock from drawing heat downward. In this way, the first flames will use all of their energy in spreading the fire upward.

Gather several handfuls of pencil-sized debris for feeding the fire, put it within reach of the pit, then collect some fine, burnable litter— match-sized sticks, dead grass, dry pine needles, pieces of pitch or bark—and place in a pile on top of the insulation material. Try to leave a hole or space underneath to insert a match.

There is nothing wrong with using toilet paper or other material to start a fire, but one should not rely upon it. Pitch oozing from the bark of pine trees is an excellent fire starter, and forest floors abound with litter. Match-sized twigs may be broken from trees without defacing them.

After the litter is well started, add pencil-sized sticks, one by one and not too fast, since each new piece will absorb heat before it starts to burn and too many might extinguish the starting flame.

When the pencil-sized sticks catch fire gather larger pieces of wood. Add enough to make a bed of coals as the wood burns down. Start with a small flame and feed it gradually. With patience, a fire is generally possible under any conditions.

Burn only debris that can be found on the ground. After the fire is started, almost anything organic will burn, such as sticks, half-rotten logs, old roots, and litter of all kinds. No matter how generous the nearby wood supply, use it sparingly.

Be prepared for unexpected storms in the mountains. Dry wood can be thoroughly soaked overnight, so put some dry twigs in a plastic bag, even on a starry night. If twigs are already wet, they can be dried in a pan over the fire for use the following day.

As the fire stabilizes, try to keep flames at one end of the pit so that coals may be raked toward the opposite end. This provides a choice of flames or coals for cooking and baking. Usually an ample bed of coals provides the best cook fire, as open flames are too hot and tend to burn food or blacken oils used in cooking.

Care must be exercised in placing cooking pots directly on logs that might shift and topple their contents. In fact, a camper is on constant duty when he is chef. A fire, no matter how small, must never be left unattended for more than a few minutes.

Too much activity around the campfire can cause damage to vegetation and root structure. Clean water poured on the outside edges of the pit from time to time will prevent the area from becoming too hot and dry and damaging nearby plants.

Waste food and dirty water can be disposed of in the firepit's deeper end, where the solids will be burned during future cooking. If there is so much liquid that the fire might be extinguished, a small sump hole can be dug nearby. (See page 118.) These methods of waste disposal will not attract flies, and refuse will be burned or absorbed into the soil.

Campers tend to dry shoes and clothing around fires. Leather is easily ruined by such practices; therefore, shoes are best left damp. Wool placed too close to the heat might burn, and nylon apparel melts easily and is subject to sparks.

The last cooking fire in the pit should be made of small pieces of burnable material so that a minimum of ashes and coals will be left after the final meal. Stir these remaining coals to give them a chance to burn out, and let the fire smolder to the last possible moment before dousing it generously with water. A great amount of water is necessary to be sure that coals are completely out and to cool off and remoisten the ground underneath and around the pit.

Some burned ashes and soggy, water-soaked coals may remain forever in the bottom of the pit, but excessive material must be removed to permit regrowth of vegetation. Ashes and coals may be disposed of in the following ways:

1. They may be buried in a separate place.
2. In western pine forests, where there are always indigenous coals visible from years-old fires, coals and ashes (if completely out and dead) may be scattered in the grass, where they become part of the natural surroundings.

Soil or sod originally taken from the pit must be carefully replaced. Then sprinkle soil in cracks and holes to bring everything back to ground level. Pour additional water over the top to give disturbed vegetation an extra boost, scatter some natural litter and debris over the whole area, and put anything previously removed from the seven-foot circle back into its original setting.

If more firewood has been gathered than was needed, do not leave the pile intact. Scatter the wood before leaving camp.

The small pit fire described above is not very useful for warming, and is certainly not suitable for huge bonfire gatherings of large groups. But if one is properly dressed, warming fires are not necessary, and no one has the right to build a fire that leaves a scar many feet in diameter and visible for a lifetime.

There are other methods of making a fire without leaving scars or destroying the ecosystem. About three inches of mineral soil placed on a flat rock will provide a safe base for a campfire. With careful handling, the rock underneath the mineral soil will not be blackened or exfoliated, and even colorful lichen on its surface will not be destroyed.

Upon deserting the campsite, remaining ashes may be scattered or buried and the mineral soil returned to the ground before rinsing the rock with water.

There might be emergencies when a somewhat larger fire is needed for warmth or survival. Build it a short distance away from a large reflecting rock. In this way, a person between the fire and the rock will derive heat from both sides, and there will be no ecological damage to the boulder. A fire built directly against the rock not only harms its surface but restricts the camper's warmth to a single direction.

If one camps at timberline or where wood is scarce, a mountain stove with fuel may be necessary. For brief overnight trips in such places, food cooked at a lower camp where timber was plentiful can be packed and eaten cold.

The Cooking Area

We have stressed that food preparation must take place at least six feet away from the firepit. Accident prevention is important in the cooking area. Hot cookware should be handled with cotton gloves and sturdy pot grips. Remove pans or billy cans from the fire before adding ingredients, and never pass pots of hot food over other persons. Cut bread and solids on a hard surface such as a log, not against the body.

Use only what is needed in preparing a particular meal. After each ingredient is selected and measured, retie its plastic bag and replace it in the larger nylon sack.

When students learn that we advocate not using *any* soap or detergent for dishwashing in the wild outdoors, they often worry about sanitation and illness. Strict adherence to our NOLS methods makes this unlikely. While there have been isolated cases of upsets to individuals who have been careless about sanitation, we have never had an outbreak of illness or diarrhea in one of our courses. This is unusual in group camping, as stomach ills generally affect an entire party.

One's own germs rarely make one sick, although they might affect others. Develop the habit of washing hands after eliminating and before handling food. Keep fingernails short and clean. Pick up cups by the handle, not the lip, and refrain from using someone else's dishes or spoons.

In the wilderness, it is impossible to keep eating and cooking utensils so sterile between meals or on the trail that some bacterial action does not occur. Traces of grease or food particles always remain, and millions of germs may develop during the heat of the day. It is senseless to worry about this. Instead, after meals wash the dishes tolerably clean, and wait until *before* the next meal to sterilize. Do not wash dishes in or adjacent to streams, lakes, or other natural water sources.

Sterilize cups, bowls, cutlery, and pans by immersing them in boiling water. If there are any remains from the previous meal, remove them before rinsing or after the first dipping and then dip again. Cooking pots will be sterilized by the boiling. Metal spoons may also be sterilized by holding over an open flame, but let them cool before using.

Macaroni and cheese and many other favorite campfire dishes may stick to pots like glue. Attempting to wash them with hot water only compounds the problem. Instead, fill the pots with cold water and let them stand for several hours or overnight. The "paste" will come off the sides and bottom, or be easily coaxed.

Many beginners instinctively bang their pots against rocks to remove food particles. Since most outdoor cookware is made from thin metal, this often causes dents which not only harm expensive merchandise but make it more difficult to clean.

When billy cans are used for cooking, seams on the interior bottom may be cleaned by running a sharp twig around them.

Grease and other remains in a frying pan are eliminated by covering the bottom of the pan with water, placing it over hot flames or coals, and allowing it to boil vigorously. Swish the water around and scrape the pan with a stick. The dirty water can be carefully poured into the deep end of the fire pit or the sump hole.

Natural debris is an ideal substitute for scouring pads. It is almost always possible to secure small ends of live pine boughs, pine cones, grass, gravel, or sand for cleaning cooking utensils. Exercise care and judgment in securing live boughs, and dispose of them in the sump hole or fire after dishwashing. Many household scouring pads contain chemicals, soaps, or detergents that not only pollute lakes and streams but could contribute to diarrhea and stomach illness. Pads devoid of these additives are also not advocated, as they become messy and form breeding grounds for bacteria. In addition, most pads are not burnable or biodegradable, so must be packed out of the mountains.

Remember to remove dry pots from the fire. They can be completely destroyed in a matter of minutes.

The Sump Hole

There are times when a sump hole is necessary. If excessive water has been used for dishwashing or there is an abundance of garbage, for instance, it is well to have a special place for disposal. Keep in mind that waste should be burned whenever possible, as animals sometimes dig up sump holes.

A hole ten to twelve inches deep and about one foot wide is dug approximately ten feet from the cooking area. The process of digging, refilling, and relandscaping the site is the same as for the campfire pit. If a large hole is not needed, a good-sized rock may be toppled and its cavity used as a sump. The rock should be rolled back into its original place upon breaking camp.

Pitching the Tent

A camper should know his equipment before starting a trip. Never take off with a new tent without getting complete manufacturer's instructions. Set up the tent at least once at home to be sure you can do it quickly, and ascertain that there are no missing parts or damaged merchandise.

While the art of making lean-to shelters from trees and limbs or soft beds of pine boughs may appear in old-fashioned camping manuals or survival books, no one has the right now, or in the future, to indulge in such destructive practices. One might argue that these skills are valuable in emergency situations, but the best survival technique is to *avoid* survival situations through proper Time, Climate, and Energy Control Plans.

There are many styles of outdoor tents and shelters, but those most generally carried beyond the roadhead are the two-man mountain tent, or a rain fly that gives protection only from above.

When using a waterproof nylon fly strung between trees, one needs only enough flat space underneath for a comfortable sleeping surface. Part of the ground can be rocky or brush covered.

Obviously, for a tent one must select a fairly large flat area. The waterproof floor should not rest on sharp rocks or sticks that might puncture it. (After some use, the floor will unavoidably develop some pin-point holes that will admit running water, but ground moisture will be eliminated.)

Unlike the fire, which is placed well away from duff and burnable trees, a shelter can be pitched on soft duff in thick timber, protected from wind and rain. Some leveling of the duff will not harm the ecosystem. Sticks, small logs, and debris may be removed from under the tent site and the soil may be leveled if plant roots are not destroyed. Of course, one has the moral responsibility of relandscaping the setting in a natural manner upon departing.

Wind is often a problem in the mountains. Sudden gusts of great force may come up unexpectedly. This dictates care in the placing of tents.

Shelters, especially those of nylon, should be placed thirty to forty feet away from the campfire to avoid sparks, and should be up-wind from the firepit, if possible.

Most tents have small tabs at strategic places to accommodate supports. These tabs are apt to be torn off by continual flapping in high winds. There will be less flapping if the back of the tent, rather than the side, faces the prevailing wind. The entrance is down-wind.

Stakes should never be driven through tabs directly into the soil, as this pulls the fabric too close to the ground and might injure it. It is better to tie short pieces of nylon string on the tabs before driving stakes.

One of the most common camping mistakes is made in tying tent-support strings. Whether they are tied to trees, brush, logs, or pegs, they should be fastened with a knot that will come undone as easily as a shoelace. Knots less easily untied often tighten in wind and rain so that they are tedious or impossible to loosen, especially with cold fingers.

Never pitch shelters where they might be blown against sharp twigs or abraded on rough rocks or tree trunks. Such friction can puncture the fabric and leave the camper with a damaged tent for the remainder of his trip. Rocks or dirt piled on wall flaps to anchor them also shorten a tent's life.

If a tear does start, there is generally little that can be done in the field. Temporary repairs to prevent enlarging can be made by tying off the damaged portion with string or covering the rip with tape. The residue left on the fabric when tape is later removed hampers machine sewing, however, so tape should be applied sparingly.

When leaving camp for a day or more in windy country, it is best to drop or take down the shelter rather than risk having it flap and strain in the wind. Nylon strings that will break before the fabric receives enough pressure to rip are advised.

Mountain tents to be used in snow or wind should have nylon sleeves in which tent poles can be inserted. The sleeves should have an enclosed bottom of reinforced, heavier nylon. Metal rings are no substitute for sleeves, since strong winds can whip the poles out of their mooring and cause the tent to collapse.

Digging a trench around one's shelter to prevent flooding in case of unexpected night rains is against all practical conservation ethics. Such unsightly scars require years to heal.

Bathing

Bathing is essential on backpacking trips. Besides making one feel better, a bath every day (if possible) contributes to standards of expedition behavior, sanitation, and good health. In cold, stormy weather, frequent bathing might be precluded; however, germs do not multiply as fast under frigid conditions and odors do not bloom so quickly.

One is able to keep clean in the outdoors by washing without soap or detergent. True, bathing in cold water will not eliminate all of the natural oils from the body, but this is not necessary in the wilds. Bathing the feet every day, washing hands after eliminating, and cleansing the face and body frequently will assure that one meets good outdoor grooming standards.

If soap and detergent *must* be used by a camper, they should be used in a special way. Perhaps if we regarded all wild waters—lakes, rivers, streams—as swimming pools, we could better understand the respect an outdoorsman should give them.

Rinse feet with a can of water before lathering them with soap or detergent, then rinse well in a place where soapy water will not harm the vegetation or drain back into the water source. Final soaking in a lake or stream is then permissible.

At times when one really needs a good bath, don't lather up and dive into the water. Soap up a distance from the lake, rinse off with a can of water, and take a final plunge after suds have been eliminated.

Laundry

If the outing is extended enough to make laundering necessary, clothes may be washed in cold water (without soap or detergent), hung in the wind and sun to dry, and made fresh enough for wearing. One will not have the "bright" wash so essential to television viewers, but perspiration and germs will be removed.

If one carries three pairs of wool socks and wears two at a time, one pair is free for washing each day. It is best if socks are not washed with soap or detergent. Soap is especially difficult to rinse completely from wool, and if some remains, it might irritate or infect the feet. Such irritation sometimes makes people think they are allergic to wool.

Socks washed in plain cold water will retain some discoloration, but such laundering will eliminate perspiration and dirt and make them clean enough for practical use. The same is true in the case of other apparel.

Be sure to wring out excess water over the ground and not directly into a body of water.

Axemanship

A beginner who uses an axe before receiving careful instruction is taking an unwarranted chance of injury to both himself and the equipment. Obviously, it would be impossible to teach the novice all the things that an expert commercial woodsman must know. In the past, when house logs were axe hewn and railroad ties, fence posts, and many other necessities were shaped by axes, axemanship was an art. For our purposes, here are some "must-knows" for limited use of axes on a camping trip.

Special precautions are necessary when using the short-handled axe popular with campers. If one misses the object being chopped, the axe will swing toward the axeman, and the shortness of the handle causes the axehead to swing toward the feet or legs. A clumsy amateur swing with a longer-handled axe will place the axehead in the ground—hard on the axe but easier on the body. Axe handles are short-lived with beginners, since one blow that misses the log is apt to crack the shaft. It takes practice to hit where one aims.

Hard-toed shoes are essential when using an axe. One who wears tennis sneakers or lightweight footwear is inviting serious injury.

The beginner is usually tempted to cut a stick with a blow that sends the blade clear through and into the ground. One such blow is generally enough to ruin a cutting edge and, should it strike a rock, a nick large enough to permanently damage the axe might result. Place sticks or logs to be chopped on top of another log so that the blade will hit wood instead of rocks or ground.

Don't lean wood for chopping against a rock or log. Besides possibly ruining the axe blade if it hits the ground, the breaking stick is apt to fly up and injure the person using the axe.

A small file is necessary for sharpening an axe blade. Press the file hard against the cutting edge and push downward. This can be hazardous to fingers, so always wear gloves when sharpening an axe. One can drive the small, sharp end of the file into a short length of wood to provide a handle that will decrease the chance of accident.

The duller the axe, the greater its tendency to glance off a log rather than penetrating it. An axe glancing off might hit a careless bystander, or the woodsman might lose his grip entirely and the axe strike some-one several feet away.

Stand on the opposite side of a log when removing a limb. If glanc-ing occurs, the intervening log will protect you from injury. Look around to ascertain that all is clear before hefting an axe. Many ac-cidents occur when onlookers walk into the swing arc or the axeman swings without warning.

The only safe way to store an axe is to lay it flat on the ground, preferably in a protected, untraveled place. Axes left stuck in trees could be hit by passers-by and knocked out of place, causing injury. Axes sticking out of stumps or logs are also potential hazards.

Carry an axe by grasping the handle immediately back of the head, never by balancing it on your shoulder. Then, if a fall occurs, the arm that is instinctively thrown out for balance takes the axe away from the body. An axe must never be carried on backpacking or horse packing trips unless the blade is encased in a sheath. (This can be purchased with the axe.)

Horse Packing

Though we teach horse packing in some of our NOLS courses, we can only touch briefly on it here. Our purpose will be to discuss the "must-knows" for the backpacker who might use horses to transport his gear, or part of it, into the wilderness, or use saddle horses on a portion of the trip into hiking or climbing country.

In my youth, I directed and owned pack outfits, and set up semi-permanent base camps and more lasting hunting camps as some outfit-ters still do. In recent years, while developing techniques for conserva-tion, I realized there were many changes that would have to be made. The old-time camps had nails in trees for hanging gear, poles wired high upon which to string game, logs around tents, axe scars, and badly trampled ground. New methods must be employed to enable us to use horses without damaging results. And since it is more difficult to camp with large numbers of animals without semi-permanent facilities, it is necessary to take as few horses as possible and limit the amount of gear to be carried.

Wild regions were grazed by animals long before man arrived, so if they are carefully grazed, vegetation will grow again. A good rule is not to allow your horses to graze more than half of the vegetation. That is all the environment can stand in one season.

Horses do cut up trails and cause some erosion, yet compared to scars left by trail builders who have blasted out rocks that could easily have been skirted, this damage is insignificant.

If horses are tied to trees overnight or for long hours, they may trample the undergrowth or kill trees by exposing roots. If they are roped to unusually small trees, they might pull them out by the roots. If staked or tied to logs in a meadow, an unnatural appearance will result if these anchors are not later scattered. Little damage results when horses are hobbled and allowed to graze.

When a mountaineer or backpacker plans to use horses for all or a portion of his trip, there are certain things he must know for his own protection.

Don't be too eager to help when horses are hired and their packing is under the supervision of an outfitter or his cowboys. Tell the person in charge whether or not you are familiar with horses. Even if you are a horseman, wait until you are told what to do.

For your own safety, if asked to hold or lead a horse, grasp the rope without a loop or hold it doubled in your hand so that if the animal jerks back, the rope will slip clear. A loop could tighten around the hand or fingers, pulling you toward the horse and possibly panicking him. Such accidents have caused rope burn, dislocated bones, and even amputated fingers.

Never walk backward when attempting to lead a horse; he is likely to retreat rather than follow. Face the direction to be traveled and walk naturally. The horse will follow behind.

Do not put fingers in a half-tied knot when tying the horse to a tree, as he might rear back and tighten the knot. Tie the rope at least five feet from the ground and leave less than three feet of slack between horse and tree. This will prevent the horse from getting tangled in the rope.

It is hazardous to ride horseback while wearing climbing or hiking boots, especially if they are wide or lug-soled, because it is difficult to manage stirrups easily. One might be caught and dragged by one foot in case the horse falls or if he "spooks" while the rider is dismounting. Of course, you will have to deal with the consequences if you wear soft-toed shoes and the horse steps on your foot. Hard-toed footgear is recommended.

Ride with reins untied (not tied together). This will make dismounting easier and facilitate holding the horse afterward.

Ask the packer how he wants you to ride uphill, since leaning backward at such times can put strain over the horse's kidneys and harm or overtire him. Find out whether you are to let him eat while you are mounted or riding. Doing so might make him more difficult to manage.

Keep a close watch for hikers and backpackers along trails. Persons on foot should move *at least* twenty-five feet *below* the trail when they see horses approaching. If they move above the trail, a horse might panic and charge downhill, possibly falling. If he bolts up the hill, it is usually not as serious. Sudden movements and brightly colored packs and clothes may also frighten horses. Realize beforehand that these possibilities exist. Ask for advice when you need it, and follow the instructions of the cowboy unless you are absolutely certain of your ability and he knows it.

7

Expedition Behavior

High on the glaciers of Alaska's Mt. McKinley some time ago, two men started bickering over a minor disagreement. Because neither of them had developed conscious emotional control, the argument grew so violent that they actually attacked each other with ice axes.

Another battle erupted on a mountain in South America when a couple of climbers tried to divide their last remaining sardine into two equal portions. Despite intellectual achievements as Ph.D.s, these outdoorsmen failed to realize that special efforts must be made to insure compatibility under trying physical conditions.

It is easy to understand why extended or even short outings often explode into verbal or physical confrontations between members. Extreme fatigue because of unrealistic Time and Energy Control Plans, discomfort caused by lack of workable Climate Control Plans, misunderstandings, and annoying personal idiosyncrasies become magnified when a planned system of Expedition Behavior is neglected.

Expedition Behavior is a basic, teachable skill. Yet, over the years, there has been little emphasis on developing methods to help persons get along with one another in the wild outdoors. This need has long been unrecognized, and the result has been much unnecessary tragedy, especially in the field of high-altitude mountaineering.

Human nature influences the success or failure, comfort or discomfort, safety or danger of an outdoor experience as much as equipment, logistics, trail techniques, rations, and other basic organizational concerns. Although a breakdown in personal relations between individuals is encouraged by poor pre-planning, even the well-thought-out and well-equipped outing might face failure, injury, or death if good Expedition Behavior practices are missing. In high altitudes or during adventuresome, energy-draining endeavors, outdoorsmen must make a concerted effort for the consideration of companions in addition to securing their own personal comfort and safety.

Many climbing trips and expeditions sponsored by clubs, societies, or nations select participants on the basis of competition, daring exploits, and extraordinary feats of skill or endurance. Often, such outdoor "prima donnas" care only about fame, reaching the summit, being first, and are unconcerned that their personal success may be attained at the expense of the enjoyment, companionship, and even safety of others.

Himalayan expeditions have been full of examples in which poor Expedition Behavior has promoted failure and disaster. The early Germans on Nanga Parbat, the French in the Karakoram, the English on Everest, Americans and Italians on K2, the French on Annapurna, all had disappointments and tragedies that might have been prevented.

The attempt to plant a United Nations flag atop Mt. Everest in 1971 was a classic example. Thirty-two persons representing eleven countries and speaking eight different languages led an army of four hundred low-altitude porters and forty-two Sherpas to the highest mountain in the world. Renowned climbers from the United States, Great Britain, Switzerland, France, Italy, Norway, Japan, Austria, and India were brought together for the assault.

Because it was deemed impractical to accommodate so many varied national diets in the rations allotment, it was decided to compromise by purchasing Central European food. But no one realized that the Austrian appointed to be in charge of commissary was a vegetarian and health-food faddist. His five tons of supplies included a venison substitute made of chopped nuts, dried fruit bars, a Swiss herb and yeast "Biostreth Elixir," sauerkraut, pickled cucumbers, and five hundred family-sized tins of whole-meal pumpernickel (which he was the only one to even taste). The remainder of the party grumbled over meals and suffered from inadequate nutrition.

A French political hopeful, an Italian, and a Swiss woman were bent on becoming the first Frenchman, Italian, and woman on top of Everest. However, when progress was slowed to the extent of their being asked to assist the Sherpas in carrying supplies to upper camps, they claimed insult to their native countries and abandoned the expedition. The leader attempted to coax them back, but the woman responded by pelting him with rocks and snowballs.

Death struck an Indian representative of the party when he attempted a difficult rope traverse during a storm. He was moving to a lower camp with the Austrian commissary chairman. The Austrian negotiated the tricky ledge, but when his companion did not appear behind him after twenty minutes, he returned to camp and sent rescuers. No one was able to reach the victim. His body dangled from ropes for six days before it could be retrieved. The Indian had been too proud to admit that he had had no previous experience with such a rope traverse and delayed calling for help until it was too late.

Someone broke out a bottle of whiskey in hopes of relieving growing tension; this only provided a catalyst for a monumental row with invectives shouted in four languages. The entire undertaking was tragic and unhappy because Expedition Behavior skills were lacking. (For a detailed description of the 1971 Everest assault, see "Ordeal on Everest," by Murray Sayle, in *Life,* July 2, 1971.)

Such conflicts are much more common than the reader of articles and published journals would suspect, since incidents that might cast doubt on the stability or unselfishness of members are generally omitted from post-mortem accounts. Traditionally, it has not been "good form" to admit that such situations occur. Scores of mountaineering books close by depicting the expeditioners returning to civilization "with lifelong friendships cemented by the trip."

Annapurna, a book by Maurice Herzog, honestly describes a negative situation. Members of the party not only had trouble getting along under normal circumstances, they hated one another when their mountaineering abilities failed to match the demands of their mission. Ailing companions were deserted, and some persons were so affected by high altitudes and emotional pressure that they completely lost their judgment.

Naturally, the longer the trip or harder the circumstances, the greater the strain on individuals in the wild outdoors, but one must not neglect Expedition Behavior standards on any sojourn. Such concerns even affect the weekend hiker.

Achieving Good Expedition Behavior

Previous chapters have already mentioned some factors which promote better relations in the outdoors. Eating greens on summer outings prevents irritability triggered by lack of vitamin C. Taking salt regularly promotes body moisture to fight dehydration. Eating continuously maintains energy. Selecting clothes and shelter to meet a Climate Control Plan assures physical comfort. Using an Energy Control Plan prevents overfatigue. Scheduling a Time Control Plan enables people to reach destinations and realize goals. All of these relate to Expedition Behavior because as long as everyone is having an enjoyable time, feeling well, comfortable, and unworried, human nature is at its best.

But when the storm strikes, food runs short, an accident happens, or time schedules go awry—whenever the chips are down—people without conscious control can become like animals in the jungle. In Kipling's words, ". . . the white man and the savage are but two short days apart."

Simply, poor Expedition Behavior is a breakdown in human relations caused by selfishness, rationalization, ignorance of personal faults, dodging blame or responsibility, physical weakness, and, in extreme cases, not being able to risk one's own survival to insure that of a companion.

Good Expedition Behavior is an awareness of the relationship of individual to individual, individual to the group, group to the individual, group to other groups, individual and group to the multiple uses of the region, individual and group to administrative agencies, and individual and group to the local populace. It is this awareness, plus the motivation and character to be as concerned for others in every respect as one is for oneself.

Individual to Individual

Tentmates represent the closest one-to-one relationship of persons on an outing. Living in close quarters with another, often a complete stranger, and under expedition conditions, requires extra thought and consideration.

As a rule, the delicate balance of human relations is better maintained by limiting two persons to a tent. Usually, people are able to adjust to one other individual easily. Large tents housing four or more campers are so crowded that they threaten the compatibility of occupants, besides being heavy and difficult to pitch. Three-man tents invite the proverbial "triangle" with someone feeling left out, imposed upon, or misunderstood.

During winter mountaineering, high-altitude expeditioning, or adverse weather in summer camping, it is often necessary to spend extra time in the tent or sleeping bag. Long nights and blustery days of winter might force members to spend over half of the expedition under cover. I know of no way to guarantee selection of a tentmate who will remain enjoyable under such close, prolonged personal contact, but there are some pointers that help in choosing a partner.

Campers are happier when allowed to select their own tentmates. But everyone should have an understanding before leaving civilization that these pairings can be changed if original combinations make for conflict or other problems.

Tent companions near the same age or mental maturity are best. They are better able to understand each other's personality, enjoy easier conversation, and possess greater mutual tolerance.

Persons from the exact environment and social structure should be discouraged from camping together, especially in youth groups. Close pals should be separated. Learning, adventure, and enjoyment are enhanced when one meets new companions, and it is often easier to start out being a more considerate person with a new companion.

There are times when coed partners get along best. People are often on their model behavior when associated with the opposite sex.

A little special consideration makes it possible to live amicably with almost anyone. Respect another's privacy; he might wish to be alone at times. There will be more space and comfort dressing, undressing, and changing clothes in a tent alone. Maximum opportunity to perform private grooming is welcomed by everyone.

Tolerance and understanding of another person's moods and consciousness of one's own moods are necessary. A companion's wish to sleep or lounge in tent or sleeping bag should govern one's own movements and activities.

Borrowing or misplacing someone else's personal equipment is a quick road to unpopularity. In the outdoors, each item is essential for safety and comfort. Leave another's belongings alone. Snooping into personal gear, diaries, or letters is inexcusable.

Maintain a neat camp. Piles of soiled clothing, discarded equipment, and items not in use invite accidents and are a source of irritation to associates.

It is preferable to distribute rations to cook groups of two or four persons, rather than to each individual. While the work of preparation and cleanup is divided among the group, there is no need to apportion food equally, as one person may not have the same energy output as another. A thin person will need more food than one who is receiving hundreds of calories a day from his own fat as he starts to reduce with excessive activity. Therefore, individual daily food rationing is impractical. Everyone consumes as much as he wants. But it must be understood that no one takes along his private "goodies." Hoarding food is one of the most contemptible violations of Expedition Behavior.

Pitching tents, cooking, and other chores are mutual responsibilities. If a partner does not do his share, avoid direct confrontation or emotional arguments; switch tentmates if the situation becomes unbearable.

Switching tentmates can be a delicate matter. It is best to avoid blaming either party or inventing reasons for the move. Be understanding and honest. If one camper wishes to team up with a different person, let him; their former partners can do likewise.

Essentially, the good expeditioner is willing to put his own comfort and safety on the line for that of another. In extreme cases, this might involve risking one's own life to rescue someone else.

If an individual is taught to become conscious of himself on an extended trip, it is an opportunity to really get to know himself. After a few days away from civilization, everyone starts to change. Values change. The veneer, the bluffing, artificiality, and crutch of family wealth or prestige are no longer valid in the natural environment of camping. Suddenly, people must make their place in a new society based upon what they can actually do and what they really are. Attempting to use former prestige to promote expedition prestige is a serious error. If one is aware of this change and the fact that he must be real, sincere, and unselfish to gain the respect of his peers, adjustment without confrontation is much easier.

Individual to Group

One must be aware of one's weaknesses and idiosyncrasies when going into the outdoors with companions. Before leaving home, one should sit down and analyze these habits and resolve to modify them.

Neatness has special significance in the wild outdoors. Unwashed dishes attract flies. Carelessly filled packs cause delays and irritation along the trail. Clothing and gear scattered throughout camp are not only irritating to other campers; the chance of loss or damage to essential items could affect the success of the entire outing.

It is unfair to one's companions to neglect personal cleanliness. I do not mean that one must have hair slicked down and buttons closed in a military fashion; practical cleanliness is all that is required on an outing. However, clothes must be free of grime and body odors. Even though mountain water is icy, one must bathe often.

Dress in accordance with standards set by the group. Outdoor apparel that is warm, comfortable, and practical takes precedence over contemporary faddish styles that often sacrifice these qualities for appearance.

Try to be conscious of offensive habits. Some years ago, I was called upon to train Peace Corps members going to Nepal. One otherwise attractive young man had the unfortunate habit of picking his nose—aggressively. Naturally, this was most upsetting during my lectures or around the campfire. Although all mannerisms are not as distasteful as the above, everyone does little things that might grate on the nerves of others. Correct them, if possible.

Dwelling on personal accomplishments or interests is also irritating. We had a boy in a course who talked continuously about his home town and his exploits. After a few days, I noticed that every time he started talking, the group would dissolve and he would be left to himself. He became very lonely until his instructor told him the facts about himself. The boy was somewhat shocked and remained silent for a few days, but he soon bounced back and only mentioned his home town at acceptable intervals.

Joining an expedition is like signing a contract; after the commitment is made and the trip has started, one cannot back out or become surly and uncooperative because one thinks one has made a bad deal.

Outings are sometimes ruined by one selfish individual who refuses to cooperate because he "didn't know what he was getting into." Rationalization is easy under such circumstances, and one can conjure up all kinds of reasons why the expedition should be sacrificed or adjusted to suit his wishes.

It is the individual's responsibility to determine before starting out what the goals and standards of the trip will be. Not every climb must make the summit to be successful; some are for educational or reconnaissance purposes. Some outings are for pleasure; others seek competitive glory. A person aware of Expedition Behavior should be able to judge if the trip would be to his liking.

In the summer of 1971, we sent an expedition to Mt. McKinley in Alaska. This was a six-week trip involving much physical exertion and danger. A letter establishing and stressing the importance of behavior standards was sent to all participants before the starting date. In part, the letter said:

Mood and Tone of NOLS McKinley Expedition

OUR INTENT

This is no first ascent. It is an expedition for experiment and learning. We believe that people can and should be as relaxed as they are at home, while climbing a high peak. Careful preparation, good technique and expedition behavior should eliminate mountain sickness, pulmonary edema, and exhaustion. There is no need for rational people to become unhinged and start to chase each other with ice axes at 19,000 feet. A climb is to be enjoyed; it is demanding work, but it need not be grim. We would like the McKinley Expedition to be a happy one, just as we try to make every outdoor experience a happy one. We want to find out if the techniques and principles set down here can accomplish this. We believe that they can, with your help.

Comfort and enjoyability are essential to all phases of the expedition.

1. Hiking: Practice of rhythmic breathing is essential to conserve energy and avoid exhaustion. Breathing controls movement: learn to shift gears so that the beat of the heart remains constant.
2. Short days: To prevent fatigue. *Everyone* goes slowly. No race horses.
3. Everyone doesn't have to do the same amount of work. Work to your capabilities, not above or below. Graduated scale, according to strength and ability. Avoid heavy packs. There is no weight lifting competition.
4. Sun: Watch out for sunburn. It drains your energy.
5. Control of temperature: Never be too hot or too cold hiking, sleeping, or resting. Take food and drink to bed with you. Keep your digestive system going.
6. Salt and water: Drinking lots of liquids and keeping salt intake high assures proper body functioning. Water loss is extreme at high altitudes.
7. Sleep well: Adds to physical and psychological security. Relieve yourself before hitting the sack. Have food and water available for midnight snacks.

Exemplary expedition behavior adds to enjoyment.

1. Be tolerant and considerate of all others.
2. Avoid arguments.
3. Keep a pleasing appearance.
4. Don't take offense.
5. You must realize that at high altitude you may think that you are the only one right, and all others are wrong.
6. Maintain a "cow-like" nature. Don't worry; relax; have fun. This is no big deal.
7. Personal hygiene is important to avoid sickness. Wash yourself whenever there is such an opportunity.
8. Switch tent-mates if you don't get along.

Basically, one helps maintain the integrity of the group by thinking about the other guy. The expedition is no obstacle course; individuals should have no reason to compete. Excitement and stress are a drain on everyone. A relaxed and confident attitude toward reaching a realistic goal is more helpful than a fierce, aggressive drive forced upon one's companions.

Any venture in the wild outdoors presents danger. One cannot climb, hike over primitive country, or ford rivers without taking some chances, and isolation from hospitals and technical medical help compounds the threat. One should realize before joining a group that physical risks and the possibility of moral or financial responsibilities resulting from a rescue, illness, death, or other unusual occurrence are shared. Each member should have medical insurance or other proof of his ability to pay emergency expenses.

Some people hesitate to join an expedition because they are afraid of heights or dread the unknown. This is a normal reaction but no reason to stay home. The person who should not join a group is the one without fear. He could endanger the entire party. The natural fear of a normal person is the element that prevents him from attempting the dangerous feat until he has learned necessary techniques of safety. Fear is the basis on which to train the best outdoor leaders.

An individual has the responsibility to avoid dangerous activities not sponsored by the group and strictly adhere to safety standards that have been established. Neglect of this practice generally results in trouble.

For example, after a demonstration of river crossing and warnings about wearing boots in the water to protect feet, one of our students forded a stream barefooted. He slashed his foot and had to be evacuated.

One very superior student disagreed with his fellow hikers when they became confused about how to reach the roadhead by reading a topographical map. The intelligent young man knew that the route he selected was correct, but the majority insisted on going another direction. Our individualist refused to go the wrong way and hiked to the roadhead alone.

He made two serious errors. First, he traveled alone through the mountains. Had he suffered even a slight injury, he would have been stranded without help. This could have resulted in the necessity of a search party, an expensive and grueling task for the local sheriff and citizens. Secondly, regardless of the fact that his companions were mistaken, he should not have deserted them.

Horseplay has no place in the wild outdoors. Danger is present in the most innocuous situations. A severe accident occurred when a group of young people were having a water fight. Some boys were dousing a girl when she unwittingly grabbed a billy can that happened to be full of scalding water and poured it down one boy's back. His burns were extremely serious.

Anticipating possible results of one's actions and sublimating personal preference to majority rule will help the individual contribute to the general welfare of his group.

Group to Individual

Individuals must bow to majority rule, but the group has an equal responsibility to consider the needs of every member. When a group accepts a person, it must be willing to adjust to his ability; he might be doing his best but be unable to carry his share or keep up with the rest of the party. If an individual is unable to manage all of his pack, stronger hikers should share the load and do so good-naturedly, without belittling or blaming him. Walking pace and activities should be geared to the slowest member's capactiy.

Occasionally, outings are delayed or abandoned because illness or injury befall a single member. I have seen persons unskilled in Expedition Behavior take out their frustration and disappointment at such times by making the victim feel as if he had done a deliberate, unfriendly act. Misfortune might strike anyone. Everyone should feel a commitment of loyalty to associates in this event.

Every group must have a designated leader. When there is an emergency, when there are conflicting wishes as to activities, when nonconformists endanger health, safety, or conservation standards, someone must have the right to make decisions. A leader must be selected by the group before leaving civilization. It is then up to every member to respect this leadership.

Individuals with strong, domineering personalities might find it possible to depose someone already designated to head the group. Such actions do not belong in the wild outdoors and should not be condoned by associates.

Conversely, the "führer" type of leader is not compatible with an enjoyable outing. General activities and standards of an expedition should be discussed democratically.

Group to Other Groups

Respect for other groups should be expressed in a sportsmanlike manner. Those who arrive at an area first should be skirted with no personal contact except by invitation.

I once had a patrol located in a campsite when another party appeared and accused us of intruding because they had camped at the spot the previous year. Despite such ridiculous reasoning, I told them that we would move the next morning because it was too late in the afternoon to break camp. While I was out fishing, one of the newcomers relieved himself behind a bush near one of our tents. When he left, his used toilet tissue blew into our cooking area. An incensed student threw it in front of the offender's tent so that he "could smell his own crap." Had the late arrivals observed the "first-come principle," this incident could have been avoided. The student also used bad judgment in magnifying the already uncomfortable situation.

Some people come to the wilderness to be alone. Although most tend to be more gregarious, when two groups meet, a "hello" and friendly answering of questions is all that is needed. Ask no unnecessary questions and don't engage in extended conversation. Be careful about accepting hospitality that may be offered from a feeling of obligation rather than from the heart.

Except in emergency, do not impose on others to borrow the proverbial cup of sugar or use equipment.

Respect divergent behavior standards. At NOLS, where we go to extremes to protect the beauty and ecosystem of the wilds, it is always heartbreaking to see another group destroying. After we have been careful not to leave fire scars, it is annoying to see others building giant bonfires that make ugly marks. However, we have no right to confront or advise such persons.

If one wishes to clean up litter, bury human manure, or correct other errors made by the uneducated, Expedition Behavior demands that one wait until the camp is deserted and the people out of sight.

If one wishes to swim nude, remember that such practices, especially in mixed groups, might be offensive to others. Use judgment. Youth has a right to freedom of behavior, but Expedition Behavior also consists in recognizing the values of less flexible, conservative older groups.

Another source of irritation in the mountains is the misunderstanding between horse trains and backpackers. Some backpackers, through ignorance or laziness, will not move downslope off the trail and stand still while horses pass, as courtesy demands. If walkers stay close, stand on both sides of the trail, or make sudden noises or movements, animals might shy, causing injury or inconvenience.

Individual and Group to the Multiple Uses of the Region

Inexperienced outdoorsmen might not realize that there are many different kinds of laws and regulations governing use of the wild outdoors. It is impossible to successfully plan an expedition without understanding these requirements and limitations, such as the use of horses, fire permits, game laws, and so on.

Many people argue that all federal public lands should be under one governmental department, but this is not the case. Most of these areas are administered by the Department of Agriculture or Department of the Interior. While the two agencies cooperate with one another, each has its own rules, regulations, and local administrators.

The Department of Agriculture, through its Forest Service, controls most of the timbered mountain country in the United States (except Alaska). These are "lands of many uses," or "multiple use." The same areas at the same times may be used for timbering, mining, grazing, oil drilling, game habitat, watershed for irrigation, horse packing, dude ranching, hunting camps, and mountaineering. These are areas for the hunter, fisherman, and rockhound. They are training grounds for outdoor schools and recreation spots for scouting, church groups, and families. So many uses of a single region often trigger irritation between competing interests. An outdoorsman must modify his activities with good Expedition Behavior by realizing that his interest has no preference over others.

Officially designated Wilderness areas are subject to limited multiple use. Road construction, permanent buildings, and motorized vehicles are prohibited; mining claims and oil leasing are being phased out. The Forest Service is authorized to restrict use of lands being investigated as possible wilderness areas.

The Department of the Interior contains four bureaus designed to administer lands used by outdoorsmen: the Bureau of Land Management, Bureau of National Parks, Bureau of Indian Affairs, and Bureau of Reclamation.

The Bureau of Land Management controls vast acreages of public lands on the plains and deserts and some mountain terrain below the higher U.S. Forest domain. Nearly all of these BLM lands are under grazing, oil, and gas leases or mining claims.

In order to permit better grazing and access to water, the BLM has allowed some leases to be fenced. Since private and BLM lands are often intermingled, the outdoorsman might not be able to distinguish between them. Some ranchers have taken advantage of this fact by illegal posting and fencing to bar outdoorsmen from using what is rightfully theirs. While it is advisable for a camper to check at the local courthouse or BLM office for accurate maps designating proper boundaries, Expedition Behavior demands that the lessee be given every courtesy and legitimate consideration.

Various national parks and monuments are used extensively for outdoor recreation, and Park Service officials are experienced in offering information and policing their lands. Boundary lines, regulations, and rules of use are readily available from Visitor Center staff or other permanent employees.

Indian lands merit special consideration, as local tribes have major control over their usage. Such areas are not public lands. They do not belong to the state or federal government. They belong to the Indians and must be treated as private property.

One has no right to travel on Indian lands except by special permission from the governing body of the tribe. Two sets of rules prevail; one for the visitor, another for tribal members. It is likely that Indians do not need hunting and fishing licenses or recreational permits required of outsiders.

The Bureau of Reclamation controls land and water around lakes, dams, and reclamation facilities.

State lands involving school sections and state parks may also have special requirements for outdoor use. Information and maps are available from the state concerned or local sources.

It is possible for an expeditioner to pass through several of these divergent regions on a single outing. Adequate advance knowledge of what is expected and adherence to laws in spirit as well as in practical interpretation will promote good Expedition Behavior.

Individual and Group to Administrative Agencies

Administrators of federal lands need our sympathy. Every group, recreational or industrial, using these lands is in some conflict, and each expects the local ranger to give him the advantage. The outdoor leader should adhere to regulations and refrain from requesting special privileges which the official will need to deny.

Be sure that necessary permits or licenses are obtained and carry them at all times while in the wilds. If a ranger asks to check these papers, be prompt and courteous about allowing him to do so.

When registration is required in primitive country, sign in and out so the authorities will be alerted as to users' locations. Decisions concerning rescue operations are often made on the basis of these records.

Do not embarrass a local representative by expecting him to discuss skilled outdoorsmanship or techniques involved in recreational activities such as fishing, climbing, or backpacking. His education has probably not prepared him for this, and his job has not allowed field time for self-education.

Do not expect the ranger to know all of the terrain in the interior of his region. Bureau employees are transferred frequently and little time is available for exploration. Federal employees administering public lands are hard working, public spirited individuals. They are doing more than one should expect, and are handicapped by lack of funds and personnel.

Individual and Group to Local Populace

There are certain relations with the local populace that must be carefully considered by the visitor. Standards of dress, morality, and conservation must not be offensive.

Knowledge of regional problems and conflicts of interest is extremely helpful. For example, if one knows in advance that an area is under a grazing lease and the lessee has experienced previous trouble with hikers or horse packers who have disturbed livestock of left drift-fence gates open, one can be doubly concerned about the good Expedition Behavior of one's party.

Many ranchers who hold such leases are practical conservationists, and they resent tourists messing up their leased federal land. Although the area actually belongs to the American public and is administered by government officials, these persons might have had the parcel handed down through family generations, and their interests look to preservation for their children's use as well. They do not want water polluted, meadows overgrazed by horses, or fire hazards.

I knew a rancher from Dubois, Wyoming, who was the involuntary host of a family from Casper who camped on his lease one weekend. When the visitors left, there were fire scars, cans, paper plates, tinfoil, broken glass, and unburied human manure littering the entire area. The rancher was furious.

The next weekend, he drove to Casper, parked his pickup truck in front of the offender's home, and proceeded to camp on his lawn, throwing cans, papers, and other trash at random. The suburbanite summoned the police, but the rancher had already notified the press, so the resultant publicity was a bonus for conservation.

The backpacker is a newcomer to the wild outdoors and presents a physical and political threat to the unchallenged custody enjoyed in the past by the livestock grazer, dude rancher, horse packer, and professional hunting-camp outfitter. Out-of-state backpackers must realize that these local users have more than a cursory interest in the region. Their livelihoods, life savings, and the tax base for local schools and government depend upon their continued access to these federal lands. Their priority use, economic needs, and place in the political structure deserve special consideration.

Many dude ranchers and outfitters have certain places where they camp several times during the season. These spots are generally recognizable by repetitive use. One might be tempted to stop at such a camp only to have the outfitter arrive with his party. His right of "being there first" must be respected.

We all know that a vital part of the outdoor experience is "getting away from it all" and developing a sense of isolation. But there are times when involvement with others is unavoidable. The continuous practice of good Expedition Behavior will contribute to everyone's enjoyment.

8

Outdoor Leadership

Every group that ventures into the wild outdoors should designate a leader. Even among close friends, one responsible person must have the final say. The democratic process might be workable under ordinary conditions, but in the out-of-doors, when there is a conflict of opinion, an unexpected storm, or an accident, someone must be in authority. If a leader is appointed before the outing, he can take such responsibility and delegate to others.

Handling emergencies is the exceptional responsibility of a leader. More common is his obligation to organize and guide an expedition for the ultimate safety and fulfillment of all its members and conservation of the ecosystem. This demands a great deal more than just taking one's place at the head of the line.

There are hundreds of combinations of character, personality, and knowledge that make for good leadership. A qualified leader in one field would not necessarily be capable in another situation. There are leaders for get-together groups in which most decisions are made through mutual agreement. There are club leaders who merely direct pre-planned schedules or have the primary goal of motivating or educating members. There are leaders for scouting, church, and civic organizations, where the wish to help and donate time might be the only requirement, and there are commercial packers, hunters, and guides whose leadership is predicated on the comfort and entertainment of clients. For our purposes, leadership is defined as the ability to plan and conduct safe, enjoyable expeditions while conserving the environment.

Qualities of Leadership

Knowledge of the outdoors, technical ability, and actual experience are obviously desirable prerequisites for good expedition leaders. One who has learned from instruction, demonstration, reading, and personal practice under field conditions before attempting to direct others is the ideal person to lead.

Yet there are those who have not had time or opportunity to be *taught* and then also *experience* total outdoorsmanship who are also capable. As long as a person possesses the judgment and unselfishness to limit his activities and those of persons under his direction to areas of his own actual capabilities, he can conduct expeditions with reasonable safety.

A lifetime of experience does not necessarily prove ability to lead others. Nor does a reputation for daring feats. Climbing the North Face of the Eiger or scaling Yosemite's perpendicular walls could indicate either a skilled climber or one who took unwarranted chances and luckily lived to tell about it. It does not say a thing about leadership.

Conversely, a qualified leader might not be the group's most proficient climber or camper. The important point is that a leader be a pragmatic realist about himself and his abilities, know his limitations, and not be over- or falsely confident. I have known leaders with very little technical skill whom I would trust to take a party into the wild outdoors. Perhaps activities or instruction might be rather limited, but the leader would not attempt dangerous things he did not know how to do.

One aspect of outdoor leadership is absolute and unquestionable. A leader must never bluff. If there is any point of technique that he does not know, he should frankly admit it. Trying to bluff under the dangerous conditions of mountain climbing, wild-river crossing, first aid, or map reading can endanger the entire party and will certainly lessen members' trust and respect.

A wise leader will make use of others who are more skilled in certain activities. He will openly recognize their superiority and call upon them for guidance. He might delegate temporary authority to the best climber to conduct the day's climb, the talented fly caster to advise other fishermen, and so forth.

One should be forewarned, however, that on occasion someone with a strong personality may attempt to take over. Probably the best way to avoid such action is to tell the challenger frankly that he is not to try to assume control. Many times, the aggressive person may not even realize he is doing so.

When expeditioners disagree over pre-established plans and haggle among themselves, a delaying tactic is sometimes useful. Naturally, an emergency demands quick decisions, but in other matters a leader will do well to listen to suggestions and relate his own past experiences and knowledge to them before reaching a conclusion.

In vital situations, the leader is "captain of his ship." He is responsible for the ultimate safety and success of the trip. The group is as secure as its leadership.

A talent for judgment can be taught. I have seen persons make the transition from poor judgment in the outdoors to good common sense.

However, a leader is different from a general member of the group. He must have demonstrated his ability to make valid decisions before assuming responsibility. If he draws unworkable plans, is ignorant of possibly dangerous situations, is unable to assess the different purposes, personalities, technical skills, and desires of those under his guidance, he is no outdoor leader.

Perhaps he can read a topographical map with ease. But can he select a route compatible with the ability and stamina of his party?

Maybe he has successfully climbed a particular peak and is setting out to lead the expedition up another route. His previous knowledge would count little. The piton cracks would be different, the belays not the same, the handholds, weather, personnel, altitude, length of day, approach to the summit, morale and spirit of the party, would all be changed. Everything he had learned in the past, every situation he had previously faced, would have to be modified. Ability to do this with rewarding results is good judgment. A leader with limited knowledge and superior judgment is better than one with vast knowledge and little judgment.

No matter how skilled or experienced a leader may be, he cannot be effective if he is selfish. I have seen the selfish person select a mountain route unsuited to the ability of his group just because he wanted to make the climb. He might select rations for the trip based upon his special likes or dislikes, or allow activities and pace to be oriented to his own taste. Just as a good cowboy will feed his horse before preparing his own meal, one in authority must think of the welfare and enjoyment of his party before satisfying his own wishes.

Sympathy and understanding are related to unselfishness. One who is in charge must not feel more companionable toward the strong member than the weak one. He must tolerate mistakes of beginners or those below his own level of intelligence and refrain from criticizing those who are trying to do their best. Such compassionate behavior will reduce disharmony in the group.

A sense of humor and the ability to laugh at oneself and recognize one's own human weaknesses is a desirable quality of leadership. Sometimes the light approach is a tactful way of correcting others.

Rationalization is a luxury a leader cannot indulge. He must be a realist, face facts no matter how disagreeable, and convince his group that he knows what he is talking about. He cannot fool himself into thinking that a climb is easier or shorter than it actually is just because he wants to make the attempt. Group plans and activities must be carried out realistically.

Sometimes one is tempted to excuse rationalization by calling it optimism. The positive attitude is commendable. But a leader's optimism must be based on fact, not wishful thinking. The more confidence his group has in him, the less chance of panic or haphazard overreacting.

Good outdoor leadership includes the ability to study planned activities in advance and anticipate any problems or dangers and their possible solutions. Each evening, the leader should check the following day's schedule and mentally test its practicality. Anticipate accidents and evacuation needs and evaluate the group's ability to cope with such emergencies. Many times, such anticipation will dictate modification of plans to insure safety and enjoyment.

Few groups will not need some instruction in techniques and conservation. A leader must be able to assume the role of teacher in such circumstances.

There is no reason why members of an expedition should not be happy, companionable, natural, unstrained, and eager. The difference between a good and a terrific job of leadership may depend on one's ability to consciously set the tone of a course. The skilled leader will do so at the onset when members seek guidance and are anxious to co-operate.

Be certain that everyone is familiar with accepted Expedition Behavior standards before starting. Each person must recognize weaknesses and faults in others and tolerate them with patience unless they interfere with the safety or rights of companions.

In the first few days, expeditioners learn something about individual and group responsibility, but it isn't until they begin to climb, cross wild rivers, or engage in other vital group activities that they grasp the true essence of cooperation. After a few days, the leader can encourage a tone that will make it easier to teach principles of tolerance, self-control, and mutual consideration necessary to keep things running smoothly. The atmosphere must be open and honest. No one should hesitate to express himself, register complaints, or ask questions. Each person assumes personal responsibility for the group's spirits, but the leader must be alert for any problems and help to adjust them.

While leadership qualifications might be more demanding in the wild outdoors, many attributes generally expected of persons in charge also are desirable. Honesty, a certain degree of intelligence, pleasing personality and appearance, and dependability are expected.

Demands made upon the group hold doubly for the leader. Punctuality, cooperation in meeting schedules, ability to carry out extended orders are not matters he can require of others and shirk himself.

Duties of a Leader

Unfortunately, there are some who contend that an outdoor experience implies being cold, having blisters, suffering from diarrhea, quarreling with companions, being exhausted, accomplishing only half of planned activities, and having "close calls." In reality, such conditions indicate poor leadership.

All of the information in this book is designed to promote enjoyable camping trips or expeditions. It is incumbent upon a leader to have such knowledge so that he is qualified to approve plans and equipment of those in his charge to insure their protection and that of the environment.

One of the first duties is to formulate an expedition itinerary by outlining Time, Energy, and Climate Control Plans. If an outing has already been organized by a club or other leader, one must be sure that the schedule is realistic. It is my firm belief that a person who will assume leadership without being satisfied as to the safety and practicality of an itinerary is being negligent.

Be sure that all permits and licenses have been secured and that the proposed route meets the approval of the administrative agency or agencies controlling the area to be traveled.

Approve a logistics plan of how the group is to be assembled and transferred to and from the take-off point, and how equipment is to be transported and resupplied (if necessary). A method for ending the expedition and disposing of equipment must also be understood and agreed to by all involved.

Avoid including individuals whose health, physical stamina, or special physical or mental handicaps might endanger or impair the expedition.

Insist that each member of the party, or the group as a whole, has medical insurance to meet expenses that might accrue for rescue, evacuation, and medical care in case of illness or accident. Make a financial plan concerning ability to pay the balance that might not be covered by these policies.

Be sure that every member understands and has agreed to any behavioral restrictions involving cigarettes, alcoholic beverages, prescribed medication, drugs, coed tenting, mixed nude bathing, or other controversial matters that might be disputed.

Know that all persons have signed statements (or have had statements signed by parents, if under age) accepting the possibility of dangerous activities and releasing the leader from responsibility.

Form an understanding as to use and exchange of photographs taken during the expedition and release in event of possible publication.

A leader must also check the clothing brought by those in his party to be sure that all items meet minimum requirements. If he finds a person in base camp who lacks proper footgear or longjohns, he sees that the necessary items are provided or refuses to allow that person on the trip, for his own safety and that of the group. His knowledge about clothing must be such that he can make this decision without equivocation.

A limitation must also be put on the amount of personal gear carried, since the weight of everything contributes to a realistic over-all plan.

Tents, shovels, special-activity equipment, and other items must be properly packed and distributed to be carried by stronger members. Individual backpacks should be adjusted and fitted to the wearer.

Check that all rations have been repackaged in plastic bags so that no metal, glass, or foil containers are included.

Distribute maps, compasses, notebooks, and pencils for making Time Control Plans, logging, and note taking. A few books on local flora and fauna may be packed in waterproof plastic bags and distributed.

The leader will carry a few special items for first aid and equipment repair. Medical supplies are kept to a minimum. (See Chapter 12, pages 217–18.)

In my experience, I have found that the need for repair of equipment in the field is limited. In a freak situation, the leader must use judgment and improvise solutions, but on most outings the following extras will suffice:

1. Thread and needle and a small amount of fabric for mending and patching.
2. Nylon string (parachute cord) to replace broken straps or buckles on backpacks.
3. A few horseshoe nails to repair separated soles on climbing or hiking boots. Place boot on a log and drive the nails with a piton hammer along the edge of the boot through the sole, and then bend back around edge of the shoe. This will usually hold the sole in place for several days.
4. If fishing is planned, extra microfilament line for casting rods and a small screwdriver or wrench for fishing-reel repair.

9

Basic Climbing

This chapter will not cover all of the technical skills and specific rock-climbing techniques that have been developed over the years. It is my purpose here simply to touch upon some of the techniques that I have developed and used at NOLS to teach beginners how to enjoy rock climbing with safety and common sense. Other books, such as those listed in the Bibliography, should be consulted for more advanced study.

Aside from judgment, balance is the basis of all climbing. We have already explained how to maintain balance while walking up, down, or across slopes; now we will explain how to coordinate such movements with the addition of handholds, footholds, and the use of various climbing aids.

Nearly all mountain climbing is concentrated on the feet, the hands being used merely to pull the climber toward the cliff so that his foothold will be more secure. Obviously, on a cliff one does not have the abundance of footholds available on lesser slopes. The climber cannot stand upright or lean into the cliff; his feet might slip out from under him. He must bend over from the hips with buttocks well away from the wall. Thus, he can reach the lower handholds that will make him secure and his feet will be at an angle to insure purchase against the rock and gain the friction that will help him push his body upward.

The angle of the feet determines their ability to hold. I call this method the High Hip Technique.

It is difficult for the beginner to do this. Exposure to heights is apt to frighten him and cause him to cling with his whole body to the mountain. This instinct actually makes a fall more likely. His feet are not solid on the rock and he becomes dependent upon his handholds, a dangerous and exhausting situation. We sometimes refer to these novices as "rock huggers."

Pitches that are difficult to climb are generally descended on a rope by rappelling. (See pages 180–90.) In easier spots, one can climb down by facing outward, bending forward with hips kept close to the rock, and pushing with the palms of the hands against handholds that are below the shoulders and near the waist. Thus, one can maintain balance and see where to place the feet. The only energy expended is to brake the downward movement.

If extreme steepness necessitates descending with face toward the cliff, study possible footholds before starting. One should only back down short pitches when there is no other alternative.

Rhythmic breathing adjusted to movement of hands and feet is just as important in climbing as in hiking. The inexperienced often tend to hold their breath on challenging pitches.

Handholds and Footholds

There are as many different kinds of hand- and footholds as there are cracks and indentations on the mountain. While no two are ever the same, it might be helpful to explain a few principles. Then, when one is actually on a climb, he can observe and analyze the holds encountered and make his own judgments.

In ascending a cliff, it is less tiring to find handholds below shoulder height and push the body upward than to pull oneself up from a higher hold. The hand can be turned sideways or completely twisted away from the wall so that the palm will be flat and retain maximum contact with the rock. In this way, the force is on the palm and there is little strain on fingers and arms.

On extremely steep pitches when such push handholds are not available one might have to pull from a hold above the shoulders. Pull handholds place more strain on the fingers and require extra energy.

Counterpressure is another principle of handholds. Just as the hands bring the body toward the cliff to afford the feet more traction to push upward, one hand braced against one side of a wall and the other hand braced against the opposite side achieve the same result. Counterpressure can also occur when the hands pull sideways on opposite sides of a crack to create a friction hold.

Footholds rarely accommodate the entire boot; therefore one must adjust the foot's position to assure the greatest leverage. On narrow rock ledges, the boot may be turned sideways, but this tends to bring the body close to the cliff. One can use toes on small outcroppings, and in vertical cracks that are wider than the boot the foot may be turned sideways to place pressure on both edges. The feet can also gain purchase with counterpressure if they are placed against opposite footholds and pushed outward.

Weight Distribution

One can be in a safe climbing position without good solid handholds or footholds if one learns to transfer weight from one limb to another in a smooth, flowing motion. In this manner, the climber releases one hold at a time, maintaining the other three points of contact.

For instance, a climber might have one foot against a rock that will withstand 90 pounds before slipping, the other foot against a rock that will take 70 pounds, one hand holding an outcrop that will stand 30 pounds, and the other holding on to a rock with 50 pounds' capacity. The total weight that could be held is 240 pounds. If the climber weighs 140 pounds, he has a hundred-pound safety margin. However, were he to place all of his weight on one handhold or foothold, he might fall. Obviously, he must move only one limb at a time and transfer that weight to the remaining three points in a way that will not endanger him. While he will not analyze this process mathematically, he will accomplish it by "feel." A skilled climber will appear to flow up the mountain rather than move with jerks and lunges. I call this technique "weight distribution," and it is one of the most important aspects of hand and foot climbing.

The Rope

In technical climbing, life literally depends upon equipment. It follows that a rope should be selected carefully, cared for meticulously, and proffered the same respect that one would give a lethal weapon.

When I first started climbing in the 1920s, we used rope made of Manila or Indian hemp, commonly called "hay rope." Before World War II, we had progressed to somewhat stronger Italian hemp or English linen, which was considered the ultimate in those days. The latter was very soft and pliable but became rotten and moldy if it was stored wet.

During World War II, the Tenth Mountain Division started to use the new nylon rope, which was superior to hemp. Today, most American climbers prefer twisted nylon ropes that are manufactured especially for climbing. They have a great deal of strength and stretch, and although extremely slippery when new, will abrade slightly after use and become fuzzy as tiny fibers are severed by contact with rock. This in no way weakens them but increases friction and helps retain tension on knots.

Europeans manufacture an untwisted, single-strand rope of a synthetic similar to nylon with a woven protective covering. While its strength is comparable to nylon, it has less tendency to lose its smooth surface, thus cutting down appreciably on the drag (friction). Not all of these ropes are as dependable as nylon. A superior quality is acceptable, but poorer grades have been known to fail in the stress of a serious fall. (However, accidents due to a rope's breaking are extremely rare.)

There are standardized specifications for climbing ropes in both the United States and Europe. They are as follows:

UNITED STATES	EUROPE
150 feet x $^3/_8$ inches diameter	45.72 meters x 8 or 9 millimeters
150 feet x $^7/_{16}$ inches diameter	45.72 meters x 11 millimeters
120 feet x $^3/_8$ inches diameter	33.58 meters x 8 or 9 millimeters
120 feet x $^7/_{16}$ inches diameter	33.58 meters x 11 millimeters

Individual preference and proposed usage determine the selection.

The American $^3/_8$-inch rope has a diameter in between the European 8- and 9-millimeter types, and all will hold approximately 3,000 pounds. These lighter ropes are adequate for average climbing expeditions, when the climber generally does not drop far enough to put excessive strain on the rope.

The $^7/_{16}$-inch diameter (11-millimeter) rope tests at about 4,000 pounds and is recommended for practicing because it will retain its strength after much abrasion from rocks and stretching. The heavier line is also used in situations that might result in long falls and unusual demands.

A climbing rope should be inspected before each ascent and after any fall. The strand might be partially cut by a falling rock, worn thin over sharp edges, or slightly weakened by stretching or prolonged exposure to direct sunlight. No rope should be used for climbing if it has a bad nick in one or more strands.

Ropes should be kept away from fires. Nylon is very susceptible to heat and may melt at extreme temperatures. During normal use, the sun is no problem, but it is better to store ropes in the shade.

Rinse ropes occasionally to remove dirt and tiny abrasive rock crystals. Dry in the shade.

Contact with oil or gasoline could dissolve or severely weaken synthetic fibers.

A twisted nylon rope will unwind unless the ends are secured. Tape the last two inches at each end, place the rope on a hard surface, and, with a sharp knife, cut off about one inch to make a smooth, neat edge. Then hold the taped ends over a flame until the nylon fibers melt and adhere to one another. Do not allow rope to burn or drip. Remove tape and apply a liberal amount of epoxy glue to the melted ends and remaining inch of rope.

Retape both ends of the rope in separate colors to differentiate them when climbing. If two ropes are carried, tape the four ends in varying colors.

It is also important to mark the middle of the rope. This may be done with tape, although sometimes tape will work loose and slide out of place. A colored piece of nylon one-half inch wide and three inches long may be pushed between the strands with a small screwdriver or nail. Avoid separating strands by excessive twisting.

European ropes with cloth sheaths are usually two-toned. Such ropes make for easy identification of ends and middle.

Rope handling must be mastered before other skills are possible. Although the subject can be vast and complex, a beginner would do well to concentrate on a few simple procedures that will be easily remembered in times of pressure or fright—the "must-knows." To achieve spontaneity, a great deal of practice at home or in camp is necessary.

One hundred and fifty feet of tangled rope is a nuisance. With practice, a rope can be coiled and uncoiled quickly with few kinks or snarls.

Throw out the rope in random loops on the ground before starting to coil. Grasp rope about one foot from the end with left hand. Sit to the right of the pile and rest the left hand, palm up, on left knee.

Right hand holds rope at arm's length, flips it under left toe, then brings it across left palm to be clasped in left hand. Run right hand out again, flip loop under toe, bring rope across left palm, and grasp. Repeat these basic movements—out with right hand, under toe, across left palm, and grasp—until a tail approximately five feet long remains.

Clasp coiled rope between the knees. With both hands free, make a loop with the first foot of rope and place on top of coil. Wrap the tail around the coil with a half hitch once. Then several times without half hitches. Finally bring this end through the loop and tighten.

This is not the fastest way to coil a rope, but it is a practical method for beginners and takes little practice. Instructions are given for right-handed persons; movements are reversed for left-handers. (This will be true for all instructions.)

To uncoil, hold coil between knees and remove binding wraps with both hands. This is a much faster method than holding with one hand and untying with the other. Speed is essential in all rope handling.

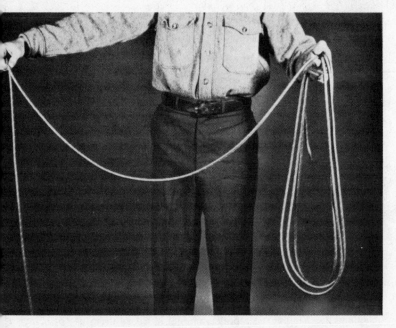

Uncoiling rope one loop at a time and dropping at random.

When ends are freed, hold the coil in left hand at waist level, remove consecutive loops with right hand, and throw rope out at random. Make no effort to pile neatly, as this will usually cause tangling.

If rope is twisted when uncoiled, it should be restacked to remove kinks. To do this, grasp rope with left hand and pull it through the palm with right hand. If kinks appear, they can be whipped out by whirling the right hand in the appropriate direction. The number of kinks will increase as the end is approached, therefore much whipping with the right hand is necessary.

Beginners' Knots

One could become fascinated with the variety of knots and mathematical theories behind them, and climbers often disagree on their preferences, there are several basic knots that a person must know in order to climb any mountain. While each of these knots could be tied in a number of ways, a novice should concentrate on learning one method perfectly, so that he will not forget it under stress of actual climbing. For this reason, I will again bow to the priorities and explain only the bowline, half hitch, overhand, and fisherman's knots—the "must-knows." (Manuals on more advanced knots and various ways of tying them are listed in the Bibliography.)

What About the Square Knot?

The beginner may have been advised that the square knot is safe, and he might be tempted to substitute it for those recommended here. The square knot is very dangerous to use in climbing. It can be easily undone by snagging on a projection and has been the cause of many mountaineering accidents.

Bowline (Bo'lin)

A bowline is the simplest way to tie oneself into the end of a rope. Run rope behind the back and hold separate ends in front with hands, leaving about one foot of tail in right hand. Right hand crosses over to left side and grasps that rope near the waist. Keep palm down and thumb toward the stomach. Make a loop by turning the right hand away from the body. (The rope encircling the body is on top of the loop.) Pass the tail end *up* through the loop, around behind the main rope, and back *down* through the loop, from top to bottom. Tighten the knot while taking up slack so that rope is snug around waist.

There are many ways of tying the bowline. We prefer this method because an instructor or guide can tell from a distance if the beginner has tied it properly and safely. This method also leads to the double bowline with little new instruction.

Tying the Bowline.

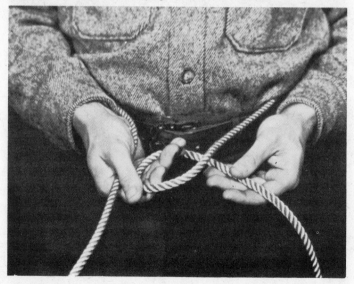

Double Bowline

A double bowline is similar to the single bowline, except that two consecutive loops are made. Make the first loop by twisting the wrist as described above, and then bring the rope around into a second loop underneath the first. This knot will not loosen with continuous climbing and is used when one will be on the rope for long periods.

Half Hitch

The half hitch is not a knot. It is merely a wrap around another rope or an object with the rope running under itself with each turn. A series of half hitches can be made after another knot such as the bowline has been tied, in order to secure ends extending beyond the knot.

Bowline with Half-Hitch backup to prevent knot from loosening.

Fisherman's Knot (or Fisherman's Bend)

This very simple knot is used in fastening together two ropes of nearly equal size. Face the rope ends in opposite directions. Wrap one end completely around the other rope and then forward through the resulting loop. Repeat with other rope end. The knot will tighten itself. It is advisable to place knots a few inches from the ends in case of minor slippage.

Fisherman's Knot

Overhand Knot

The simple overhand knot is used by beginners for tying into the middle of a rope.

If the rope has not been previously marked, double it to locate the center, then mark. Hold doubled rope and make a basic simple knot near the midpoint to form a single loop. The middleman steps into loop and pulls it to his waist, fitting it snugly. Always step into the loop, since putting it over the head might catch it on packs or hinder balance. To remove, pull loop down over hips and step out of it.

Overhand Knot. Loop in Overhand Knot must be large enough to slide up over waist before tightening.

Three Men on a Rope

Although two persons on a rope are a frequent combination and sometimes larger numbers tie in, the techniques involved with three men on a rope are productive to teach since they may be adapted to all other combinations.

Two persons tie into opposite ends of rope with bowlines and the third into the middle with an overhand knot. For long periods on the rope, a double bowline is recommended for end men, as it remains stable with sustained climbing.

The technique of three men on a rope involves some leadership and voice signals. Before roping up, a leader must be appointed by the group to make decisions that will activate the team and protect its members.

The leader first hands the rope to the person designated as "end man." When he has tied in, the leader runs the rope through his hands, whipping out any snarls, until he reaches center. He then has the middleman tie in. Ridding rope of additional snags, he himself ties in at the other end.

Formerly, some climbers thought that people should rope up whenever they were on the mountain. My own experience has taught me that this is neither necessary nor advisable. Only use rope on potentially dangerous pitches. However, on short traverses between cliffs and other obstacles, it may not be practical or convenient to remove ropes. Therefore, one must learn to walk and scramble while tied into a rope although not using it for protection.

End man and middleman coil the rope in their left hands at full arm's length from the waist. Coils are approximately fifteen inches in diameter. The last coil lies between thumb and forefinger so that if the rope becomes taut, consecutive coils can be released as necessary. As the party moves, the interval between climbers will vary. Coils which have been released may be recoiled by the right hand while the climber is still moving.

Since the leader is in danger of being pulled without warning by those on the rope below him, he carries a "leader's loop," holding it far enough from the body to maintain freedom of movement. The loop lets him "feel" the person behind and avoid being jerked off balance. The leader's loop is similar to that used by a good cowboy in leading his horse; the hand is not put through the loop but holds it at its base so that a sudden tug will pull free rather than tighten around wrist or fingers.

The Belay

The belay is a rope technique used in climbing to prevent a fall. As a sailor belays, or makes secure, his ropes by winding them around cleats or pins, a mountaineer belays another climber by bracing the rope around his body or a fixed object such as a boulder, tree, or artificial aid.

One should not climb on a rope without first learning to belay. This is accomplished only through practice and the grooving of a particular set of movements. When these basic moves become familiar, one may learn the feel of a belay by catching a practice fall. Only when one feels secure in this should he rope up on an actual climb. In time, a natural feeling will suggest other methods and positions in belaying, but these should be attempted only after one has spent some time in the mountains.

The belaying movement may be practiced anywhere—in one's room, on the lawn, or on a gentle slope. All one has to do is stretch out the rope and imagine a climber is on the lower end.

The belayer sits facing the climber, with the rope to his left. The rope is brought around the belayer's back, resting snugly just below the belt, and the end is grasped with the right hand. The left hand holds rope leading to the climber. In this position, the belayer can arrest a fall with his right hand, but most of the pressure will be absorbed by the rope around his body. The left hand cannot hold the fall, nor is it supposed to.

Belayer grasps rope with left hand fully extended toward climber, gripping with right hand close to the waist near the belt line. This is the *starting belay movement*.

Pull rope up with left hand and, at the same time, push forward with right hand. This will cause the rope to slide easily around the hips and body. When the left hand has pulled up one arm's length and the right hand has pushed out that length, left hand is grasping rope near waist on the left and right arm is fully extended. This is the *ending belay movement*.

Notice that from the starting belay movement to the ending belay movement the right hand was gripping rope at all times and was ready to stop a fall. Now the problem is how to return to the starting belay movement without endangering the climber.

Loosen the left-hand grip without releasing the rope and slide hand forward until it is slightly ahead of right hand. Left hand temporarily grasps both ropes to maintain the belay in case of a fall during the instant it takes the right hand to slightly loosen its grip and slide back to

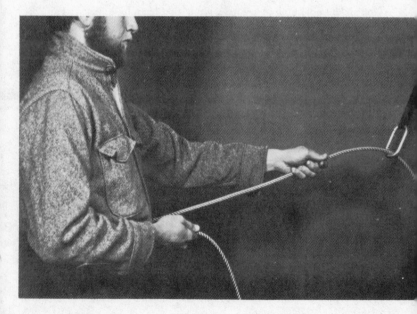

Starting belay movement. Right hand is the brake hand. Left hand is guide hand.

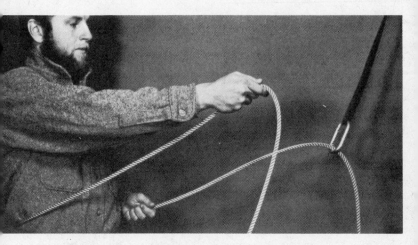

Ending belay movement. Left hand pulls in, right hand is out-stretched.

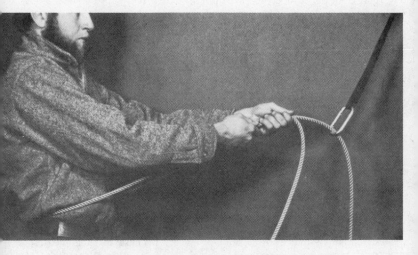

Shifting belay movement. Left hand is in position beyond right hand, grasping both ropes. Right hand can then return to the starting belay position.

starting position at the waist. With the belay secure once more, left hand can regrip line leading to climber at extended arm's length. The starting belay position is in effect. This movement, from ending belay to starting belay, is called the *shifting belay movement*. In a repetition of these movements, the climber is safely belayed. The rope being brought up by the belayer is dropped at random on his right side.

Belay movements must be rehearsed until some coordination is developed and one can belay without having to focus attention upon the mechanics, for there are other things one must think about while belaying. One of them is the *belaying position,* or way in which the body will be held securely in place if the climber should fall.

There are many belaying positions and, since no two climbing situations are identical, judgment must be exercised. The belayer may sit and brace his feet wide apart (possibly against a rock or tree) with knees stiff or locked so that they do not buckle under pressure. The rope will cause least discomfort around the body if kept just below the belt. It should lie between the belayer's outstretched feet so that pull from the climber will not tip him to the side.

The belayer and climber must be in constant communication. For instance, when the belayer is ready for the climber to proceed, he must let him know. In practice sessions, he could merely say, "O.K., Bill. I'm all set in a belaying position up here, and I think I can hold you if you fall, so why don't you let me know if you're ready to climb?"

This would not work on an actual climb. In many cases, the words would be muffled. So Bill would yell back, "What did you say, Pete? I can't understand you." And Pete would answer, "I can't hear you, Bill. What are you doing?" A third man on the rope might confuse the issue by adding, "What's going on up there? I'm getting cold. Get the lead out, you guys!" Bedlam, confusion, and perhaps a dangerous situation has developed.

The human voice is difficult to hear and understand on a mountain. The belayer might be out of his companion's sight, words do not carry well around rock projections, wind and rain sometimes make conversation impossible even at short distances. Because of such interferences, I have developed voice signals that are brief and intelligible, even when faintly heard.

When a belayer is ready to belay a climber, he calls, "On belay." The climber then knows that his companion is in a belaying position and has the rope ready for belaying movements. Climber yells, "Climbing," to let belayer know he has heard the signal and is ready, too. Both persons want to make sure that there is complete understanding, so if the belayer has heard the signal and is absolutely ready, he yells, "Climb." The climber then proceeds, certain of a safe belay.

When proper signals have been given and acknowledged, climber can walk very slowly toward belayer (or climb, in a real situation), and belayer will take up slack. Remember, taking up slack does not mean a tight rope that will pull the climber or disturb his balance.

When climber reaches belayer, he might wish to get on a ledge or other safe area before relinquishing his belay. The belayer does not know when the climber feels absolutely secure, so he stays on belay until climber says, "Belay off." Belayer registers understanding by responding, "Thank you." Only then does he leave the belaying position.

There are additional signals to practice. After the interchange "On belay," "Climbing," "Climb," the climber starts up. Perhaps he notices that there is too much slack in the rope, a dangerous situation on the mountain as this will allow too much momentum to build before belayer has a chance to stop a fall. Also, the belayer may not be able to "feel" movements of the unseen climber, as the rope might catch in cracks or other impediments. Therefore, the belayer needs to be told if he should take up slack. To accomplish this, the climber yells, "Up rope." The belayer acknowledges hearing the signal with "Thank you."

Conversely, the climber might wish to drop down a few feet to rest on a ledge or select a different route. In this case, he yells, "Slack." The belayer responds, "Thank you," and cautiously feeds out some slack by slightly loosening his grip and allowing rope to gently slide through his hands. The belayer remains in belaying position, prepared to stop a sudden fall at all times. When climber has enough slack or wishes to resume, he calls, "Climbing," and belayer, if ready to start belaying up, replies, "Climb."

A climber seldom falls without prior warning. If he senses a fall, he yells, "Falling," to warn belayer to brace his position and grip the rope with right hand fully or partially extended and crossing over body toward left side. This brings the rope almost completely around him, causing so much friction that the rope will not pull through right hand.

If climber feels he might fall, he may yell, "Tension." With this signal, belayer will take up slack quickly while replying, "Thank you," literally holding climber in place. When climber recovers, he signals, "Climbing," and after hearing response "Climb," can proceed.

Sometimes a climber will need a helpful pull on the rope. For this he yells, "Climbing with tension." After answering, "Climb," belayer pulls as hard as he can with left hand, helping climber over the *mauvais pas* while still protecting the belay with right hand and proper movements. For a return to normal belay, the signals are "Climbing" and "Climb."

"Slack with tension" will accomplish the reverse of the above when climber must retreat with help of the rope to hold him.

Notice that all signals in which rope will normally be taken up by belayer are composed of two syllables—"Up rope," "Climbing," "Falling," "Tension." Signal for letting out rope is monosyllabic—"Slack." There can be no serious misunderstanding even if signals are only heard faintly because merely determining the number of syllables dictates proper action.

"Hardware"

Artificial climbing aids such as pitons, carabiners, and piton hammers are referred to as "hardware."

The carabiner is an oblong metal link with an automatic spring gate to allow insertion of a climbing rope. When fastened to a solid object, a carabiner acts as a belay point between belayer and climber.

Sometimes carabiners are secured by slings, six- to twelve-foot lengths of rope or webbing that may be tied around a fixed object such as a tree or boulder. The carabiner can also be snapped into a piton, an iron spike with a hole, or "eye." Pitons are driven with a special piton hammer into cracks in rock to provide belay points, furnish footholds and handholds, or anchor rappel ropes.

Snap a carabiner into a piton or sling with spring gate on lower side, the opening forward. Then turn the carabiner over so that spring gate is on top, ready to receive the rope.

The beginner invariably asks, "How do I know that a piton will hold? Isn't the crack likely to spread? Won't the piton pull out if I fall?"

The answers are not too reassuring. There is no guarantee that a piton will hold, but there are certain principles that can be taken into account.

Pitons are generally graduated in width. As a rule, the crack must be as wide as the widest part of the piton. A piton driven into a crack that is likely to spread will give a dull ring, while that driven into a solid, non-spreading wedge will ring like a guitar string, becoming higher and higher in tone as it is hammered further inside.

A vertical crack running straight up the mountain forces full pressure of a pull directly on the piton, and a secure hold is less assured. A horizontal crack running level across the mountain protects the downward pull against the lower lip of rock and provides a much safer anchor.

Piton in a horizontal crack slanting downward.

The ideal crack is one running horizontally and downward into the mountain. A ringing piton driven into such a place is most secure, as the downward pull will tend to force it further into the crack. Cracks, of course, are likely to be at any angle, but the closer to the horizontal the better.

Mountain hardware can be carried on a special sling that fits over the shoulder. The shoulder sling should be short enough for hardware to hang above the belt. Carabiners may be snapped into the sling and into pitons for transport. Extra slings are tied around the waist or over the shoulders. Piton hammers, carried by leader and end man (for retrieving hardware), are tucked into the belt or placed in a special carrying scabbard.

Belaying Through Carabiners

Novices can learn how to belay through a carabiner by tying in three men on a rope and going through a simulated exercise on gentle terrain. Instead of tying slings to rocks or pitons, as would be done on the mountain, tie them to trees. Because ropes are generally 150 feet long, trees for the practice course should be no more than 65 feet apart for a three-man team. Climbers will also need four slings and four carabiners.

A leader is appointed and participants tie into the rope. The leader carries hardware.

Before detailing the mechanics of belaying through carabiners with three men on a rope, it might be helpful to visualize the process in simplified steps. Imagine three trees as three levels of a mountain, with tree No. 1 at the lowest level. Initially, the trio of climbers is together at the base, about sixty feet below tree No. 1.

Obviously, on exposed pitches and rugged terrain, climbers cannot move simultaneously; they must move in tandem, each person being belayed by a companion as he takes his turn. In outline form, it would be as follows:

1. Leader climbs to first tree while middleman feeds out rope.
2. Leader belays middleman to first tree.
3. Middleman belays leader to second tree.

4. Middleman belays end man up to first tree. At the same time, leader belays middleman to hold him at first tree and as an added security.
5. Leader belays middleman to second tree while end man also belays middleman for added security.
6. Middleman belays leader to third tree.
7. Leader holds middleman on belay while middleman belays end man to second tree.
8. Leader and end man belay middleman to third tree.
9. Middleman belays end man to third tree.

As can be seen, the three climbers move ahead in an accordionlike motion until all are together at the final destination.

Now let us review the exercise in more detail, including judgment factors and proper voice signals.

Starting at the base, leader hands middleman the climbing rope and says, "Climbing no belay." This indicates that he is in no danger of falling but wants middleman to feed out rope carefully so that it does not tangle or catch on obstacles. Middleman replies, "Climb," when he is prepared.

On actual climbs, the leader must know how many feet of rope remain. Therefore, middleman calls out, "Fifteen—ten—five," as he feeds out the rope. As each footage is called, leader responds, "Thank you." These signals prevent the leader from running out of rope in a difficult climbing position or impossible belay site.

In our simulated exercise, the leader reaches the first tree and ties one sling around it with a fisherman's knot. He snaps one carabiner into the sling and then snaps the rope running down to middleman into the carabiner.

If middleman has not yet given the "Five" signal, leader knows there is more slack, so he brings up the rope hand over hand until middleman yells, "Five." Leader then knows that he has five feet of slack with which to assume the sitting belay position and starting belay movement.

The leader could face the middleman on the opposite side of the tree and brace his feet to effect a sitting belay. However, we want the carabiner to hold most of the imaginary fall. In order to accomplish this, leader sits below tree on same side as middleman and belays with his back toward climber. If middleman should fall, belayer would be pulled toward carabiner and much of the strain would be on the sling and carabiner rather than belayer.

Standard "On belay," "Climbing," and "Climb" signals are given. End man prevents rope from catching behind middleman as he proceeds.

When middleman has joined leader at first tree, he says, "Belay off," and is answered, "Thank you." Leader unsnaps the rope from the carabiner near middleman's waist and snaps the rope at his own waist into this carabiner. He gives ropes near his waist to middleman, who assumes belaying position previously taken by leader. This shift of rope in and out of carabiner allows climbers to switch rope position without having to pull sixty-five feet of slack through the carabiner by hand. This saves both time and energy and is repeated each time a belay is so shifted.

Standard belaying signals are given, and leader proceeds to second tree as middleman signals footage. At "Five," middleman takes rope from around his body, since there is no more slack. He has a solid belaying position without having his hands on the rope. He indicates the end with "Zero."

On the mountain, belay points depend upon availability of rocks, cracks, and so forth. One does not always have the ideal choice. Therefore, it is wise to practice several belaying positions. At the second tree, our leader will place an overhead belay.

He ties a sling around the tree as high as he can reach and fastens in a carabiner. The rope runs from the leader up through carabiner and down to middleman. The leader may stand and perform belaying movements around his upper back, rather than the hips. The belay can be kept from slipping upward if the leader keeps left elbow down. As in all belay positions, it is a matter of noting direction of pull and bracing accordingly.

Signals between middle and end men do not confuse leader since he has already exchanged signals with middleman and is aware of the situation. The middleman knows leader is still on belay after he has brought up end man, so when he is ready to ascend, he yells, "Climbing," and leader answers, "Climb." Middleman proceeds to next position, belayed by leader above and end man below.

When middleman reaches leader, he snaps another carabiner into the sling and snaps rope leading to end man into that carabiner. Thus, he is belayed by end man while he belays leader upward. The shift of rope in and out of carabiner and signals between middleman and leader are the same as at tree No. 1.

There are times when the leader will want to place extra carabiners on slings or pitons as he climbs above the middleman. Theoretically, if he climbed twenty feet above the middleman, a fall could take him those twenty feet plus twenty additional feet before the slack would be used up. To avoid this possibility, he could place belay points every ten feet or so to drastically reduce the length of his plunge and resulting strain on belaying pitons, slings, and carabiners.

Three on a Rope Using Pitons

When three men on a rope use pitons instead of natural anchors, there are a few additional techniques and signals.

As before, leader signals, "Climbing no belay," and middleman responds, "Climb." Leader travels about twenty feet, hammers in a piton, and snaps in carabiner and rope. If middleman is able to see leader, he immediately gets on belay and they exchange standard signals. However, if leader is out of sight, he shouts, "Belay through piton," and middleman replies, "On belay."

The leader may go ten feet higher and drive another piton. No additional signal is necessary unless indicated by judgment.

It is vital that ropes slide through carabiners with the least amount of friction possible. Since pitons might not be in a straight line, rope will bend in passing through carabiners. Each bend will increase friction on the rope and the leader might have to pull up the rope with his hands to obtain enough slack.

Often, a piton is driven into a crack near a rock projection that would cause extreme friction on the rope. In this case, insert a sling with carabiner into the piton, so that the rope will run freely.

A belayer must be unusually careful to avoid injuring his left hand should any climber fall. If one holds on to the rope with the left hand during a fall, the rope might be jerked forward enough to take the hand into the carabiner and cause injury.

If a leader must turn to look downward, he should always turn back in the same direction, so that the rope will not twist but pass freely through the carabiner.

Experienced climbers who have climbed together might find some of these signals superfluous, but beginners should use them until they are instinctively understood and no longer need be voiced.

The Rappel

Often a party can climb down a mountain by belaying in the same way it ascended. At other times, this is impossible or dangerous because a descent might be more difficult, sudden storms may have left rocks wet, snowy, or glazed with ice, or progress may be too slow to avoid threatening weather or darkness. At such times, climbers may descend a cliff by sliding down a rope. This technique is called rappelling ("abseiling," in England).

The novice might assume that one could merely secure a rope to a rock, throw the end over a cliff and descend hand over hand. But this would necessitate an exceptional grip and, if one started to slip, one could not control the body's momentum or prevent hands from being severely burned or skinned. Also, it would be impossible for the last climber to retrieve the rope for further use.

In rappelling, however, the rate of descent is controlled by rope friction against the body and/or carabiner, rather than by the hands, and a special double-rope technique allows the line to be retrieved.

One must anticipate the length of rope needed to reach the bottom of a pitch and allow rope to be doubled for retrieval. If a descent is under seventy-five feet, one 150-foot rope is sufficient, but if the elevation is higher, two ropes must be carried. A second rope is also advisable for belaying inexperienced persons on a safety line while they rappel. Thus the leader will have his party rappel on one rope, using the other rope as a belay to protect the rappeller. The leader will then descend, rappelling on both ropes, without a safety rope.

Hazardous, exposed conditions which necessitate a rappel make accidents common in this phase of mountain climbing but, with good leadership and sensible precautions, rappelling can be safe. Once again, repeated practice on gentle slopes is indicated before one attempts to negotiate cliffs.

The Guide's Body Rappel

The Guide's Body Rappel is a safe, easy technique recommended for beginners, here explained in terms of practice on unexposed terrain.

Tie a sling around a rock or tree, insert rope through sling, and stretch double rope down the grade. Face uphill and straddle rope. Reach backward with left hand to lift both ropes, bring them around left leg and up over left shoulder. Then reach back with right hand, grasp ropes, and hold them with arm near right buttock. Extend the left arm, palm up, and partially close fingers over ropes. Do not grip.

Place feet slightly apart for balance, stiffen knees, then push backward on double rope. The rope will slide up through right hand, over left shoulder, around left leg, and through the crotch. Remember, do not grip with left hand, as this will prevent body from moving backward as rope slides.

One stops the rappel by closing the right hand on the rope. With so much friction around the body, a slight grip will act as a brake. The descent is controlled by the right hand as it grips and releases the rope.

Rope will run with less friction when right hand pushes it up toward left shoulder, slides back down the rope, then pushes up again. This is called "pumping the rappel."

This Guide's Body Rappel is practical for short pitches where rock is less than perpendicular. It has the advantage of being easy to get in and out of; however, unless one is wearing heavy clothing, there is a problem of rope burn. It is advisable to slide rope over the left buttock rather than directly through the crotch.

The Swiss Body Rappel

The Swiss Body Rappel places more friction around the body than the Guide's method.

Face uphill and straddle rope. Reach back with right hand, bring rope around right leg, across chest, up over the head, and down over left shoulder. Grasp rope in back with right hand and gently hold front rope with left hand as in Guide's Body Rappel.

Action is identical in both body rappels. The only advantage of the

The Guide's Body Rappel. Rope passes through legs, around to front of body, and over same shoulder to hand on opposite side. By simply dropping the rope from his shoulder, the rappeller is free.

Swiss style is that it creates extra friction. Disadvantages are that one must lift rope over the head in getting in and out of the rappel position, which can be awkward and use more energy, and beginners are apt to become tangled in the ropes.

The Carabiner Rappel

Since rope burns in the crotch are apt to occur on long, steep body rappels, most difficult rappels are executed with an immovable sling running around hips and through the crotch. The sling is fastened to a carabiner in front of the body.

While there are several types of rappelling slings, I consider the diaper sling the most practical. Tie ends of an eight- to twelve-foot sling together to form a loop. (Length of sling depends upon climber's girth.) While standing, place loop behind hips, then pull sides to the front, and snap a carabiner into both loops in front of belt. Keep upper side of loop belt-high. Lower edge will be hanging down in back of body.

Reach between legs and pull lower part of sling up to snap into the waist carabiner. The diaper sling should fit snugly but not be uncomfortably tight. (Some climbers tie a sling in the proper size and use it exclusively for rappelling. The fisherman's knot is sufficient for fastening the ends of the sling together. Leave at least six inches beyond the knots to allow for some tightening.)

Snap rappel rope into carabiner and run it up over left shoulder and down to right buttock, holding it as previously described.

While friction on the body is drastically reduced, there still might be some discomfort on the left shoulder. A felt hat or other padding under the shirt will protect the area from burns.

One carabiner is adequate for practice, but on actual climbs two carabiners should be snapped side by side to hold diaper sling and rappel ropes. Snap both carabiners into the sling with gates down and facing the abdomen, then turn them until gates are up and on the outside in order to insert double rappel rope. Before proceeding, turn one of the carabiners halfway around so that gates lie in opposite directions. This will prevent the rope from accidentally opening both carabiners and creating a dangerous situation.

The Carabiner Rappel (with Diaper Sling). Rope clipped through carabiners attached to diaper sling passes over shoulder to hand on opposite side. When two carabiners are used, the gates should be reversed for safety.

Climbers rappelling with sling and carabiners must be warned that the rope sliding down from the shoulder, across front of body, and through the carabiners will tend to catch loose clothing or long hair. This could bind clothes and rope together in the carabiner and stop action. Without a safety rope, a survival incident is possible.

The Overhang Free Rappel

A free rappel occurs when an overhang causes the rope to dangle in space at a distance from the cliff. Since the rappeller cannot make contact with hands and feet, he must slide down the rope in mid-air.

The most difficult part of this rappel is getting past the lip of the overhang. When feet can no longer reach the cliff and the left hand holding the rope is still above the overhang, the hand will be pressed against the rock by the rope and may be skinned. If the climber lets go with the left hand, he will topple backward because he has no other safeguard.

A good way to negotiate the overhang is to slide over it on the stomach. This will allow a conscious transfer of left hand from above to below overhang before body is suspended.

During the rappel, left hand remains on the rope above the head and upper body. Leaning back away from the rope will increase strain on the left hand.

Twists in rappel rope tend to untwist with weight of a body in free rappel. Since there is no contact with the rock, the climber might be slowly spun around, causing the safety rope to wrap around the rappel rope, preventing further descent. In this event, loosen rappel rope from above and have belayer lower climber.

Last man down should slide down overhang quickly to lessen chances of twisting, which might tangle ropes and prevent their retrieval.

Setting Up the Rappel

While techniques described for practice are usable in exposed rappels, there are many factors to be considered in choosing actual rappel sites on the mountain.

One of the greatest dangers is falling rocks, which might be loosened by ropes or belayer and strike the rappeller or those standing below. Also, the upper ledge must be large enough to accommodate successive rappellers or spectators. One member of the party might back into another and push him from the cliff. I know of one instance in which someone excitedly pointed out a soaring eagle and tipped a companion over the edge. Leaders must exercise judgment to prevent such tragedies.

The stability of trees, boulders, or other rope anchorages must be ascertained. When such natural supports are not available, pitons are used.

In beginning rappels on an exposed site, it is wise to belay the climber from above on a separate rope. The chances of both the rappel and belay failing are almost nil.

If pitons are used to hold rappel rope, drive two of them into separate cracks (preferably no more than a couple of feet apart). A second piton in the same crack might loosen the first.

Snap a carabiner into each piton, uncoil rope, run end through both carabiners, and tie it back to itself with a bowline a few feet below carabiners. Rope is now looped through both carabiners. If one piton dislodges, the rope will still be held by the other. Note direction of pull on pitons, as the loop will tend to bring them toward each other as well as downward.

Drive two more pitons in new and separate cracks for the belayer. Snap in carabiners, uncoil rope, and run end through both carabiners. While belayer gets into position, climber ties into other end of rope.

Belayer and climber exchange standard belaying signals. Belayed climber is now ready to take rappel rope to the edge and throw it over cliff. (Experienced climbers may not need a belay when throwing rope.) My method of throwing rope has proved very satisfactory and has been widely used by climbers.

Grasp rappel rope close to pitons where it is fastened. Make a series of loops about one and a half feet in diameter, holding each loop in left hand, palm up. When approximately half of the rope has been so looped, transfer to right hand. Hold portion leading to unattached end in left hand. Then, with an underhand swing of right hand, throw coils horizontally out into space as far as possible and let rope fall down the cliff. The remaining rope is now held by left hand and a loop runs from left hand down the cliff and back to pitons.

Coil the remaining rope in left hand, trying to keep coils parallel. Transfer to right hand and throw out, as before. When throwing, pressure of hanging rope will be reduced if left hand holds the line in back of loops, releasing grip with the toss. As this second coil is thrown, it pulls the hanging loop away from cliff walls, and the full length has a good chance of reaching bottom untangled.

In a variation of the above, instead of being coiled, the rope may be laid in loops about two and a half feet long across the upturned palm of the left hand. Loops can then be transferred to right hand and thrown out as described for coils.

Rappelling Techniques

With the first rappeller tied into the end of a safety rope, belayer takes up slack and assumes position. They exchange standard belaying signals and climber snaps rappel rope into double carabiners on his diaper sling, reverses carabiner gates, and starts down.

Rappeller's feet should be about twelve inches apart, with knees straight, and body bent forward from the hips, somewhat like a formal bow. As much weight as possible is placed on the feet, which are kept low. Even on perpendicular cliffs, the feet can hold part of the weight by pressing against the rock at a point lower than the waist. At no time should the feet be higher than the buttocks or the rappeller might be upended.

The right arm is kept straight, except when pumping the rappel. It swings toward the front for more friction, and back for less.

Signals for rappelling are the same as those used in belaying. (See pages 172–74.)

The first rappeller should inspect his route for rocks which might be loosened as he passes. He signals, "Tension," and is held in place if he wishes to discard rocks and loose debris or seek another route. Care must be exercised when dislodging rocks in order to avoid injuring those below or cutting the hanging rope. When ready to resume rappelling, he signals, "Climbing."

Left hand is guide hand, right hand the brake hand. Note that boot soles are flat on the rock, knees are slightly bent as rappeller steps down cliff. This beginner is gripping too tightly with upper hand and not bending forward from the hips.

At the bottom of the cliff, climber removes rappel rope, making sure that it is not tangled around his body. He takes off diaper sling if it will hamper walking, then unties safety rope, steps aside to a safe position where rocks dislodged by subsequent rappellers cannot strike him, and signals, "Belay off and all clear." Belayer answers, "Thank you," gets out of belaying position, and brings up safety rope hand over hand.

When it is impossible for a climber to move out of line of falling rocks, his signal is merely, "Off rappel." This indicates that he is free of all ropes but still in danger of falling rocks. Subsequent rappellers must be extra cautious.

Last man down must redo the setup, as there will be no one to belay him and he must arrange to retrieve both ropes. It is not possible to salvage pitons used for rappel. The safety rope is now dangling where preceding climber left it beside rappel rope.

Last man runs a sling through the two rappel-rope pitons, tying the ends to form a loop. It will be necessary to remove the carabiners so that the eye of the pitons will accommodate the sling. The bowline knot on the rappel rope is untied and the rope is run *down* through the sling loop and tied with a fisherman's knot to the end of the safety rope.

The rappel rope must be run *down* through sling loop before being tied to safety rope so that it will slide over the top of the sling without pressure and not press the sling against the ledge and bind the lower rope.

One can readily understand why the ends of the ropes should have been marked with different colors before the climb. If the wrong rope is pulled, the knot would be brought back to the sling. At best, the knot will not slide around the sling and may be caught in it, perhaps lodging there even if the correct rope is pulled. Inability to retrieve ropes from the bottom is a common and dangerous error made by climbers. Scaling the cliff to get them loose may be impossible and at the least is a waste of precious time.

The next-to-last rappeller should test the setup before final man descends to be sure that ropes will slide through sling.

Needless to say, the last man down must have ability and judgment to make a safe rappel although unprotected by belay. He must prevent ropes from catching in cracks, and must be sure that they can run parallel above him as he descends. Should the ropes become twisted, they might not pull through the sling. He can keep a right-hand finger between ropes to maintain their parallel position.

Roped River Crossings

Most river crossings may be accomplished by wading, boulder hopping, or using logs as a bridge, but in cases where one is apt to be swept away should he fall; a climbing rope is used.

The safety line is carried across the river by the first man, who is belayed by another rope so that he may be pulled in or swung around to the downstream bank in case of trouble.

When setting up a safety line, fasten the end on the opposite bank downstream from the starting point so that the current will carry a person cross-stream if he falls. The first man over may take an extra belay rope in cases of extreme danger so that subsequent crossers may be belayed from both shores.

The wader is connected to the safety line by tying a sling around his waist and fastening it to the rope with a carabiner. Two carabiners with reversed gates are used in very dangerous crossings.

If conditions are very treacherous, the expedition leader may decide that a Tyrolean traverse is necessary: method of crossing above water on ropes strung up in a pulley system.

The first crosser must be a strong person and an accomplished swimmer who is capable of setting up the traverse on the opposite bank. He can be helped by the current if the crossing is made at the bend of the river. He should be belayed from above to let him arc across the water and also belayed across the current to return him to the starting point if necessary. The upper belay should be around a tree or fixed point, since a strong current makes a direct body belay impractical.

Ropes for the Tyrolean traverse may be attached to any solid base such as a boulder or tree. If trees are too small to safely bear the entire pull, the rope may be placed high on one tree through a carabiner and sling, and fastened at the base of a second tree. In this way, the first

Tyrolean Traverse. Climber is fastened to Tyrolean traverse with diaper sling. In this photograph, an extra sling is used around chest for increased safety. The rope is anchored to tree on either side.

tree will hold the rope high and the pull from the traverse will push down on the carabiner sling, with no tendency to yank the tree from its roots. All forward strain will come at the base of the second tree.

The rope must be taut and high enough above the stream to offset the sag caused by the weight of the person crossing. The rope may be tightened by a pulley system using double carabiners at several points. The carabiners can be attached by simple overhand knots. Since the knots might become so tight that they will be difficult to untie later, small sticks may be placed in the knots before tightening.

Persons crossing are fastened to the traverse rope by a diaper sling with two reversed carabiners, and they are belayed from one or both riverbanks, depending upon the danger. Sometimes a second sling is placed around the chest and fastened to traverse rope with a carabiner to make crossing easier and safer.

Only those who are experienced in using ropes and climbing hardware should attempt the Tyrolean traverse. Practice on dry land between trees or fixed points should precede actual attempts. One should remember that when crossing wild water, communication may be impossible. Make plans for transferring people and equipment beforehand, and be sure that there is complete understanding among all persons involved.

10

Summer Snow Techniques

High up in the mountain peaks there are snowfields and glaciers which challenge climbers all year long. One might think that mountaineering techniques used in winter would be the same for summer in this snowy terrain, but there is little relationship between seasonal skills required for the two situations. A major factor is snow conditions.

Winter snow is soft. One needs snowshoes or skis to keep from sinking with every step, but if one falls, the body will stop naturally in the deep snow.

When summer comes, these same snow slopes become heavy with moisture and harden. They might freeze into a solid mass at night. One can walk on the surface without skis, but a fall might cause one to slide out of control and be injured on protruding rocks or boulders below. Special skills are needed to traverse summer snowfields and glaciers and to stop oneself should a fall occur.

Walking on Snow

It is difficult and often dangerous to perform snow techniques when wearing smooth-soled shoes or sneakers. Only boots with cleated soles should be used, and they should be laced tighter than when worn on the trail, since one needs more control in edging boots into the snow.

Learning to walk on snow takes practice. Because footing is likely to be treacherous, cautious and deliberate moves are necessary.

In the discussion of trail techniques, we mentioned various ways of maintaining balance and conserving energy while walking. Going uphill, one stands straight because a slip will throw the body forward; descending, one leans forward from the waist with chin over feet to avoid being pitched backward; traversing crosswise, one drops the downhill shoulder and slants out over the slope. These positions to make recovery possible after a slip are even more vital on summer snow.

In walking up a gentle snowfield, plant the boot flat on the snow with weight partially on the heel. Do not lean forward or weight will tend to be put on toes and push the feet backward.

When going downhill, lean upper part of body out over the toes and throw weight on toes with each step. This will cause the boots to slide a few inches forward with each step. One might even wish to exaggerate these movements as in skating or cross-country skiing. Slipping is stopped by throwing weight more to the heel.

To travel at an angle upward and across the slope, lean upper body downhill. Do not bend forward, however. Stand upright. It is helpful to place some weight on the heel. If the foot tends to slip, edge the entire side of the boot into the slope with each step.

When angling downward and across the slope, lean upper body out and down. One may skate on the edged boots with weight toward the toes or heels.

When the grade becomes too steep to climb flat-footed, "step kicking" is necessary. A step is kicked by swinging the foot backward, then swinging it forward to drive the toe into the snow. The foot is nearly level as it goes into the slope, making a platform to support the body.

Do not waste energy pushing into the snow. The swing's momentum is sufficient. On hard or steep surfaces, lengthen the backward swing of the foot to get more power in the forward thrust. Do not try to increase the force by making a short kick more violent. Relax leg muscles as the toe contacts the snow.

In descending steep slopes, we use the "plunge step." Lean forward from the waist, lift one leg straight with locked knee, raise the toe, and then shift all of the weight to this leg as the heel is driven down into the slope. As the heel penetrates the snow, shift weight forward and lean from the hips; leaning backward will make the heel slide forward out of its step. Repeat maneuver with other foot and continue in a rhythmic descent.

The Self-Arrest with Ice Axe

Slipping out of kicked or plunged steps on steep slopes may send one skidding downhill out of control. To avoid this, everyone climbing on snow must know how to make a "self-arrest" with an ice axe.

"Ice axe" is not a very descriptive term for a climbing aid that is used almost exclusively on snowfields. The tool, something like an old miner's pick, has a head with a sharp "pick" at one end and a flat blade, "adz," at the other. At the bottom of the stock, or handle, is a metal point. A wrist loop attached to a ring that slides up and down the stock secures the axe to the climber. The movable ring allows the hand to slide up or down the handle as needed for step cutting, walking, or self-arrest.

Climbers on steep terrain must be able to place the ice axe in a self-arrest position quickly in case of a slip or fall. For the self-arrest position, grip the axehead with right hand, plam down and thumb under the adz. Grasp the stock near the point with the left hand.

In a fall, make a self-arrest by rolling onto the stomach, facing uphill. Position the axe diagonally under the chest with right hand above the shoulders and left hand below them. Push the pick gently and gradually into the snow. This movement plus friction of the body will brake the descent. Jabbing with the pick might jerk the axe from the hands.

Preparing for self-arrest. Note that climber has positioned hands for self-arrest and the pick of the axe is held away from the body.

Self-arrest position. Climber's body is positioned over the ice axe, with toes dug in, and the pick of the axe securely in the snow.

Legs and feet may also be used as brakes. Spread the legs, maneuvering them to keep the body facing uphill, and dig in with the toes.

Whenever possible, practice self-arrests on slopes having a safe runout of rock-free flat snow at the bottom. If such conditions are not available, set up a fixed climbing rope as a precaution. Secure the rope on rocks or ice axes at both ends, leaving a little slack. The rope should fall slightly diagonally across the slope or "fall line." This position is sometimes termed a "J-line," since the rope now resembles the letter "J." The climber is fastened to the line by a sling with a carabiner. Thus attached, with the sling sliding freely, the climber may practice self-arrests and other techniques without danger. Even when the ice axe is being used as a cane, one should be prepared for the self-arrest by keeping the right hand in self-arrest position. After a fall starts, one can position the left hand quickly, but it might be impossible for the right hand to assume its proper position. The self-arrest is the most important snow technique and must be mastered.

Other Uses of the Ice Axe

Sometimes one will have to make steps with an ice axe. In brittle ice, the pick end will break out chunks, and steps may be finished by chopping with the adz. In hard snow, however, such chipping is impossible; the axe point will bury itself with each chop. Steps are made in hard snow by "pulling" them—that is, striking the snow with the adz and pulling at the same time.

It is easier to pull steps toward the side of the body rather than above. The resultant step accommodates the side of the boot in an upward traverse. With practice, one can learn to pull steps that slant downward into the snowfield, assuring a more secure footing.

When pulling steps, keep both hands on the axe handle. However, in case of a slip, the right hand moves to self-arrest position on the head. It is advisable to disengage the wrist sling and hold it while pulling steps in case the sliding ring does not move freely enough to allow an immediate self-arrest.

When not using the wrist sling during hiking, belaying, or when storing the axe, fasten it to the head by inserting the pick through the loop, making a twist in the loop, and securing it over the adz. Pull down on the ring and the loop will fit snugly.

When there is little danger of losing control or sliding into obstacles, glissading is a fast and exhilarating way of descending snow slopes. Here one skis on one's feet, using the ice axe as a third leg, or rudder.

Hold the ice axe ready for self-arrest, with its head near the left knee and its point in the snow behind the left foot. Squat down slightly and place some weight on the axe point. Glissade, or slide, down the hill on the feet, balancing with the ice axe. For more speed, move weight forward over the toes and off the axe point. To slow down, move weight back over the heels and press down on axe point. To stop, force weight on the axe point and turn both toes left, digging heels into the snow, a maneuver similar to a Christie in skiing. In case of a fall, the ice axe is already in self-arrest position.

Climbers who are also skiers can ski down slopes without skis. Speed is controlled by a series of Christies, or sharp turns. Hold the ice axe in front of body in self-arrest position. Stopping is accomplished by a heel-weighted Christie, which generally throws a spectacular "rooster tail" of snow into the air.

One may alternate the various methods of descending, switching from skiless skiing to the plunge step and then into a glissade, and so forth, as one's ability and conditions of the terrain dictate.

Using the Rope on Snow

There are times when one would not feel secure in relying upon the self-arrest alone. For instance, when there are exposed rocks or crevasses below, a party may rope up and belay one another. However, the belay should be used only as a backup to a self-arrest, not a substitute for it.

It is easy for a falling climber to pull his belayer from his stance on a snowfield. To avoid this, the ice axe can be brought into use as a belay point. In hard summer snow that has not yet turned to ice, the axe handle can be inserted all the way into the slope by placing both hands on the head and pushing the point into the snow. Sometimes it is necessary to pump the axe up and down to embed the axe securely.

When a belay pulls on an embedded axe, several things may happen. Pressure exerted by the handle may cause surrounding snow to melt and become slick. Also, as the stock bends under pressure, the axe may "jump" upward, disengaging itself as a belay point.

In order to avoid this dangerous "jumping ice-axe belay," the axe must be embedded into the slope at an angle slightly uphill, opposite the pull of belay. The counterforce will thus drive the axe farther into the snow.

If the axe is plunged properly, there will be only an inch or two of snow to brace the lower side against the belay. It is a good idea to scrape a platform before driving the axe in order to accumulate additional snow for extra bracing.

There are ways of belaying a rope to a fixed ice axe. Some are complicated, old-fashioned, and unsafe. I recommend two methods for the beginner: the simple ice-axe belay and the axe-carabiner belay. Other techniques may be tried after these are mastered.

In the simple ice-axe belay, the belayer holding the rope stands slightly below the fixed ice axe. The rope runs around the upper side of the axe stock and down to the climber being belayed. A body belay incorporating the movements described in Chapter 9, pages 169–72, can be accomplished. In some instances a simple hand belay may be safe and proper, since a climber sliding on snow creates his own braking effect, with further aid of toes or self-arrest.

If one is belaying a climber who is above the ice axe, two precautions are necessary. The belayer must determine the fall line of the climber and belay from the side of the ice axe opposite that line. The belay cannot take effect until the climber has slid past the belay axe. The belayer must be sure that the rope remains in place under the axehead and around the stock when the climber slides past. If belayer takes in rope as climber descends, he can lessen the sliding distance before the belay takes effect.

In more exacting circumstances when more strain on the belay can be expected, the axe-carabiner belay is advised. A short sling with carabiners on each end, about one and a half feet apart, can be used.

The axe point is pushed through one carabiner before the axe is pumped into the snow. (Most carabiners will not snap over the stock after an axe is embedded.) The second carabiner hangs below the ice axe, and the rope is belayed through it.

The axe-carabiner belay has many advantages. The belayer, after kicking a platform to stand on below the belay point, can use a body belay with security. The axe may be fully embedded, since the rope slides through the carabiner and does not touch the ice axe or become encrusted with snow, as in the simple belay. The carabiner around the stock tends to slide down under pressure, minimizing the danger of a "jumping" axe.

In the sling-carabiner belay, a variation of the axe-carabiner belay, the belayer ties a sling around his waist, leaving a tail about five feet long. He attaches a carabiner to the end of this tail and another about a foot from the end, through which the axe handle is driven. The end carabiner is used to belay the rope. The climber has an axe-carabiner belay and is also secured to the axe by the sling. In effect, he is "tied in."

This sling-carabiner belay can be used when climbers travel three on a rope on snow, in an adaptation known as the Sliding Middleman Technique. With two end men tied into the climbing rope and the middleman fastened to the rope with the belaying carabiner on the end of a sling, the middleman can climb along the rope fixed by belays from the two end men using either a simple ice-axe belay or the sling-carabiner belay. When the middleman goes on belay, both end men can move simultaneously up the mountain with the rope sliding through the middleman's belaying carabiner. Regular mountaineering signals are adaptable to this technique. We invented this Sliding Middleman Technique in order to move more quickly up snowfields. Former methods, whereby climbers were belayed one at a time, were slow and exhausting.

Snowfields and Glaciers

Special judgment is required in traversing snowfields and glaciers because of the serious dangers of snow bridges and crevasses. Crevasses, cleavages of considerable depth and width, generally occur horizontally across glaciers. When visible, they should be avoided, or climbers can protect themselves by roping up. However, at low temperatures drifting snow can bridge the crevasses, leaving a thin, smooth, deceptive surface. The unwary expeditioner may traverse what he considers safe terrain and suddenly drop through a bridge that will not support his weight. Never go on a glacier without expert leadership.

Bergschrunds, deep and often broad crevasses occurring near the cliff heads of mountain glaciers, pose the same hazard. In approaching a bergschrund, one should watch for scars on the snow, indicating rock falls from the cliffs.

Snow-filled gullies, or *couloirs,* extending like fingers above snowfields, could also be dangerous roadways for falling rocks or surface avalanches of new-fallen summer snow. These passages are narrow and confined, and make it difficult for a climber to stop a slide with a belay or self-arrest before hitting the side-wall rocks.

Such gullies that have filled with winter snow might contain hidden streams. In early summer, heat from the buried stream might melt the snow from underneath and leave a dangerous snow bridge or "moat" above.

Even when roped, a single person's chances of rescuing a companion who has fallen into a crevasse or through a snow bridge are slim. A rescue rope will cut into the snow with the victim's weight, and one person is unlikely to be able to pull out another singlehanded. No party should venture on snowfields without a minimum of three persons.

Climbers of Alaska's Mt. McKinley or other heavily glaciated areas carry elaborate rescue equipment and perfect many advanced techniques. Those crossing glaciers in the Rocky Mountains and similar ranges will probably not carry such gear. However, if the victim is not seriously injured and if the party has an extra rope, a simpler method of rescue is often possible.

The spare rope with a loop tied at the end is lowered to the victim. This rope is run under the climbing rope already circling the climber's waist. The victim places a foot in the loop and raises his knees. The belayer on the rescue rope takes up the slack and the victim raises himself slightly by straightening his leg. Then the third person on the climbing rope takes up that slack. The victim bends his knee again, and the process is repeated until he slowly makes his way to safety.

A better safeguard, however, is accident prevention. Change the route if snow terrain appears to be dangerous.

11

Winter Mountaineering

Winter mountaineering is a new sport and can be a hazardous one. Little margin for error can be allowed when one is in the mountains for an extended period of time, and likely to encounter temperatures of forty degrees below zero, seventy-mile-per-hour winds, and the threat of avalanches.

No one should attempt to lead a winter outing until summer camping has been mastered. While many skills involved in summer and winter camping are similar, small mistakes in Climate, Time, and Energy Control plans that might only prove annoying during the summer season may be fatal in winter. Trail techniques, logistics, and Expedition Behavior must be near perfect.

Winter mountaineering as we envision it is quite different from Scandinavian-style cross-country skiing between villages on designated trails, or from its American counterpart, where one skis between rest huts or from a lodge and back again. Mountaineering in winter as discussed in this chapter is a wilderness experience beyond the roadhead. Shelter and food and other appurtenances of civilization are not available along the way or at day's end.

Equipment and clothing for winter mountaineering require special consideration. Heavy packs are necessary, and with such loads the narrow cross-country ski sinks too far into unpacked powder snow. Regular ski bindings are too fragile to hold a ski boot in place on sidehill slopes or under lateral pressure. Boots and other wearing apparel appropriate for normal cold weather do not provide enough warmth for prolonged sub-zero outings during our American winters. Many tragedies have resulted because uninformed persons have attempted winter camping with garb and equipment designed for milder European climes.

Gear that is satisfactory for downhill skiing is equally inadequate for the winter camper. One cannot tour in boots with soles that do not bend or with bindings that hold the foot solidly to the ski. Contemporary ski clothes are manufactured with more emphasis on styling than on warmth and comfort, and some have moisture barriers that could become dangerous on overnight outings. Most ski apparel is tight and restrictive, which makes it cold and energy-draining.

Winter Clothing

The general theories relating to dressing for summer in the wild outdoors also hold true for winter. We have found no substitute for 100 percent pure virgin wool as a first layer of clothing next to the body. All garments must be loose and permeable so that air can circulate and carry dampness away from the skin. After the first layer or two of wool, other clothing may be of synthetics such as nylon; and outside layers of padded Dacron or Fiberfill II are acceptable.

It is especially important for the winter outdoorsman to be able to make clothing adjustments easily in order to avoid overheating or chilling. Knots tend to freeze in laces, and laced closings require too much finger dexterity to be practical in sub-zero temperatures. Elasticized or tight-fitting bands at wrists, ankles, or waist are not recommended, as they might hinder blood circulation and cause frostbite.

If one expects to face cold sixty-mile-per-hour winds, one must have wind pants and parka of finely woven nylon. The fabric must never be waterproof. Windbreakers of more permeable, looser-woven nylon may be used on milder, less windy outings. Remember, chilling will depend upon the amount of air that penetrates the nylon, not necessarily on the force of the wind. Nylon garments do not insulate, they only protect undergarments from the elements and allow them to be the insulating agencies. With proper clothing and windbreaking outerwear, the chill factor of the wind is no longer crucial.

Wind pants may be pajama style, with a drawstring, or zippered, just so that they are easy to put on or remove. Parkas may have a nylon hood insulated with Dacron or Fiberfill II which is zippered to the collar.

A nylon parka insulated with Dacron or Fiberfill II is used in extreme cold, for emergency bivouac, or in the sleeping bag on extremely cold nights. The wind hood described above can be used interchangeably on the wind parka and padded one.

It is convenient to have parka sleeves removable by zipper, also. In this way, several combinations may be utilized: full parka with hood and sleeves, full parka without hood, vest parka with hood and no sleeves, or vest parka minus hood and sleeves.

Matching padded pants for extreme weather are also desirable.

Face masks form an effective barrier against the elements. They should be made of woven wool cloth. Knitted masks become impregnated with snow and frozen breath. Leather freezes and is damp and cold. Be sure that eye, nose, and mouth openings adjust for proper fit. It is a good idea to practice putting on masks before the outing, since making adjustments in a blizzard may be impossible.

One pair of light wool gloves should be kept handy and dry for emergencies, adjusting ski bindings, or performing other jobs that require touching metal. Contact of bare hands on frozen metal will cause surface frostbite and blisters.

A pair of wool mittens is worn on warmer days. Try to dry them out each night in the sleeping bag or tent.

At lower temperatures, an outer pair of nylon mittens will act as windbreakers and keep woolen mittens dry. These nylon shells extend above the wrist and prevent snow from entering.

Large padded mittens should be taken along for extreme cold, and padded bootees with non-skid soles can be worn around camp or at night in the sleeping bag.

Though air temperatures might rise to twenty degrees during the day, snow underfoot might remain at sub-zero temperatures. When considering footgear, there can be no restriction to blood circulation carrying warmth to the feet. Boots must be very loose, with no strings, cuffs, or other tightness around ankles.

An insulated area of trapped air pockets between foot and outer boot is necessary. But there must be enough circulation to remove moisture from the feet. The insulating material around the foot must not hold wetness or prevent rapid evaporation. Also, ski bindings, snowshoes, or crampon straps cannot press tightly on any spot to destroy insulation. Outside moisture should not enter the boot.

No boot on the market is satisfactory for all aspects of winter mountaineering. Rubber, or Korean, boots with permanent air pockets between rubber layers will prevent feet from freezing; however, they will be constantly damp because evaporation is impossible through rubber. Moist feet become white, wrinkled, and soft, and create a breeding place for fungus. Also, Korean boots can only be used with snowshoes or crampons. They do not fit into ski bindings.

The boot with a rubber foot and leather upper is permissible for snowshoeing, but this too does not fit ski bindings.

Double mountain-climbing boots composed of a felt-lined shoe inside a leather outer boot fit some ski bindings, but they are very heavy.

Boots made entirely of felt with cleated rubber soles are good for climbing or lounging in camp, as feet are kept warm and dry. Yet their efficiency is limited to temperatures colder than twenty degrees above zero Fahrenheit. In warmer weather, melting snow will dampen the outer felt and lessen its insulating power. Felt boots can be used with snowshoes or crampons but not with skis.

Since there is no perfect solution, we have solved the problem by wearing a large summer hiking boot for skiing and changing into felt boots while climbing or in camp.

Two pairs of heavy wool socks are necessary. A wool felt innersole can be added if it will not cause toes to push against the top of the boot.

Gaiters are essential in winter to prevent snow from entering boot tops.

(A checklist of winter clothing appears in Appendix 2.)

Winter Equipment

There are some additions and modifications for the NOLS Minimum Equipment List (Appendix 3) in the case of winter mountaineering.

Bulkier cold-weather clothing calls for a special pack bag. There should be extra-large pockets on top and sides for easy access, and zippers must be of heavy nylon that will not freeze. One should be able to tie, untie, put on, take off, and handle the pack without having to remove one's mittens.

The pack bag must be well organized and all items replaced in their proper spot after use. Rummaging for misplaced items in a storm, exposing contents to snow, removing mittens to find something, are inconvenient. Items carelessly strewn around camp might be lost in the snow.

For any outing, it is important to select sleeping bags that will maintain their loft and dry quickly. This is essential in winter. As previously stressed in Chapter 3, Fiberfill II has proved superior to down.

Winter sleeping bags should be roomy enough to accommodate the user when he is wearing padded parka, pants, bootees, and mittens. Stuff bags must also be spacious, because it is awkward to stuff a bulky bag while wearing mittens. The stuff bag may be of waterproof material.

Sleeping-bag zippers should operate easily and be installed so that they will not jam or catch on cloth. Zippers must remain usable even when ice freezes on them; heavy nylon is the best material.

Extra-long straps with fasteners that are easily manipulated by mittened hands should be used to attach the sleeping bag to the bottom of the pack frame. It is a good idea to affix straps permanently to the frame so that they will not fall off and be lost in snow.

To accommodate bulkier equipment, winter tents should be larger than those used in summer. While tent floors can be waterproof, tops should be permeable for ventilation. There should be a zippered opening in the floor where stoves can be placed when cooking. See page 211.) The extra waterproof fly suggested for summer is not necessary unless warm weather with melting snow or rain is indicated. Wind will automatically ventilate tents and keep them frost-free, but on quiet nights the ends can be opened for ventilation.

Since the winter tent will be pitched on snow rather than solid ground, it is imperative to have tent poles that are held in place by tent sleeves with firm nylon bottoms that prevent the poles from penetrating the snow. When poles are secured to the peak of the tent, they will remain firmly in the sleeves even though supporting strings are broken in the wind. Jointed tent poles, when fitted together, must still have some play; under freezing conditions, those fitting too snugly are almost impossible to dismantle.

Nylon is preferable to cotton for tent cords, as a knot will loosen with a single pull, even when wet or frozen.

Lightweight laminated wood skis are best for winter mountaineering. The heavier the load to be carried, the longer and wider the ski should be. For instance, the average person carrying a pack will require a ski approximately three inches wide and six and a half feet long. I must have a ski that is approximately three and a half inches wide and seven and a half feet long in order not to break through the trail made by companions ahead.

Beartrap toe plates and cables are very satisfactory. New types of bindings for winter mountaineering are being developed. One should test them and ascertain that they are durable enough for backpacking.

Ski poles must be long and have large baskets (about eight inches in diameter) so that the climber can more easily propel himself uphill in deep, soft snow. Generous wrist straps are necessary with bulky mittens. Ski poles are also handy when one is snowshoeing, or they can be used as walking sticks when climbing without skis.

In steep terrain, "climbers," formerly sealskins, strapped to the bottom of skis help in gaining altitude. Although these are still referred to as "sealskins," they are now manufactured of cloth with a hairlike nap. Skins should be fitted to skis before use and their straps checked against interference with bindings. It is essential to have a notch cut in the back of skis to hold skin straps in place.

Climbing waxes may be substituted for skins. Instructions for use of these various waxes are on the product labels. In steep terrain, however, rather than gambling on selecting the proper wax for the current conditions or reapplying wax in a blizzard, climbing skins are recommended.

Snowshoes are sometimes superior to skis for traveling in rolling, timbered country. Snowshoeing should not be attempted, however, without pre-conditioning before the trip to strengthen muscles not ordinarily called into play in normal daily activities.

Crampons, iron spikes attached to boots, will prevent slipping when climbing or walking on ice. They have little use in winter mountaineering, since the snow is soft and there is generally insufficient melting and refreezing to develop ice. Some experts use crampons for steep winter rock climbing. If crampons are carried, be sure that they are large enough to fit boots and that fastening straps do not interfere with blood circulation to the feet.

Contrary to popular belief, ice axes and ice pitons are seldom used in winter mountaineering. Large grain scoops or snow shovels are carried for digging snow caves.

A well-stocked repair kit, including pliers, screwdriver, screws, wire, binding parts, stove parts, clovis pins for pack frames, and extra baskets for ski poles, might be included in winter equipment.

(A checklist of winter equipment is in Appendix 4.)

Trail Techniques

Winter trail techniques are similar to those practiced in summer, with some variation. Breaking trail, whether on foot, snowshoes, or skis, can be very exhausting, since the first person may sink a foot or two with each step. One should lead only for a short distance and then step aside for another person to pass in front. A rotating system is a good idea, so that all members have an opportunity to head the line.

The pace must be organized to prevent front skiers from leaving those following too far behind. The repair kit for ski bindings is carried by the end man so that it may be used by anyone dropping out of line. Those stopping must stand far enough to the side of the broken trail to allow others to proceed.

One of the great dangers of winter mountaineering is the possibility of avalanches. The sojourner will seldom have the instruments, time, or ability to make the observations of avalanche experts in populated resorts. Nevertheless, there are some basic "horse sense" precautions he can take in order to recognize and avoid dangerous terrain.

Do not cross steep slopes where snow lies upon smooth ground or slick rock. Here the slab of snow has little adherence to the ground and may break loose, causing a slide. Where the ground is covered with trees or large boulders, this does not happen.

Do not cross steep slopes where an unstable layer of snow is not bound to those above and below it. A combination of weather and temperature might create a layer of unstable, or "rotten," snow sandwiched between layers of stable snow. This layer has little substance and can act as a roller skate in allowing the upper layer to slide. A ski pole punched through this rotten layer will encounter little resistance.

New snow, especially light, powdery snow, will slide over the surface of old snow. Do not cross steep slopes of new snow immediately after a storm. A day or two later, this snow will become more stable.

Drifting snow will often form a hard crust on top of stable snow. This "wind slab" may become brittle and break off, triggering an avalanche.

Cornices, or overhangs of snow, on the leeward side of ridges may break off and avalanche also.

Any snow lying at an angle steeper than thirty degrees is potentially dangerous and should be judged according to the above considerations.

A slide from a steep slope can avalanche a low-angle slope below, and the resulting momentum might carry it over long stretches of flat terrain. I have even seen avalanches plunge up opposite slopes, then reverse themselves and slide down into the valley.

Timbered hillsides often contain treeless gullies that stretch the full length of the mountain between the ridges. These bare corridors, from which the trees have been eliminated by previous slides, are called avalanche troughs. Crossing such troughs is extremely risky.

Steep *couloirs* (ravines) above timberline that are filled with snow are also avalanche troughs and should be avoided.

One can judge snow conditions by careful observation. Frequently, probing with a ski pole can give some indication of the stability of various layers. But even if one learns to recognize potentially dangerous areas, one must never risk crossing them. The winter mountaineer must be psychologically set to limit his movements to non-avalanche terrain.

Winter Camping

Camping on deep snow requires special techniques and conservation practices. Since it is no longer permissible to break branches from trees or chop down dead growth in the wild outdoors, finding a supply of firewood in snow-covered areas is difficult. If timber fires are built, they must be small, and any charred remains should be scattered before one breaks camp. As in all seasons, one should dress adequately and not depend upon fires for warmth except in emergencies.

For cooking on winter outings, gas or kerosene stoves are preferable to the campfire. Only stoves that have pumps for pressurizing the fuel chamber are recommended. Those requiring hand-warming to create pressure are impractical at sub-zero temperatures. Stoves fueled by canisters of propane or butane gas are also very undependable in cold weather because they do not develop enough gas pressure to function properly. Be sure gas containers are leakproof, and carry a funnel for use in filling stoves. Keep moisture out of the stove fuel tank.

Cooking with or filling gas stoves inside of nylon tents is hazardous. It is almost impossible to avoid spilling gas while funneling it, and such accidents could ruin the nylon tent, trigger fire or explosion, or at the very least cause sickening fumes.

If it is necessary to cook inside of the tent, fuel the stove and get it burning uniformly before bringing it into the tent. Be sure the tent has a stove hole. Place the stove on snow, not the nylon tent flooring. A special piece of cloth or square of Ensolite could be carried to act as a platform for the stove and keep it from upending as the snow melts underneath it.

The winter camper should not rely on sweets for quick energy, because continued endurance depends upon a combination of starches, proteins, and fats. Fats contain more calories per pound than the other foods and can be used liberally to generate extra heat.

Pre-cooked roast beef, steak, bacon, and poultry or semi-nonperishable foods such as salami can be kept for long periods of time on a winter trip. Hot drinks of Jell-O, juices, cocoa, coffee, tea, and soup make nutritious and convenient additions to meals.

Each member of the party needs a water bottle that he can take into his sleeping bag for a drink during the night or as a starter for breakfast next morning. The bottle may be filled with hot water at night and used to pre-heat the sleeping bag or placed inside of damp mittens or socks to hasten their drying. Aluminum containers are most efficient; when frozen inside, they can be thawed by heating over stoves. Plastic bottles are difficult to thaw without ruining them.

Conservation of energy through frequent eating and drinking is especially important. Have snacks and drinks available when awaking in the night. This will prevent early-morning chill. Extra salt with plenty of liquid is essential to avoid frostbite.

People often ask how elimination problems are handled in wintertime. World War II ski troops were taught to stand sideways to the wind and urinate cross-wind and slightly leeward. Women find the safest position is squatting close to the ground with face or back directly to the wind. In timbered areas, one may urinate against a tree on the leeward side.

Take a shovel to bury feces and yellow stains deep under the snow. Burn toilet paper and bury unburned portions.

At night, or even in daytime when one wishes to avoid outside weather, campers may urinate into plastic bags, seal them with a knot or rubber band, and set outside to freeze and be disposed of later.

The Snow Cave

One of the happy rewards of winter camping is living in snow caves. The wind might be howling, but inside the snow cave the air is calm and clear, the room is insulated from outer sounds, and the temperature is a comfortable few degrees below freezing. Snow crystals glisten in candlelight, companions lounge on sleeping bags and pass hot soup and drinks.

Snow caves are dug with small shovels and aluminum scoops such as the No. 12 or 14 grain scoop available at hardware stores. Drifts on the leeward side of ridges or gullies make fine locations. Snow must be several feet deep. One must not walk on top of the area before or after the cave is dug, as this might cause the roof to collapse.

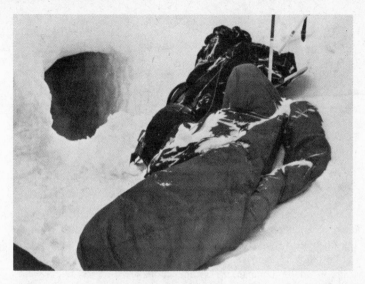

Snow cave entrance. Note that Dacron Fiberfill II sleeping bags have been left outside to dry.

Two sleeping chambers in a large snow cave.

Organize the cave's design before starting. An excellent four-person plan has a center aisle four feet wide and high enough for persons to stand upright. The aisle runs the length of the cave and has a slightly higher bedroom alcove on either side and a cooking area in the rear. The entrance is only about four feet high, with a floor a foot or two below that of the aisle. Thus, a person must stoop or crawl through the entrance, but may walk in the aisle and sit up in the bunk-type bedrooms. The small, low entry prevents whirling snow from gusting inside.

Dig the entrance four feet square and far enough into the drift to enable you to dig upward until you can stand erect. The roof must be domed, with at least two feet of snow above the highest point of the curve. Standing up, continue to dig the aisle four feet wide, maintaining the domed roof. The aisle is approximately ten feet long.

Snow that is removed is thrown into the entry and shoveled away from outside by companions. Grain scoops are used for digging and a small shovel for doming and chipping out pieces of hard snow.

Bedrooms are at right angles to the aisle. For two occupants, each room should be at least five feet wide and seven feet deep. The highest part of the domed roof must be about four feet above the bedroom floor.

The kitchen shelf is four feet above the aisle floor. A venthole to allow fumes and heat to escape may be poked above it with a ski pole.

When living in a snow cave, one can dig a smaller cave nearby with a hole to be used as a toilet.

Regardless of temperatures outside, the cave interior will be twenty to thirty degrees above zero. However, because of heat from cooking, candles, and the presence of several occupants, the temperature will rise. At thirty-three degrees (about freezing), the roof will start to drip. Clothing and sleeping bags will become moist, and humidity will increase. All precautions should be taken to keep the cave from further heating; cooking activities may be interrupted or the cave temporarily vacated.

It does not matter if the entrance drifts completely shut, as there is always ample air coming through the porous snow. Occupants will not suffocate. The only such danger occurs when the cave starts to melt and then glazes over. In this case, the glaze can be scraped off to make it safe again. However, special care must be taken to avoid inhaling fumes from stoves.

The cave as described here is an ideal one, but there are times when the depth of snow or time limitations make such a plan impossible. One must then improvise. Perhaps one cannot stand upright in the aisle, or the bedrooms cannot be benched above the floor. Two factors remain vital, however: the roof must be domed under all circumstances, and the entrance must be small and low to prevent snow from blowing inside.

One major point must be stressed about all winter camping, in or out of a snow cave. There must be a designated place for every item of equipment, and it must be put back in place immediately after use. To do otherwise will invite disaster. A knife, for instance, laid down momentarily on the snow, may be covered and never found again. Loss of essential items will handicap the entire trip. Winter campers must be super-organized.

Winter camping and mountaineering must be near perfect to be enjoyable and safe. The skills and judgments are only briefly discussed in this chapter. Those planning winter climbing and camping expeditions are encouraged to contact NOLS if advice concerning a specific trip is desired. This is offered as a public service.

12

Mountain Medicine and Evacuation

There is little correlation between mountain medicine and what we term first aid. In the hills, illnesses are generally caused by excessive fatigue, chilling, or inadequate sanitation procedures, and accidents usually result in burns, cuts, and broken bones. The backpacker is not equipped with numerous medical supplies and so has two choices: simple treatment or evacuation. The reader should familiarize himself with the excellent first-aid handbooks compiled by the Red Cross, Ski Patrol, and others, but it is not the purpose of this chapter to duplicate the detailed material in them. Here we will only cover the most frequent and potentially dangerous situations.

Through years of experience, we have learned to have little faith in pills and medication in the wild outdoors. Medicines that destroy germs in wounds also destroy flesh and slow down healing. Antibiotics can cause violent reactions in some people. In our opinion, the only first-aid materials needed are tape, a small roll of gauze, moleskin, Band-Aids, pain pills, and sleeping pills.

On the first eager days of an outing, one is apt to drive oneself too far too fast without adjusting to the new altitude, new diet, and unfamiliar sanitary obligations. Overfatigue often results in carelessness, which in turn can cause minor accidents such as cuts and burns.

Cuts and deep scratches from sharp rocks, tree branches, and knives are common in the mountains. If the wound contains dirt or debris, wash it with drinkable water. Knife cuts need not be washed. Quickly close cuts with tape, Band-Aids, or butterfly tape without addition of salves or disinfectants. More severe cuts requiring stitches should be closed as well as possible and the victim should be evacuated.

Minor burns around campfires, generally caused by careless handling of hot utensils or liquids, are best treated by submerging the hot spot immediately in cold water or snow. If burns are serious enough to become infected, evacuation to medical help is essential.

Since the demise of the kerosene lamp, kerosene has been relatively unavailable. Most mountain stoves are fueled with gasoline. Gasoline stoves can explode; spilled fuel can ignite clothing and tents. Resulting burns are usually serious and demand evacuation, but immediate treatment is immersion in cold water or packing with snow.

Serious fatigue is a frequent complaint on an outing and can cause loss of appetite, vomiting, chills, lack of judgment, irritability, and general weakness. The patient must be allowed to rest and regain his strength before continuing expedition activities. As soon as he is able to eat, feed him frequent small amounts of food fortified with salt and vitamin C from greens. Keep him at a comfortable temperature and restrict physical activity.

Stomach and bowel upsets occur in the mountains owing to improper sterilizing of dishes and utensils or the amount or type of food consumed. Freeze-dried foods, dried fruits, nuts, and cheese can produce an unusual amount of gas, and stools are softer than usual. Cramps in the lower abdomen or chest pains may develop. This is not serious unless vomiting and diarrhea lead to dehydration. A light diet, liquids, and avoidance of spices and acidic juices will usually remedy the situation. No one who has recently suffered amoebic or germ-induced dysentery should be included in an expedition. A victim of any persistent or severe abdominal pains indicative of appendicitis should be evacuated immediately, and a leader should familiarize himself with the symptoms before starting.

Mountain sickness (with symptoms similar to seasickness) can occur at high altitudes because of fatigue, dehydration, lack of salt, moving too fast, fright, or a combination of these factors. The illness can be prevented by continuously eating and drinking in small amounts, moving within one's energy capacity, and remaining calm. If one does become ill, do not try to continue. The victim should be removed to a lower camp for rest.

The nausea, dizziness, and vomiting associated with mountain sickness are annoying but not dangerous. However, pulmonary edema, which may start with some of the same symptoms, can become fatal, because in this illness the lungs fill with fluid. Therefore, whenever fatigue, headache, or stomach upset are accompanied by ragged breathing that might indicate moisture in the lungs, emergency procedures should be initiated.

As in all mountain aid, the patient must be kept comfortable but evacuated as quickly as possible to lower elevations and medical attention. Death can occur within a few hours.

A good friend of mine, a skier and climber in excellent physical condition and well versed in first aid, died of pulmonary edema on an expedition. I have helped evacuate two college athletes who specialized in long-distance running. My experience indicates that even those in good shape should never push themselves in high altitudes. Going slowly and allowing the body to become acclimated is the fastest and safest way to reach a destination.

Hypothermia (or exposure) occurs when the body core temperature drops below 95 degrees Fahrenheit. The combination of wind, cold, and wetness can cause hypothermia in temperatures well above freezing. When the body becomes cold, blood is rushed to vital organs, extremities chill, and chilling spreads throughout the body. The victim shows progressive symptoms of shivering, slow reaction, stumbling, clumsiness, confusion, difficulty in speaking, dilated pupils, and loss of judgment. Coma and death may develop within a few hours.

Most cases of hypothermia occur away from base camps, during storms, when inappropriate Time, Energy, and Climate Control Plans have resulted in an emergency. Under such conditions, there is little one can do because extra clothing, sleeping bags, and other equipment to make the victim more comfortable may not be readily available. Also, if one person is severely chilled, it is likely that the entire party is chilled. Therefore, when any one person experiences hypothermia, immediate retreat to base camp is essential. There, warm the patient by covering him and placing hot canteens around him, or warm him with another body. Give small amounts of food and drink with salt.

Frostbite develops under freezing conditions. While frostbite is more common when the temperature is below freezing, a person can freeze his feet by standing too long in summer snowfields when the air temperature is mild.

There are two types of frostbite: superficial and deep. Both are caused by the shunting of blood away from the extremities to the vital organs when body temperatures drop or when circulation is restricted by tight boots or clothing.

Superficial frostbite causes a sudden blanching of the skin, with tingling followed by numbness. After thawing, the flesh will redden and blister. Under freezing conditions, superficial frostbite is a danger to areas exposed to the weather or hands and fingers that have touched metal on ice axes or ski bindings.

Deep frostbite usually occurs on hands and feet. Tissue becomes waxy and pallid, the skin won't roll over the joints, toes and fingers solidify. Minor cases may heal if warmed promptly, but extreme frostbite under expedition conditions usually results in gangrene or even amputation. The only solution is retreat. Abandon the outing!

Allow the patient's foot to remain frozen. Sometimes a victim can hobble a short distance on a frozen foot, but he should walk on a thawed foot only when it is necessary to save his life. This is a judgment factor: better to make gangrene and amputation a possibility than death a certainty.

All cases involving broken bones indicate evacuation. The patient should be given pain pills according to direction of the prescribing physician before departure, and the bone should be protected by a temporary splint made of branches, ice axes, tent poles, or similar objects padded with strips of cloth. Watch patients for signs of shock and treat the symptoms.

One or two persons on every expedition should be knowledgeable about accepted first-aid procedures concerning splints, treating shock, closing cuts, and detailed symptoms indicating appendicitis, pulmonary edema, and hypothermia.

Evacuation

When we come to fast, efficient, and safe evacuation, we must be well prepared with techniques and judgments not found in first-aid manuals. Primarily, a party should maintain a minimum of four persons so that two may go for help and one remain with the victim, know their location on a topographical map at all times, and be aware of places on the edge of the wilderness where help and communication facilities can be reached. These factors should have been researched during the pre-planning stage of the expedition.

There are no set rules to follow when an accident happens. If I knew the exact terrain where the incident took place, the nature of injuries, the number of people in the party, the time of day, weather, and temperature, the amount of clothing and equipment available, the fatigue of group members, their experience and knowledge, the distance to communications and help, availability of a helicopter, landing spot for a helicopter, and urgency of the evacuation—if I knew all this and more, I could formulate a plan. But the random combination of circumstances in each emergency precludes rules. I can only offer pointers for making judgments.

An expedition leader must remain calm, and act promptly and authoritatively. After immediate aid has been given the victim, he must determine if evacuation is necessary, formulate procedures, and delegate responsibilities among the group.

The patient is made as comfortable as possible, treated for shock, and given constant companionship and moral support. Others can move supplies from base camp to the injured person, construct a litter, or perform similar jobs relevant to the accident. The leader should instruct specific people to do specific things instead of asking for help generally. It is important to keep the entire group busy. I have seen people keel over from shock as they watch a companion suffer.

As soon as the patient's immediate needs are met, the leader gathers everyone together and calmly discusses the situation. Do not be in a hurry. Take no impulsive action until all plans are made. Weigh factors such as condition of the trail, how long it would take to retreat or be rescued, and the time element in relation to the victim's condition and expected weather.

Put all reports and instructions in writing! These can be brief, but one should *never* rely upon an oral message. In emergencies, confused thought and garbled memories can plague the most dependable people. Written messages are not easily misunderstood if they are clear and to the point.

Reliance on oral communication resulted in tragedy for a pair of expert rock climbers scaling an unclimbed two-thousand-foot vertical north face in the Wind River range. The wife of one climber was in a camp below, but they were about eighteen miles from the nearest roadhead over a high, trailless pass.

The leader fell. He was hurt but not unconscious, so his companion tied him on a narrow ledge and hurriedly rappelled down the cliff to pick up his wife and go for help. It was the next day before they reached the roadhead and asked for assistance. Their oral message was taken by another person and relayed to the sheriff, who had charge of rescue operations.

The sheriff's office, discovering that the accident was "over the pass" in another county, phoned that county sheriff to take responsibility. But instead of reporting that the victim was "on the north side of Mt. Mitchell near Lonesome Lake," the message said he was "on Mt. Mitchell on the north side of Lonesome Lake."

After much time and expense in fruitless searching, the sheriff called on us. Local people did not know which peak was called Mt. Mitchell. The ̖ mountains were only recently named by climbers and were not identified on the maps. We knew the location and were able to spot the climber from the air. Helicopters took our instructors to the top of the peak, and they rappelled down to the climber, who was still tied in place. That was Tuesday. The accident had occurred on Friday. The man was dead. He might still be alive if relayed messages had been written.

If outside rescuers are necessary, select two runners to notify authorities. Be sure to give written instructions to those going for help. State whom they are to notify, if they are to return, if the expedition will continue or be abandoned, how helicopter, medical, or hospital bills will be covered and the type of individual or group insurance involved.

The county sheriff is responsible for all rescues and must be the first person contacted. Permission for use of helicopters, jeeps, horses, and so on is granted by the U.S. Forest Service or other administering agency.

In the report to the sheriff, write a complete but brief assessment of the situation. State the name, sex, and age of the victim, the nature of injury and your opinion of the seriousness, what kind of help and equipment is needed, and if a doctor should be summoned. If parents or friends of the patient must be informed, write special messages to them, and should a press release be required, compose it carefully for accuracy.

Send a separate report for the doctor, stating how the accident happened, the time and date, information about the injury and the patient's reactions, and what medication, if any, has been administered.

Rescuers must be able to locate the scene even if runners do not accompany them. Draw a map or send a marked topographical map pinpointing the location. If a helicopter is requested, possible landing spots should be marked on the map. Send an additional message noting how the landing spot will be made visible from the air with sleeping bags, bright objects, fire, and so forth.

Sometimes it is more expedient for a group to conduct its own evacuation. One morning at a NOLS camp, it was reported that a student had had a restless night. The boy had complained the previous day that he was having trouble carrying his pack. On examination, it was discovered that his lungs were starting to fill with fluid, and further symptoms indicated the possibility of pulmonary edema.

The group discussed the problem. We did not think that we could send out runners and secure a helicopter that same day because the nearest airport was distant and much time would be wasted making arrangements. Yet we thought it imperative that the patient reach a hospital as soon as possible. It was about ten miles to the nearest roadhead. We knew a horse packer camped there, and he would likely have an automobile. However, at least five miles of the route was over trailless country with much downed timber, and the way was mountainous.

We finally decided that we had the knowledge, leadership, and enough strong litter bearers to make the evacuation. We left at 8 A.M. Five pairs of carriers took turns transporting the litter at top speed. At

4 P.M. we were at the roadhead; by six o'clock the patient was in a hospital bed fifty miles away. We were told that he would not have survived except for the fast evacuation.

The method we use to improvise and carry litters makes evacuation a far more practical consideration than formerly. In the past, litters were carried by people walking on each side and holding the frame with their hands. On open, level ground, this process was tiring; on narrow trails and in heavily wooded areas, it was virtually impossible because there was no place for the bearers to walk.

It is feasible for two people to carry the litter by hand at front and rear for short distances, but the method is too exhausting for lengthy treks over rough country.

The method we have developed places the weight on regular backpacks, making litter bearing with two bearers only slightly more difficult than carrying a pack.

Improvise a litter by fastening three backpack frames between two poles which are about twelve feet long. In the Rocky Mountains, small pine trees can be used. If the party is not carrying an axe, green trees up to five inches in diameter can be cut down in minutes with a pocketknife. Bend the tree over and the knife will slice easily through the outward side of the bend. Dead poles weigh less, but green ones will not break easily. Lash poles together to attain the necessary length if longer ones are unavailable.

Place poles parallel to each other on the ground, thicker ends to the rear. Position a backpack frame flat across the poles one foot from the front end and tie it to both poles, securing straps so that nothing can dangle or catch on obstacles. Fasten two more frames behind the first to make a continuous surface to hold the patient. Pad the top with Ensolite pads, sleeping bag, or clothing and tie the patient in place. If a sleeping bag is used, the victim may be placed inside.

A pack frame for the bearers is fastened at each end of the litter; two bearers get into the straps and walk with the litter between them. Be sure to allow enough space for the rear man to be able to see the ground when walking. Equalize the burden by placing the patient's head to front or rear as judgment indicates.

Six is the practical number for an evacuation team, although four men might suffice. One person is appointed as leader. Carriers walk at

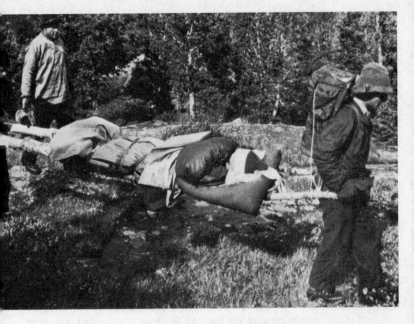

Evacuation procedures. Students, using makeshift litter made of long poles, pack frames, and slings, carry "injured" companion from injury site to roadhead.

any desired speed. When they tire, fresh replacements take over, and the group alternates in this manner. In rugged terrain, those walking alongside can help lift the litter over obstacles and balance it.

Cliff evacuations as performed by trained rescue teams are very complex and require special skills and equipment. However, when a victim must be moved to a campsite for survival or to a helicopter loading place for evacuation, companions might have to accomplish the feat. I spent many months experimenting with mountain evacuation while in the ski troops during World War II. One method proved fast and practical in nearly all instances.

Stretch a "zip line," or climbing rope, tightly from the cliff to a spot out and away from the bottom and secure it by mountaineering methods. Improvise a litter (identical with that previously described but without the two end carrying frames) and hang it on the line by tying slings to the pole ends and clamping carabiners in the knots and onto the zip line. Thus, the patient may be lowered down the rope. The rate of the litter's descent can be controlled by a separate rope belayed by a climber above. If the zip line sags under the weight and fails to clear the ground or rocks, belayed climbers can help the litter over such obstacles.

Since a zip line must be taut, there is considerable strain at both ends. Therefore, in order to equalize the pull, three separate piton points may be used to provide additional security.

At the top of the cliff, place three pitons a few feet apart and snap a carabiner into each. Hold a carabiner about four feet below the pitons and run the end of a climbing rope (a sling is too weak) through the carabiner, up through the piton carabiner on the left side, back through the carabiner in hand, up through the middle piton carabiner, back through the carabiner in hand, then up through the right carabiner and back through the hand carabiner, where the end is tied with a bowline to the original rope below the hand carabiner. Thus, equal strain is placed on the pitons with a climbing rope as strong as the zip line. An additional carabiner may be used at the foot of the cliff for more strength and the zip line tied to both.

If tying to a tree, tighten the rope near the bottom of the tree close to the roots so that the pull will not create sideways leverage against the root system. If it is necessary to tie high on the tree so that the zip line will be free in the air, reinforce that tree by another line to the base of another tree or point in back. Thus, pressure on the original tree will be straight down and the roots protected.

13

Educating Users of the Wild Outdoors

We *can* enjoy the wild outdoors and still conserve it! All of us can learn to use the wilderness with so little disturbance that signs of our passing will be healed by the seasonal rejuvenation of nature. But, unfortunately, the methods and techniques of practical conservation are known to only a few; therefore most users, no matter how well intentioned, become destroyers.

Public concern over such destruction of our environment triggered legislation in 1964. Congress passed the Wilderness Act, which set aside certain unspoiled lands as wilderness areas that they might remain forever in their wild and primitive beauty "where the earth and its community of life are untrammeled by man, and where man can have solitude as a primitive and unconformed type of recreation." In order to accomplish this, the act specifically limited use of the wilderness areas for all time. There were to be no roads, no buildings, no permanent structures. There would be no mechanized equipment such as chain saws and portable light plants, no motor vehicles such as jeeps, cars, trucks, snowmobiles, motorboats, motorcycles, airplanes, or helicopters. Timbering was prohibited. Existing grazing rights were continued, but mining claims were allowed only through 1983.

On passage of the Wilderness Act, conservationists and outdoorsmen rejoiced. A long editorial in the *New York Times* on August 21, 1964, praised Congress for "saving our wilderness heritage." On September 4, 1964, a *Times* headline read: "President Signs Wilderness Act. Land set aside for lovers of outdoors." People believed that the Wilderness Act had saved our natural heritage forever; such was the ignorance of man.

Today, the classified wilderness regions are not being threatened by mining, timbering, or ranching interests; the destruction is coming from those very people who fought so gallantly to get the act passed. All of the study, thought, and effort was devoted to putting a legislative fence around primitive areas rather than developing techniques for their proper use and conservation.

In 1972, the Secretary of the Interior launched an experiment to further protect undeveloped areas. Hikers and campers in three national parks were required to obtain permits in order to travel beyond established recreation and camping sites. By thus limiting the number of outdoorsmen, it was hoped that the trend toward destructive overuse would be reversed.

Neither the Wilderness Act nor the Secretary's issuance of permits made any provision (except by a most liberal interpretation) for the user's knowledge of outdoorsmanship and ability to protect the environment.

Restricting visitors in these terms will only lessen the rate of destruction, not prevent it. For example, if you had six campers on your property and found them cutting trees, leaving fire scars, and littering garbage, would it solve the problem to throw out three of them and let the others remain?

In certain areas, administrative agencies rule that one *must* stay on trails, *must* camp only in regular semi-permanent sites which have been prescribed and marked. This is another outdoor tragedy. Such restrictions have become necessary because users of those areas are so uneducated that they cannot be trusted elsewhere.

In 1970, I visited Mt. Katahdin in Maine. According to local rules, I went up the designated trail. That night, I stayed where all sojourners were required to stay, in a campground where lean-tos had been provided. All night long, I could hear noises from others in the closely packed shelters. I could smell human odors. The ground was scuffed beyond the possibility of vegetation. It was like a prison camp to me.

Around us were hundreds of square miles of beautiful country. I was convinced that accomplished campers could be allowed to roam at will with no threat of devastation to the environment. I wished that restrictions could be lifted at least for the knowledgeable people who knew how to care for the land.

NOLS has developed a new code of outdoor behavior, a new ethics of outdoorsmanship, a new field of knowledge, skills, and techniques for practical conservation. Studies must be made by the best available people in the field to refine these optimum behavior patterns and interpret these patterns into laws and regulations. Then, no one must be allowed in the wild outdoors until he can prove he is ecologically housebroken or at least traveling with a certified leader who will keep his group under control.

Many people feel that the possibility of restricting use of the wild outdoors to those who know how to conserve it is beyond political or public acceptance. I disagree. If informed people will take action, such a plan could be implemented. The means: a national organization that would provide for the education and certification of outdoorsmen. Then the administrative agencies could issue permits stipulating that at least one member of the party must be a certified leader who would take responsibility for the conservation practices of that group.

An Outdoor Leader Association could be created by a gathering of top figures in the field of recreation. Representatives from various outdoor organizations, youth groups, the Department of the Interior and its Bureau of Land Management, the Department of Agriculture, and other knowledgeable persons could formulate an Ecological Bill of Rights, a guideline for environmental preservation and a workable plan for practical conservation. This would not be another legislative theory; it would reach the grass-roots camper through an ongoing educational program.

The association could also advocate amending the Wilderness Act in order to reflect these standards of conservation. The group could encourage laws and regulations that would gradually introduce a permit system requiring all organized groups venturing in the wild outdoors to have a certified leader who has passed an association-sponsored test on general outdoorsmanship.

Most people who go into the wilds would welcome a chance to be taught about conservation if instruction were available. An adequate method of educating wilderness users does not exist. Organizations such as the National Outdoor Leadership School reach only a few thousand students each year. While these graduates pass on their knowledge by becoming teachers in other groups, this is a rather slow method of mass education.

If an Outdoor Leader Association were formed to operate in a manner similar to the National Ski Patrol, NOLS would initiate action by helping to set up nationwide educational and certification centers similar to the special instructors' courses operated by our school. This action would probably encourage universities and other organizations to follow suit. Even now, some colleges are giving credit to students attending schools such as NOLS, and many are incorporating classes in outdoorsmanship into their curriculum. This is a good beginning, and efforts should be expanded.

Just as the Red Cross offers courses in Life Saving, the association could sponsor a series of classes involving conservation, map reading, selection of clothing, equipment, and rations, legal regulations, and second aid and rescue procedures for prospective leaders, who would then be required to pass tests for certification. Ideally, this educational process would later expand to include the general public. In time, only parties having a licensed leader would be allowed access to the non-specified trails beyond the roadhead.

The Outdoor Leader Association certification tests could include written and oral quizzes as well as actual demonstrations of skills. The questions selected would determine a leader's proficiency in conservation practices and his capability to conduct a safe, well-organized outing. A possible examination for a leader of an organized group on a hypothetical trip could be as follows:

Outdoor Leader Certification Test

You are leading a coeducational group of ten young people, aged sixteen and over, on a ten-day backpacking trip. The area you are using is U.S. Forest land. The average minimum temperature at 8,000 feet this time of year is 28 degrees Fahrenheit at night and 65 degrees Fahrenheit in daytime. On the basis of the trail indicated on the accompanying topographical map, do the following:

1. Write a brief letter to the U.S. Forest Service requesting necessary information.
2. Make a complete list of food for the group by description and weight. For example: White flour—6 lbs.
   Cornmeal—5 lbs.
3. Make a minimum clothing list for one individual.
4. List personal equipment needs for one individual.
5. List group equipment needs.
6. List first-aid materials.
7. Work out logistics for the trip, including approximate total weight of food and equipment, its transportation to and beyond the roadhead, transportation of personnel at beginning and end of trip.
8. Outline practical conservation procedures regarding camping locations, trails, roadheads, flora and fauna, fire building, laundry and bathing, and disposal of garbage.
9. Make a tentative itinerary, selecting a campsite for each night judged by studying the topographical map and considering the group's age, weight, acclimatization, and weight of equipment.
10. Formulate a brief plan for emergency evacuation and methods of financing any medical or transportation expenses that might accrue.
11. Outline a plan for disbandment of expedition and disposal of group equipment.
12. Write a brief letter to one participant outlining plans for the trip, what items he should bring, and standards of expedition behavior.

In addition to this written test, an oral examination in map reading could follow, whereby the candidate would:
1. Orient a topographical map by compass.

2. Orient the map by ground features.
3. Explain map symbols.
4. Demonstrate how to figure elevations on the map.
5. Interpret the map in relation to the group's proposed movements over the terrain.

Finally, a candidate would demonstrate his ability to build a fire and relandscape the area without leaving scars.

Those intending to lead groups in specialized activities such as horseback riding, mountain climbing, canoeing, and so forth would have appropriate additional testing.

For the total program to be effective, hikers who are not affiliated with an organized group must not be allowed to destroy the environment. Thus, every family group or small party of friends would be required to designate someone as a responsible leader. This private leader would have to pass a less stringent test than that previously described. He would be examined on conservation and safety techniques and regulations of the region to be visited. The local administrative agency would have authority to advise or refuse admittance to those who were dangerously underequipped or unprepared for their proposed itinerary.

In general, education and certification of outdoor leaders would be under the Outdoor Leader Association's control. Administrative agencies would act in an advisory capacity and would have authority to issue their permits based upon consideration of the ability of the party.

It seems obvious that another place to start outdoor eudcation is in the institutions that teach the specialists—the Forest or Park Service ranger, the Fish and Game warden. This is not being done. Many university administrators contend that the classroom is the place to gain scientific and administrative background, not outdoorsmanship.

Recently, a college professor observed our practical conservation methods at NOLS and enthusiastically arranged a conference for me with the head of a renowned forestry school. But after hearing my presentation, the dean informed me that responsibility for teaching our methods was not within the scope of the university; a forestry graduate could learn outdoorsmanship and camping in the field.

But how can we expect the ranger to teach himself the outdoor skills? He might have been reared in New York City, received a college degree, and arrived for duty in the U.S. Forest Service with little recreational experience beyond a summer camp with log cabins and a cafeteria. Once on the job, he has few opportunities to leave an understaffed office and learn about the wild outdoors. I contend that the basic skills of outdoorsmanship should be an important part of a ranger's schooling and a prerequisite for graduation.

An additional avenue of outdoor education is through advertising. Advertising on television and in magazines—even in some conservation publications—depicts happy campers around bonfires on the shores of a beautiful lake. The public is conditioned to think there is no harm in this, or even in gaining a flawless complexion by cleaning with Brand X soap in a mountain stream. This is conservation education in reverse. The practice must be changed. Advertisers should understand the demands of practical conservation and reflect them in their photography and copy.

Once an educational program is under way and certified leaders are required for every group, restriction of movement in the wild outdoors may be relaxed. Hikers will no longer be limited to designated trails and specific campsites. They will wish, and will be encouraged, to avoid well-traveled paths and seek wild country.

Our present trail system would have to be modified. Rather than traveling crowded paths ribboned through miles of untrammeled wilderness, the certified outdoorsman could roam trackless country. After some time, this route might become a faint footpath, but the surrounding beauty would not be marred by roadlike trails, terraced hillsides, felled trees, or blasted rocks. There would be no need for markers; routes could be traced on topographical maps.

Some improved trails would remain for those who are physically or technically unable to attempt more adventurous routes.

Looking into the future, one might ask what is to prevent the wilderness from being trampled into dust by an overabundance of people who are technically and behaviorally educated and motivated to protect regions beyond the roadhead. The permit system is a possible solution. Permits would outline a general route and possible general areas for camping, and suggest maximum time to be spent in each location and the conservation practices peculiar to that area. The administrative agency could divide the territory into small use areas according to square mileage, drainages, or other practical considerations. By separating parties according to their activities and qualifications, there would no longer be 95 percent of the people using 5 percent of the area. In the past, people have been forced to travel designated trails. In the future, they will be educated to avoid such paths and discover footpaths of their own. In the past, wilderness users have been required to stop in formal campsites, shelters, or huts. In the future, they must be discouraged from stopping where others have stayed because two or three nights of careful camping may be all one campsite can tolerate each year. Shelters should be reserved for emergency use only, as they are inessential for the well-equipped traveler. Theoretically, rather than cramming visitors in a few restricted areas, we would use the region as a whole. We could have one group per square mile without harm to the ecosystem or sacrifice of personal solitude.

Overnight and trailer camps at wilderness roadheads should be gradually eliminated. There are usually only a few entrances into the interior to which one can drive with a passenger car safely. Consequently, tourists flock to these better roads and camp there without any idea of venturing further. Roadheads should be reserved for parking by those certified to take off into the wilds by foot. The combination of campground and the wilderness has proved impossible; the two should be considered as distinct and separate.

A striking example of such a bad mix is found in Yellowstone Park, in the area of Old Faithful. There are hotels, restaurants, campgrounds, gift shops, garages, sewer systems, electric generators—all the attributes of a town. This is not Yellowstone Park, it is "Old Faithful City." Travelers delude themselves if they think they are "seeing" the park by driving a car through it.

Trailer camps and places for people wishing to pitch tents in social clusters should be provided away from wilderness roadheads. Such "camping cities" would have definite boundaries, and include necessary services, nature walks on marked trails, and other desired conveniences.

I am not so radical as to suggest that we do away with camping cities already constructed. I do advocate that no more should be built or expanded near public land that we wish to remain underdeveloped. Let future organized campgrounds be placed near those already developed and at a safe distance from primitive regions, not at the jumping-off spots for those venturing inside. A few scenic roads can remain so that those incapable of or not desiring rugged travel can enjoy the natural beauty of their surroundings.

A crucial problem, of course, would be the financing of an educational program and administration of the wilderness area involved. The U.S. Forest and Park Services and Bureau of Land Management can do little to implement better practices of outdoor use because of lack of funds. Administrators can only watch hordes of people descending upon them and attempt to save what environment they can with inadequate budgets. They are unable to do much more than restrict numbers of visitors, which is a deterrent but not a solution to the problem.

Recently, federal government agencies have conducted studies on methods of preserving the outdoors, but they have been reluctant to implement these studies with action because it is safer to wait and see what the public wants. It is dangerous in the bureaucratic hierarchy to act as directed by reliable research before holding up a finger to the political wind.

Nevertheless, I have strong hopes that the top men in administrative agencies will take the lead in the conservation field. The general public appears to be ready to accept necessary controls. However, there is no way that enforcement and educational programs can be managed within the present budgets.

The situation could be relieved if all people who use the outdoors were charged a permit fee. Charges would vary according to the number of people in the group and the duration of the trip. Permits for vehicles, horses, and other means of transportation would be taken into consideration. Expeditioners would be required to appear at the administrative agency, allowing that agency to control use of the area. Fees should, at least in part, remain in the region in which they were collected, and not be absorbed into some unrelated general fund.

If the citizenry wishes to subsidize wilderness expeditions for youth or church groups, this could be accomplished by giving financial help directly to those organizations, not by exempting them from obligations to pay fees, register, and conform to permits.

There will be many who will object to paying the price for practical conservation. Yet freedom in any society has never meant freedom for the selfish, ignorant, or incompetent to pillage and destroy. If we allow the ecosystem the right to exist in its wild, natural beauty, then we must restrict some of our own rights. But it will be satisfying to know that by thus limiting ourselves, the delights of recreation in the wild outdoors will be unlimited for years to come.

Appendices

NOLS Minimum Clothing List

1. Felt hat
2. Wool hat
3. Combination rain and wind parka
4. Wool shirt
5. Wool underwear sweater
6. Second wool sweater
7. Cotton shirt and pants (optional)
8. Bathing suit
9. Wool gloves or mittens
10. Cotton gloves
11. Wind or rain pants (optional)
12. Wool trousers
13. Knickers (optional)
14. Wool underwear
15. Cotton undershorts (boxer style)
16. Belt or suspenders
17. Wool socks (2 pairs)
18. Boots
19. Gaiters

NOLS Minimum Winter Clothing List

1. Wool hat
2. Wool face mask
3. Wind parka
4. Insulated nylon parka
5. Wool shirt
6. Wool underwear sweater
7. Second wool sweater
8. Wool gloves
9. Wool mittens
10. Outer nylon mittens
11. Padded mittens
12. Wind pants
13. Insulated nylon pants
14. Wool trousers
15. Wool underwear
16. Cotton undershorts (boxer style)
17. Belt
18. Two pairs heavy wool socks
19. Wool felt innersole (optional)
20. Boots
21. Felt boots
22. Padded bootees
23. Gaiters

NOLS Minimum Equipment List

1. Sleeping bag
2. Sleeping pad
3. Tent or fly
4. Pack and frame
5. Group equipment
   a. Axe
   b. Shovel
   c. Topographical maps
   d. First-aid materials
      1) Moleskin
      2) Band-Aids
      3) Tape
      4) Small roll of gauze
      5) Medicated foot powder
      6) Salt pills
      7) Pain pills
      8) Sleeping pills
   e. Optional extras
      1) Extra string
      2) Flashlight
      3) Compass
      4) Repair equipment (tape, needle and thread, horseshoe nails, small screwdriver, microfilament line)

     5) Small notebook and pencil
     6) Book on flora and fauna
6. Cooking equipment
  a. Utensils
     1) Aluminum cook set or billy cans
     2) Frying pan (preferably Teflon)
     3) Metal bowl
     4) Metal cup
     5) Metal spoon
     6) Plastic water jug
     7) Pot grips
  b. Food
7. Personal equipment
  a. Toilet paper
  b. Toothbrush
  c. Toothpaste or powder
  d. Biodegradable soap
  e. Comb
  f. Large handkerchief or small towel
  g. Small knife
  h. Lip protection
  i. Insect repellent
  j. Suntan lotion
  k. Glacier cream
  l. Hand lotion
  m. Face cream
  n. Cosmetics (minimum)
  o. Razor, blades, small mirror
  p. Sanitary napkins or tampons
  q. Wooden matches

APPENDIX 4

NOLS Minimum Winter Equipment List

1. Sleeping bag
2. Sleeping pad
3. Winter tent
4. Extra-large pack and frame
5. Skis and bindings
6. Ski poles
7. Snowshoes (optional)
8. "Climbers"
9. Ski waxes
10. Crampons (optional)
11. Group equipment
    a. Grain scoops or snow shovels
    b. Topographical maps
    c. Compass
    d. First-aid materials (same as in Appendix 3)
    e. Repair kit (tape, needle and thread, pliers, screwdriver, screws, wire, ski-binding parts, stove parts, clovis pins, extra ski-pole baskets)
    f. Optional extras (extra string, flashlight, notebook and pencil)

12. Cooking equipment
    a. Optimus stove with pressure pump
    b. Cooking gear (same as in Appendix 3)
13. Personal equipment (same as in Appendix 3)

NOLS Field Ration Form

Dairy Products	Approximate Cal./lb.
Milk (powdered)	1650
Cheese	1800
Margarine	3300

Grains and Starches

Biscuit mix	1850
Flour	1500
Cornmeal	2000
Macaroni	1700
Egg noodles	1700
Spaghetti	1700
Rice, brown	1650
Rice, white	1650
Pearl barley	1700
Oatmeal	1750
Wheat cereals	1700
Wheat germ	1650
Cake mix	1950
Gingerbread	1950

Dried Vegetables and Meat Substitutes

	Approximate Cal./lb.
Freeze-dried peas	1500
Freeze-dried peppers, red and green	1500
Vegetable mix	1500
Chop suey	1000
Onions	1600
Potatoes	1650
Split peas	1600
Lentils	1550
Bacon bits	2000
Ham bits	2000

Dried Fruits and Nuts

Apples	1600
Dates	1250
Figs	1300
Prunes	1550
Peaches	1550
Raisins	1300
Peanuts	2650
Cashews	2550
Sunflower seeds	2550
Coconut	3000
Popcorn	1650

Sweets

Cocoa	1650
Fruit crystals	1950

	Approximate Cal./lb.
Sweetened gelatin (Jell-O)	1700
Brown sugar	1700
White sugar	1700
Honey	1400
Pudding	1650

Condiments and Miscellaneous

Beef base	550
Chicken base	500
Tomato base	1375

Spices and Miscellaneous

Regular salt	
Rock salt	
Black pepper	
Garlic powder	
Curry powder	
Chili powder	
Parsley flakes	
Dry mustard	
Oregano	
Cinnamon	
Nutmeg	
Extract flavorings	
Multi-purpose food	1200
Dry yeast	1300
Coffee	
Tea	
Oil (optional)	3000
Vinegar (optional)	

NOLS Recipes

An outdoorsman rarely carries measuring utensils, but in order to make these recipes more understandable, we will use standard measurements which will make it easier for field cooks to approximate amounts. Proportions are generous to satisfy mountain appetites and make it possible to provide an entire meal with one course. Recipes serve four persons.

Cereals

Granular Type Cereals (Cracked Wheat, Cream of Wheat, etc.)

1 cup quick-cooking cereal $^1/_2$ tsp. salt
4 cups water

Bring salted water to boil, slowly sprinkle in cereal, and cook 5–10 minutes, stirring frequently, until thickened. Add milk, sugar, dried fruit, margarine, nuts, cinnamon, or nutmeg, as desired.

Flake Cereals (Oatmeal, Rolled Wheat, etc.)

2 cups instant cereal $^1/_2$ tsp. salt
4–4$^1/_2$ cups water

Bring salted water to boil, slowly sprinkle in cereal, and cook 1–2 minutes, or until thickened.

Granola

2 Tbs. margarine
3 cups uncooked cereal (quick-
    cooking variety)
$^1/_2$ cup brown sugar or honey

$^1/_2$ tsp. salt
1 cup nuts and seeds
1 cup dried fruit

Melt margarine in frying pan. Add cereal, brown sugar, salt, nuts, and dried fruit. Fry, stirring constantly, until golden brown. When cool, Granola may be bagged and used as trail food, or it can be eaten immediately for breakfast.

Cornmeal Mush

4 cups water
$^1/_2$ tsp. salt

1 cup cornmeal

Place cornmeal and salt in cold water, bring to a boil, and simmer about 15 minutes, or until thickened, stirring constantly.

Fried Cornmeal Mush

Prepare cornmeal mush in the evening and let it cool overnight. In the morning, cut mush into slices and fry in margarine. Serve hot with syrup or sugar, or cold as trail food.

Soups

Beef or Chicken Vegetable Soup

8 cups boiling water
3–4 Tbs. beef or chicken
    base (varies with brand:
    some are stronger)
$^3/_4$ cup dried vegetables
    (according to taste)
3–4 Tbs. dried onions
2 Tbs. dried green peppers

Pepper, mustard, and/or
    chili pepper
4 Tbs. margarine
$^1/_2$–$^3/_4$ cup pasta or rice
    (optional)
Dehydrated potatoes
    (optional)

Boil water and add all ingredients except pasta and potatoes. Simmer until vegetables are very well done. Add pasta or rice during last 15 minutes of cooking. For thicker soup, add potatoes to desired consistency.

Creamy Tomato Soup

7 cups boiling water
$1/2$–$3/4$ cup pasta or rice
  (optional)
3 Tbs. margarine
1 cup powdered milk

1 cup water
4–6 Tbs. tomato base
3 Tbs. flour (optional)
Seasonings to taste

Boil water. Add pasta or rice and cook until done. Mix margarine, milk, water, tomato base, and flour into a paste in a separate cup, then add to soup, stirring constantly. Season to taste. Simmer 2–5 minutes.

Potato Chowder

$1/4$ cup lukewarm water
  mixed with
$1/2$ powdered milk
1 Tbs. beef base (optional)
$1^1/2$ tsp. salt (use less
  if beef base used)
6 cups water

4 Tbs. margarine
$1/4$–$1/2$ cup dried vegetables
2 Tbs. onions
Pepper, garlic powder
$1/2$ cup bacon bits or ham bits
$1^1/2$ cups dehydrated potatoes

Combine all ingredients except potatoes and simmer until onions are soft. Stir in potatoes.

Fish Chowder, Manhattan Style

Fish
6 cups water
5 Tbs. onions
$1/2$–$2/3$ cup dried vegetables

$1/2$ cup margarine
2–4 Tbs. tomato base
Salt, pepper, oregano

Cook fish in water with onions and vegetables. Remove, bone, and return meat to stock. Add remaining ingredients and bring to boil.

Fish Chowder, New England Style

Fish	$^1/_2$ cup lukewarm water
6 cups water	$^1/_2$ cup margarine
4 Tbs. dried onions	Salt, pepper
1 cup powdered milk mixed with	$^3/_4$ cup potatoes (or more)

Cook fish in water with onions until ready to bone. Remove fish, bone, and return meat to stock. Add other ingredients and bring to boil.

Fish

Fried Fish

Fish, cleaned and slightly wet	Garlic powder, curry, oregano,
$^1/_4$ cup cornmeal or flour	or dried onions (optional)
1 tsp. salt	Margarine
Pepper	

Mix cornmeal, salt, pepper, and any other spices you desire in a plastic bag. Put fish in bag and turn several times carefully to cover with mixture. Remove fish from bag. Melt margarine in frying pan and fry fish *very slowly* over coals until tender. Several cuts on the back of the fish will prevent its curling. Turning the fish when it starts to curl will also solve the problem.

Fillet of Fish

To fillet a fish, insert a sharp knife on one side of the tail as close to the backbone as possible. Slice off the meat, moving from the tail toward the head. When one side is removed, repeat on other side. Remove skin. Shake fillets in seasoned flour or cornmeal and fry in margarine until done (as in fried fish).

Boned Fish

In many dishes, you will want just the meat, no bones. Boil the cleaned fish, head and all, a short while until meat begins to fall off the bones. Remove from the water and take off meat with a knife. Don't miss the piece of meat in the cheek. Use the water as stock for soups.

Fish Patties

Fish	Salt, pepper
3 cups water	2^1/$_2$–3 cups dehydrated potatoes
3 Tbs. dried onions	^{1}/$_2$ cup margarine
1^1/$_2$ cups powdered milk	

Cook fish in water with onions until fish is ready to bone. Remove fish, bone, and return meat to stock. Stir in remaining ingredients, remove from fire, and form thickened mixture into patties. Fry in margarine until well heated. For variation, garlic powder and 1 cup of cheese chunks can be added.

Creamed Fish

Pot of water	^{1}/$_4$ cup flour
Fish	1^1/$_2$ cups water mixed with
6 Tbs. dried vegetables	^{1}/$_2$ cup powdered milk
^{1}/$_4$ cup margarine	Salt, pepper

Boil fish in water with vegetables until done. Melt margarine in a pan, stir in flour and add powdered milk mixed with water. Season. Add drained vegetables and boned fish. Cook over low heat until thickened. Serve over rice or pasta.

Pasta and Rice

Pasta: Basic Recipe for Macaroni, Spaghetti, Noodles

4 cups boiling water	2 cups pasta
1 Tbs. salt	

Place pasta in boiling, salted water and boil gently about 10–15 minutes with lid on pot. Stir occasionally, and add water if necessary.

Macaroni and Cheese

4 cups water
1 Tbs. salt
2 cups macaroni
2 Tbs. dried onions
1¹/₂–2 cups cheese, cut into
    small chunks

4 Tbs. margarine
¹/₂ cup powdered milk mixed
    with ¹/₄ cup water
Pepper, garlic powder

Boil macaroni and dried onions in salted water. Drain, stir in other ingredients until cheese is melted, add seasonings.

Rice: Basic Recipe

4 cups water
1 tsp. salt

2 cups rice

Place rice in boiling, salted water. Stir once, cover, and place on coals to simmer 30 minutes or until water is absorbed. (Time varies with altitude.)

Curried Fried Rice

1 cup rice
2¹/₂ cups water
¹/₄ cup raisins or other dried fruit
    chopped into small pieces
3 Tbs. dried onions

¹/₄ cup other dried vegetables
¹/₄ cup chopped peanuts
¹/₂–1 tsp. curry powder
Salt, pepper, garlic powder
Margarine

Cook rice with fruit, vegetables, peanuts, and spices. When cooked, melt margarine in one very large or two frying pans, fry rice with curry powder, stirring frequently.

You can also make curried rice without frying; just add curry powder and margarine when rice is done.

Spanish Rice

1 cup rice
2½ cups water
½ tsp. salt
1 tsp. beef base
3–4 Tbs. tomato base

3 Tbs. dried onions
3 Tbs. dried peppers
Pepper, chili powder
2 Tbs. margarine

Combine ingredients, cover, and boil about 30 minutes. Stir frequently.

Cheesy Rice

1 cup rice
2½ cups water
2 Tbs. dried onions
2 Tbs. margarine

1 cup cheese, cut into small
   chunks
Salt, pepper, garlic powder

Cook rice and onions until done. Take off the fire. Add salt, pepper, garlic powder, margarine, and cheese, and stir until cheese is melted.

Sauces

Tomato Base Sauce for Pasta

4 Tbs. margarine
4 Tbs. flour
2 cups water
5 Tbs. tomato base

2 Tbs. dried onions
Salt, pepper, garlic powder,
   oregano

Melt margarine and stir in flour. Add water and other ingredients. Cook until sauce is thick and onions soft. Pour over cooked, drained pasta.

Creamed Chicken Sauce

4 Tbs. margarine
4 Tbs. flour
Chicken base to taste

2 cups water mixed with
1 cup powdered milk
Salt, pepper, mustard powder

Melt margarine in saucepan, add flour, and mix well. Add milk dissolved in water and chicken base, and simmer until thick, stirring constantly. Season and pour over pasta or rice.

Vegetables

Mashed Potatoes

4 cups water mixed with
$^1/_2$ cup powdered milk
1 tsp. salt or 1 Tbs. soup base

2 cups dehydrated potatoes
3–5 Tbs. margarine

Use as much water as you want potatoes and bring to a boil. Add salt or soup base. Stir in dehydrated potatoes to desired consistency. Add margarine.

For variation, dried onions, dried vegetables, and other seasonings may be added. Add potatoes when other ingredients are cooked.

Fried Potatoes

4 cups water
3 cups dehydrated potatoes

Margarine

Make mashed potatoes (stiffer for frying). Melt a generous amount of margarine in a frying pan. Fill pan with potatoes and fry until brown. Turn and cook the other side. Cheese bits and dried onions may be added for variety.

Potato Cheese Patties

4 cups water
3 cups dehydrated potatoes
$^1/_2$ cup powdered milk
$^1/_2$ cup biscuit mix
1 Tbs. dried onions

1 cup cheese, cut into small
  chunks
Salt, pepper
Margarine
Flour or cornmeal

Mix all ingredients and add water, if necessary, to make a stiff dough. Roll in flour or cornmeal, form patties, and fry in $^1/_2$ inch of margarine.

Pancakes and Quick Breads

Pancakes

1½ cups self-rising mix
¾ cup flour or cereal grain
1–2 Tbs. sugar (optional)

1½ cups water (or enough to
    to make a runny batter)

Any self-rising mix (Bisquick, gingerbread, etc.) will make pancakes. High altitude will cause these batters to overrise, so add another grain to avoid this problem.

The best way to fry a pancake on a campfire is to lightly grease a Teflon pan (heat pan first), pour in enough batter to make a large pancake, and cook gently over coals until bubbles on top retain their shape. Flip and cook the other side. Flipping is very easy and makes breakfast a spectacular event. Shake the pancake loose by hitting the pan on the side against a rock, or loosen with a spoon. Then flip without hesitation, using mainly wrist action, and watch the pancake so you will catch it when it comes down. Practice by flipping a glove or map if you need confidence.

Variations: Oatmeal pancakes, potato pancakes, cornmeal pancakes, apple, fruit, sour cream, or cheese pancakes. You can also fry cereal grains and add them to the batter.

Plain Drop Biscuits

2 cups biscuit mix
½ cup cold water

2 Tbs. powdered milk (optional)

Mix ingredients, spoon into a well-greased or Teflon frying pan, and bake about 10 minutes.

Skillet Biscuits

2 cups biscuit mix
¾ cup cold water
2 Tbs. powdered milk (optional)
1 Tbs. soaked dried onions

½ tsp. salt
½ tsp. garlic powder
4 Tbs. margarine

Mix first ingredients, roll biscuits into balls, and fry in $^1/_2$ inch of margarine with onions and spices. Turn biscuits until brown on all sides, then cover and cook over medium flame 5–10 minutes.

Dumplings

1 cup biscuit mix
$^1/_2$ cup flour or cornmeal
2 Tbs. powdered milk

$^1/_2$ cup cold water, or enough to
to make a thick dough

Mix ingredients and spoon on top of soup that is at a rolling boil. Cover and boil gently until dumplings are fluffy (5–10 minutes).

Pizza

Crust:

1 tsp. packaged dry yeast
1 tsp. sugar
$^1/_4$ tsp. salt

$^1/_2$ cup lukewarm water
1 cup flour, or enough to make
a thick dough

Quick Crust:

$^1/_2$ cup biscuit mix
$^1/_2$ cup flour or cereal

$^1/_2$ cup water, enough to moisten

Sauce:

1 Tbs. dried onions
2 Tbs. dried vegetables and/or
green peppers
$^1/_2$ cup water
2 Tbs. margarine

4 Tbs. tomato base
Pepper, garlic powder, salt,
oregano
$^1/_2$ cup cheese, thinly sliced

Prepare sauce first. Combine dried onions, vegetables, and water in a saucepan and boil until vegetables are soft. Add margarine, tomato base, and spices. Simmer. For crust, combine yeast, sugar, and water. Place 1 cup flour in a bowl, add salt and yeast mixture, and mix until of a stiff, doughy consistency. Knead. Press crust into bottom of greased frying pan. Pour in sauce and cover with cheese. Bake 15 minutes, or until done.

Yeast Breads

Basic Yeast Bread

1³/₄ cups water	2 tsp. salt
1 package dry yeast	2 Tbs. sugar (optional)
4 cups flour	

Add dry yeast to lukewarm water in a billy can. (Include sugar, if desired.) After about 5 minutes, if yeast is bubbling, mix in 2 cups flour and salt, and beat with spoon about 3 minutes. Add another cup flour and knead on a lid or clean, flat rock for 8–10 minutes, adding remaining flour constantly in small quantities, folding and turning the dough so that all parts are kneaded evenly. When smooth, shape into a loaf and place in a Teflon or well-greased pan. Grease top of loaf and set it aside for ¹/₂–1 hour to rise. A moist, clean handkerchief on top will prevent bread from getting too dry or crusty. (On very cold days, place loaf in its pan over a billy can of warm water to hasten rising.) If there is time, punch down raised dough and allow it to rise again before shaping into loaf.

To bake, put pan over hot coals and top with lid covered with coals (see Chapter 4, page 83). After 25–45 minutes, check by touching middle of loaf. It should spring back to shape. Poke around sides with a clean, barkless twig to be sure all areas are baked. When done, turn out of pan and cool on a trivet of rocks to allow air to circulate and prevent doughy bread.

Beefy Onion Yeast Bread

3 Tbs. dried onions	1¹/₄ cups dehydrated potatoes
1³/₄ cups water	1 Tbs. beef base
1 package dry yeast	1 cup cheese, cut into small
2¹/₂ cups flour	chunks (optional)

Cook dried onions until soft. Pour water in billy can and add dry yeast. When yeast is bubbling, mix in dry ingredients and proceed as in Basic Yeast Bread recipe.

Cheese Date Yeast Bread

1³/₄ cups water
1 package dry yeast
4 cups flour
2 tsp. salt

2 Tbs. sugar (optional)
¹/₂ cup dates, cut into quarters
¹/₂ cup cheese, cut into chunks

Proceed as in Basic Yeast Bread recipe.

Peanut Yeast Bread

1³/₄ cups water
1 package dry yeast
2¹/₂ cups flour

1¹/₄ cups oatmeal
¹/₂ cup melted margarine
1 cup peanuts, chopped fine

Proceed as in Basic Yeast Bread recipe.

Cinnamon Raisin Bread

Make a Basic Yeast Bread dough, but instead of shaping into loaf, flatten to an oblong, flat piece (use a can as a rolling pin). Spread margarine on top, sprinkle with brown sugar, raisins, and cinnamon, and roll as for a jelly roll. Cut into 1-inch slices, place in well-greased or Teflon skillet, let rise, and bake as bread.

Cornbread

1³/₄ cups water
1 package dry yeast
2 cups flour

2 cups cornmeal
2 tsp. salt
¹/₄ cup melted margarine

Proceed as in Basic Yeast Bread recipe.

Desserts

Apple Crisp

1 cup dried apples
Pinch salt

2 cups water
3 Tbs. sugar

Topping:

¹/₂ cup biscuit mix   ¹/₂ tsp. cinnamon
¹/₄ cup sugar   3 Tbs. melted margarine

Soak apples in a pot of salted water. Most dried apples will take about 30 minutes to soften. Drain, leaving about ¹/₄ cup liquid. Add sugar. Mix biscuit mix, ¹/₄ cup sugar, and cinnamon and sprinkle over apples. Pour margarine over top and bake about 25 minutes until brown.

Fruit Cobbler

Bottom:

1 cup dried fruit, cut into   ¹/₂ cup sugar
  small pieces   Pinch salt
Water to cover   1 Tbs. margarine

Combine ingredients and simmer until fruit is soft. Add more water if necessary.

Topping:

I.   1 cup biscuit mix   *II.*   1 cup cooked oatmeal
       ²/₃ cup water   ¹/₃ cup melted margarine
                                        ¹/₃ cup brown sugar

Combine ingredients of topping I or II. Spoon over stewed fruit and bake about 15 minutes.

Pastries and Pies

Crust

4–5 Tbs. margarine   1 cup flour
Pinch salt   2 Tbs. brown sugar

Melt margarine in Teflon frying pan. Add salt. Mix in flour until a dry mixture is formed; it will look much like graham-cracker crust.

The flour should be moist but not greasy or lumpy. It should be fine and relatively dry. Stir in brown sugar. Spread mixture evenly, about $1/4$ inch thick, on bottom and sides of frying pan. Pat with hand or spoon. Bake without putting coals on lid, as heat from bottom will bake thin crust. Watch closely, since sugar burns easily. Bake 2–5 minutes. Let cool before adding filling.

Fruit Pie Filling

1–$1^1/2$ cups dried fruit,
   tightly packed
2 cups water
2 Tbs. margarine
$1/2$ tsp. salt
$1/2$–$2/3$ cup brown sugar (depending upon sweetness of fruit)

$1/2$ cup chopped nuts (optional)
1 tsp. cinnamon
$1/4$ tsp. nutmeg
2–3 Tbs. flour combined with
4 Tbs. water

Simmer fruit or soak overnight until soft. Drain all but $1/2$ cup water. (Save remainder of liquid.) Simmer. Add margarine, salt, and brown sugar. Stir well. Add spices. Mix flour with water or drained fruit liquid and stir into fruit mixture. Simmer and stir until thickened. Pour into pie shell. Top with Granola if desired.

Pudding Pie Filling

Mix lemon or other flavor pudding in ratio of 3 parts water to 1 part pudding. If not instant pudding, boil, stirring constantly. Pour into pie shell and cool. Add fruit or nuts for variation.

Cinnamon Thins

$2^1/3$ cups biscuit mix
3 Tbs. sugar
2 Tbs. powdered milk

3 Tbs. melted margarine
$1/2$ cup water (approximately)
Cinnamon-sugar mixture

Mix biscuit mix, sugar, milk, melted margarine, and water into a stiff dough. Shape into little balls or flat squares and roll in cinnamon-sugar mixture. Bake in greased pan about 10 minutes.

Cakes and Cookies

Plain Cake

1^1/$_2$ cups biscuit mix	2 Tbs. margarine (melted or soft)
^{1}/$_2$ cup flour or cereal grain	^{1}/$_2$ cup powdered milk
4 Tbs. sugar	1^1/$_4$ cups cold water

Combine dry ingredients, add water until mixture is runny, pour into well-greased or Teflon pan and bake 15–20 minutes, or until golden brown.

Variations (mixed and baked like plain cake recipe)

Chocolate Cake: Substitute ^{3}/$_4$ cup cocoa for powdered milk.

Cinnamon Raisin Cake: Add ^{1}/$_2$ cup softened raisins and 1 Tbs. cinnamon.

Peanut Cake: Add ^{1}/$_2$ cup crushed peanuts and extra ^{1}/$_2$ cup sugar.

Fruit Crystal Cake: Add ^{1}/$_2$ cup dry fruit crystals.

Date Coconut Cake: Add ^{1}/$_2$ cup extra sugar, 1 extra Tbs. margarine, 1 cup chopped dates and coconut.

Oatmeal Cookies

1 cup brown sugar	^{1}/$_2$ tsp. salt
^{1}/$_2$ cup margarine	6 Tbs. water mixed with
1^1/$_4$ cups biscuit mix	^{1}/$_2$ cup powdered milk
1^1/$_4$ cups oatmeal	

Cream margarine and brown sugar. Add dry ingredients, stir in dissolved powdered milk, and drop dough by spoonfuls onto well-greased pan. Bake 5–10 minutes. Cookies tend to fall apart when hot. Let cool 1–2 minutes before removing from pan.

Chocolate Nut Cookies

$^1/_2$ cup brown sugar
$^1/_4$ cup margarine
1 cup biscuit mix

$^1/_2$ cup chopped nuts (if salted, rinse before using)
4 Tbs. water mixed with $^1/_2$ cup cocoa

Cream margarine and brown sugar. Stir in biscuit mix, add cocoa mixed with water and chopped nuts. Drop by spoonfuls onto well-greased pan and bake 10 minutes. (Sometimes cookies burn on bottom but do not bake on top. In this case, flip them with a spoon or spatula.)

Frostings and Candy

Syrup

1 cup brown sugar or fruit crystals
1 cup water

Boil together about 10 minutes. For thicker syrup, use more sugar. Add soaked raisins or other dried fruit, cinnamon, or nutmeg if desired. Makes 1 cup.

Chocolate Frosting

4 Tbs. margarine
$^1/_4$–$^1/_2$ cup sugar

$^1/_2$–$^2/_3$ cup cocoa mix
2 Tbs. water, or enough to make a thick mixture

Melt margarine and add sugar and cocoa mixed with water. Stir vigorously. Simmer for a few minutes. Pour over cooled cake.

Butterscotch Frosting

$^1/_2$ cup brown sugar
$^1/_4$ cup margarine

4 Tbs. powdered milk mixed with
2 Tbs. water

Combine ingredients and heat until smooth. Add fruit, coconut, or chopped nuts for variety.

Quick Topping

Sprinkle a mixture of brown sugar, melted margarine, and cinnamon on top of cake five minutes before baking time is up. Continue to bake and the topping will melt.

Peanut Brittle

2 Tbs. margarine   1 cup peanuts (or sunflower
1 cup sugar   seeds, dried fruit, popcorn)
Pinch salt

Melt margarine in frying pan. Add sugar and salt and melt all together over low heat, stirring constantly. When a drop of the mixture forms a hard ball in cold water, add peanuts, stirring constantly over low heat. Remove from fire and cool rapidly by completely immersing pan, candy and all, in cold water or snow. White sugar makes crispy candy; brown sugar makes chewy candy. (NOTE: Sugar burns easily, so stir constantly.)

Caramels

2 Tbs. margarine   Pinch salt
1 cup sugar   2 Tbs. cocoa mix (for chocolate
1/2 cup powdered milk dissolved in   caramels)
2 Tbs. water or coffee

Melt margarine in pan. Add other ingredients and melt together slowly, stirring constantly. Caramels are done when a drop in cold water forms a soft, chewy ball. Remove from fire and beat constantly while candy cools.

Teaching in the Wild Outdoors

The most effective method of teaching outdoorsmanship is in the field, where introduction of a subject, its demonstration, and practical application are presented in close time sequence. In the first classes, do not try to cover all or even a major part of a subject. Teach only the essentials that are most needed for immediate activities to follow. Initiation of the "must-knows" and subsequent practice will prepare students for further enlargement and refinement of skills.

It is important to teach judgment along with techniques. Judgment can be taught by showing how facts are gathered and evaluated, making each decision a learning situation, and telling the "why" of everything discussed. Demonstrate and then give reasons for every process, encouraging questions as well.

Assume that the student knows nothing, because much of what he might know could be half-learned or based upon unrealistic learning. Glen Exum, one of my guides in the Teton mountaineering school, used to warn, "If they tell you they have climbed the Matterhorn, take along some extra rope." This was Glen's way of saying, "Watch out for people with some experience. They always think they know more than they do and generally get into trouble." Many times a teacher must watch persons who have climbed before more carefully than those who have never made an attempt. Perhaps they know some mechanical skills, but lack judgment to apply them.

Dealing with the "expert" who has had some experience and wants to publicize his knowledge presents a problem. He finds it more interesting to question than to listen. Generally, such situations are best handled if the teacher explains that he is only teaching one or two good, proven ways of doing things and that other, even better, ways might be found through experimentation. This avoids discussions as to the best way or someone else's techniques. In all events, students should be encouraged to test, observe, and analyze under field conditions, with the attitude that there is no best way and that improvement on any method is possible.

A teacher must be brief and exact. There is no need for long-winded lectures or generalizations.

He must be honest. Only under exceptional conditions does he teach anything that he has not physically done or personally experienced.

A factual, dignified manner coupled with a sense of humor is the best attitude. People are more easily motivated to learn when the tone of a class is frank and pleasant.

There are various ways of teaching in the out-of-doors. Organized classes might be scheduled, lessons may be given along the trail, or instruction offered whenever an opportunity presents itself.

Classes may be large for general discussion and demonstration. However, when students start participating and practicing, smaller groups are advised (six for most activities). Safety is a primary consideration in teaching climbing or mountaineering, so such sessions are best limited to four or six persons.

The Organized Class

Weather is an important matter in choosing a class site, as it is difficult to maintain students' attention if they are uncomfortable. Exposure to breezes and shade might be fine on warm days but protected, sunny areas are preferable when it is chilly. Forewarn students to select clothing that is adequate for comfortable inactivity.

Sloping ground makes it easier for an instructor to be visible to an entire group. A rock or raised ledge provides a good platform.

If sunlight or glaring reflections are a problem, face the class in the opposite direction.

Teaching is most successful in the morning before people have engaged in much physical activity. Lessons at day's end or after exertion are usually ineffective and should be avoided except when absolutely necessary.

Synchronize all watches to an official expedition time, and announce the exact hour of classes well in advance to allow students an opportunity to secure tents and equipment, clean up camp, and attend to personal grooming.

Discourage people from arriving early. Extended inactivity encourages restlessness, especially with young people, and the attention span is shortened.

Begin promptly. Let latecomers know that it is unfair for them to delay others. The instructor may do this by making a game of it. The person who is even a second late might have to stand up and state his name, home town, and excuse for lateness. Or, five minutes before class, the leader might start a minute-by-minute countdown that can be heard throughout the camping area.

Schedule ten- to twenty-minute breaks between sessions so that participants may return to tents for materials, clothing changes, and so forth.

Making oneself heard in the outdoors is a problem, especially in wind or in close proximity to rushing water. An instructor should test his voice at the beginning of class to determine what volume is needed to make him audible to the farthest listener, and he should be aware of changing acoustics as he talks. It might be necessary to request students to move in closer or even change location.

Those asking questions must also be heard by everyone, and a leader should insist that the questioner raise his voice accordingly rather than repeat the question for the class.

Trail Teaching

Two or three nights is the maximum stay for any group at one campsite, so a great deal of instruction takes place along the trail. Usually, about half of the time is allowed for hiking and half for teaching, resting, lunch, picture taking, and attending to personal needs.

The very act of backpacking is a learning experience. Rhythmic breathing, use of leg muscles, methods of going up- or downhill, and other trail techniques are explained, demonstrated, and practiced during the walk.

Expedition Behavior is learned as stronger members share the loads of weaker persons and the pace is determined by the slowest hiker.

Identification of flora and fauna is taught where varieties of species are visible. When an edible plant is spotted, the leader tells how to recognize it, lets students taste it, and explains the food value contained. General discussions may follow.

Opportunity Teaching

It is very effective to use actual situations for demonstrating various facts of outdoorsmanship. Any opportunity that arises on the trail or at the campsite can trigger on-the-spot teaching.

Someone develops a blister. While the leader treats the sore, he explains why it happened, why it should be attended to immediately, and how the situation can be avoided in the future.

A pack breaks. A tent is damaged by improper placement. A finger is cut. Someone falls, has a narrow escape, or performs well. All are opportunities for teaching while students' attention and motivation are stimulated.

Instructor's Reference Guide

No course can follow a day-to-day teaching calendar. There are too many variables. But at NOLS we have worked out an instructor's reference guide of subjects and priorities as a reminder to insure that everything vital does get covered. While our actual reference guide encompasses five weeks' training, the following suggested schedule for the first seven days gives some idea of what should be treated during that period. Naturally, only an introductory picture of the many skills can be given, with more advanced instruction coming in succeeding weeks.

The time sequence is only a model and is not designed to put teaching in a strait jacket. Rather, it should be an aid to fuller utilization of learning situations as they arise in the field. Opportunity teaching will cover many aspects of the subjects that are not mentioned in the suggested teaching outline to follow.

Pre-planning and outfitting has been done or approved by the leader. The student is not expected to know or understand these subjects until after he has completed the course and had some field experience.

First Day on the Trail

Teaching the first day is very selective. Since there are several "must-knows" to be introduced for protection of students, equipment, and environment, the leader will limit instruction to that required to get through the first night in the hills.

Instruction starts as soon as the group has left the roadhead and found an off-the-trail spot for a class. Blister control is the first lesson, and members should be impressed with the importance of requesting stops for inspection or treatment at the first hint of trouble. Do not try to cover the entire subject; further discussion will occur with opportunity teaching as blisters actually develop.

After another short walk (about twenty minutes), stop again for a brief but frank conversation about toilet procedures on the trail.

Now that students have had some experience backpacking, give a demonstration of how to put on and take off packs and adjust straps for energy conservation.

Frequent stops at approximately half-hour intervals on the first day not only allow the leader time to teach important pointers but give students opportunities for rest, acclimatization, and guarding against overfatigue.

A brief introduction to map reading can be offered at the third stop. Every person need not get out his map if it is packed away, but this is a good chance to demonstrate how to carry maps for availability and protect them against weather and damage.

Point all maps north, trace the route covered so far, and show where the group will walk that day and camp at night. Measure distances from the present location to the starting and stopping places. Do not go into further detail.

First Day in Camp

Upon reaching camp, set the general tone of the expedition and introduce standards of Expedition Behavior. Go through the basics of firepit construction and fire starting, latrine digging and related sanitary and conservation techniques, and a quick demonstration of tent pitching. Assign a latrine-digging detail, have tents pitched, and set time for a later cooking class to show students elementary dishes sufficient for dinner and breakfast next morning.

Adopt an official expedition time, synchronize watches, and announce the following day's schedule.

Here, on the first day, it was necessary for the group's protection to give instruction after a hike. Try to limit this in the future so that people may perform camping chores, cook, bathe, and enjoy spontaneous socializing. The instructor should make subtle nightly observations of fires, tents, equipment, and activities, correcting only in cases of extreme carelessness or danger.

Second Day in Camp

First class: If class is slated for 7 A.M., remember that it will take about two hours that first morning for beginners to get up, make their toilet, start fires, cook breakfast, and straighten camp. Expect mistakes and be tolerant. After more camping techniques have been taught, better results are expected.

The instructor will give his last detailed discussion about setting a tone for the course, although the subject will be pursued continually throughout the expedition by actions, example, and opportunity teaching.

Now is the appropriate time to talk about personal hygiene and sanitation. Explain how illness or giving offense to others can be avoided through proper sanitary procedures and Expedition Behavior. Problems of water pollution and conservation of the ecosystem can also be mentioned.

Doubtless, this first class will have had the frustrations of late and early arrivals and improperly dressed students. Before adjourning for a break, urge everyone to return promptly in twenty minutes, comfortably clothed.

Second class: This might be a good time for the countdown or late-arrival game described earlier.

Expand the previous night's fire-building lesson and show the difference between duff, litter, and mineral soil. Teaching recognition of these three ground covers must be continued on the trail and in subsequent classes until every member of the party is knowledgeable, in order to prevent forest fires.

Organizing the cooking area is easy to demonstrate, but it may be difficult to get cooperation of campers. People with lifelong habits of sloppiness find it hard to change. The instructor must give a good example in his own camp and offer constant reminders to others.

Display a supply of rations and explain how each food may be identified by texture or color and its possible uses. Several cooking classes will be needed before students acquire the knowledge to prepare a variety of menus; do not try to cover the entire subject too soon. The emphasis these first few days will be on conservation skills, protection of equipment, and sufficient ability to prepare basic meals.

Third class: A general orientation to topographical maps. Tracing the expedition's destination for each day of travel motivates students' interest to see what is beyond the far ridge or next campsite. Pointing out the day's hike is a gradual introduction to aspects of distance, elevation, and terrain relevant to making a Time Control Plan.

Fourth class: In a thorough, final treatment of backpacking, show how to pack the bag for balance, terrain, and availability of necessary food and supplies along the trail, how to adjust for river crossings, and the way to store, protect, and use the pack. This subject should require only brief follow-up discussions in the future.

Second Day on the Trail

As the party moves toward the next camp, trail teaching will continue. A first stop could include a review of toilet practices for conservation and possibly a standard operating procedure for the trip (i.e., men to the left of trail and women to the right). There could also be an explanation of pace and interval and a reminder of blister control.

During the second stop, orient maps and pinpoint the present location. Try to pause where there is a view and match several hills, mountains, and other landmarks to the map. Measure distances to various places and teach how to judge mileage visually. Trace the remainder of that day's hike, placing special emphasis on contours being crossed and noting whether they are up or down contours. Teach how to measure mileage already covered and what remains. Call attention to noticeable trails, swamps, glaciers, rivers, and buildings and their special markings on the map. For the time being, teach only what is seen and actually traveled; leave more complicated map reading until later.

Initiate recognition of flora and fauna during this walk.

On the third break, continue with maps as above and suggest their relationship with Time Control Plans.

Upon reaching camp, review latrine building and appoint persons to dig (and later refill) the hole. This will be standard before making each new camp.

A short discussion on general camping skills may be amplified with examples of mistakes made the previous night. Announce any changes in plans and give the next day's itinerary. Don't forget to synchronize watches.

Third Day in Camp

First class: A general review of everything taught so far. Be sure all know how to pitch tents, store supplies, and secure belongings from the elements. Possibly an instructor's tour of individual camp-sites would be preferable to an organized class for this purpose.

Second class: Reiterate cooking "must-knows" and introduce baking.

Third class: Review previous day's map-reading lessons and have students draw up simple Time Control Plans.

Fourth class: If fishing, mountaineering, or other special activities are planned for that afternoon, introduce and demonstrate use and care of appropriate equipment. For climbing, show knots and simple rope handling. More sophisticated classes in these skills will follow during the remainder of the expedition.

Third Day on the Trail

Inspection of camp before leaving is standard for all instructors. Students will tend to leave small debris or fire scars the first day or so; offenders should be sent back to camp and leave the site in perfect condition before starting the hike.

Most people have the habit of hurrying to their destination. It is difficult to reserve half of the hiking time for teaching under such conditions. The instructor must guard against this temptation and remember that the most effective teaching is done on the trail.

This day's purpose is to prepare the student for making a formal Time Control Plan. Drawing upon his experience in making a simple, imaginary plan on the third day in camp, he now must be more realistic: know his location on the map at all times, be conscious of passing time, and make estimates of arrival at various destinations.

Fourth Day in Camp

First class: The Energy Control Plan is introduced in preparation for the afternoon hike. Stress rhythmic breathing, walking, balance, pace, length of steps, eating and drinking, and body-heat control.

Second class: If fish were caught the previous evening, show several ways of cooking them so that students may experiment at dinner. Demonstrate other recipes and the preparation of trail foods which can be made that night for the following day's hike.

Third class: Conduct a lesson on conservation, placing emphasis on the environment of the immediate location and its special restrictions.

Fourth class: This could be a short walking tour to view the general ecosystem of the vicinity and identify flora and fauna. Highlight edible plants.

Fourth Day on the Trail

The Energy Control Plan and conservation procedures covered in morning classes are reviewed.

Fifth Day in Camp

As the group is farther into the wilderness now, there will be a tendency to remain in camp more than a single afternoon so that various activities may be practiced.

First class: Double-check what has been taught about cooking and organizing the cooking area, and expand on subject. Stress foods that may be prepared in advance for future meals and trail food, as the group will not be moving on today and will have time to do this. Give tips for protection of the cooking-area environment, hauling water, dishwashing, and gathering burnable material.

Second class: Discuss the Climate Control Plan in relation to the practicality of clothing, camping gear, and equipment being used. If gear has been issued to participants (as at NOLS), suggest outlets where people may purchase similar items at home for future trips.

Third class: Teach evacuation techniques in preparation for the following day's class on second aid, emergency procedures, and Expedition Behavior during emergencies. Construct a two-man litter and explain what messages and information must be sent out to authorities, families, and others. Involve as many students as possible in actual litter building.

Fourth class: Because there will be no hike, the afternoon could be devoted to special activities such as fishing and climbing. Use the teaching technique of explanation, demonstration, and student participation.

Sixth Day in Camp

First class: This is the final formal class on the Time Control Plan. Advance map reading may also be included.

Second class: The final cooking class. Orient students toward the refinement of previous discussions and trying new recipes.

Third class: Instruction in second aid is kept simple and strictly related to the wild outdoors. The discussion will include problems most prevalent on expeditions and methods of controlling group behavior in emergencies.

Fourth class: Encourage a discussion of leadership and its place in outdoor expeditioning. Constructive criticism on the leadership shown so far can be made. A leader should be ready to accept praise or criticism objectively and with humor.

Sixth Day on the Trail

When camp is broken and students are ready to leave, require each person to make a Time Control Plan for the day's hike. (This will be standard for all ensuing hikes.) Continue lessons on map reading, flora and fauna, and Time Control on the trail.

Seventh Day in Camp

First class: Demonstrate a Tyrolean river traverse and have students set one up between trees on dry land.

Second class: Explain how an expedition is planned, selection of personnel and equipment, securing permission and licenses, financing, and other matter of pre-planning.

Third class: Give a résumé of requirements for outdoor teaching. Discuss classes, trail, and opportunity teaching and encourage constructive criticism.

Fourth class: The afternoon is spent in special activities as preferred by the group.

Balance of the Expedition

After seven days of instruction and practice, the student is reasonably adept at skills and probably ready to schedule much of his own time. The group will proceed en route together but might want to split into smaller patrols to enjoy and perfect techniques that have been introduced.

Formal classes, instruction on the trail, and opportunity teaching are continued throughout the expedition to cover all of the "must-knows" of outdoorsmanship and conservation and to provide as much actual experience in those areas as time permits.

During the last part of the course, small groups of students should plan and execute their own activities.

Bibliography

Accidents in North American Mountaineering. American Alpine Club, 113 East 90 St., New York, N.Y. 10028. Published yearly.
> Analyses of mountaineering accidents in the United States.

Bonington, C. *Annapurna South Face.* New York: McGraw-Hill, 1971.
> A well-organized, successful expedition; interesting appendices on equipment, etc.

Brower, David R., ed. *Manual of Ski Mountaineering.* San Francisco: Sierra Club, 1942; paperback ed., *The Sierra Club Manual of Ski Mountaineering.* New York: Ballantine, 1969.
> Good standard guide to winter mountaineering.

Chouinard, Yvon, and Tom Frost. *The Chouinard Catalog* (1972). P.O. Box 150, Ventura, Calif. 93001.
> Excellent for use of modern American technical climbing equipment.

Craighead, J. J., F. C. Craighead, Jr., and R. J. Davis. *A Field Guide to Rocky Mountain Wildflowers.* Boston: Houghton Mifflin, 1963.
> Standard reference guide; includes both edible and non-edible plants.

Davidson, Art. *Minus 148°: The Winter Ascent of Mt. McKinley.* New York: Norton, 1969.
> A disastrous expedition, showing drawbacks of ubiquitous "modern" equipment.

Fishbein, Seymour L., ed. *Wilderness U.S.A.* Washington, D.C.: National Geographic Society, 1973.

Fletcher, Colin. *The Complete Walker*. New York: Knopf, 1968.
> An interesting way of looking at precise, weight-conscious backpacking; not an expeditioner's approach.

Greenbank, Anthony. *The Book of Survival*. New York: Harper & Row, 1968.
> Tongue in cheek; more practical than others.

Harrington, H. D. *Edible Native Plants of the Rocky Mountains*. Albuquerque: University of New Mexico Press, 1967.
> Complete, detailed reference guide for the Rocky Mountain area.

Herzog, Maurice. *Annapurna*. New York: Dutton, 1952.
> Another disastrous expedition.

Howard, Jane. "Last Mountain Man? Not If He Can Help It!" *Life,* Dec. 19, 1969.

Kjellstrom, Bjorn. *Be Expert with Map and Compass: The Orienteering Handbook*. New York: Scribner, 1972.
> Good for orienting maps by natural features and by compass.

Lathrop, T. G. *Hypothermia: Killer of the Unprepared*. Portland, Oreg.: Mazamas, n.d.
> Reveals the insidious nature of "exposure"; note recommendations on clothing.

Manning, Harvey. *Backpacking, One Step at a Time*. New York: Random House, 1973.
> A publication of the Seattle Mountaineers; same style and depth as *Mountaineering: The Freedom of the Hills,* but with emphasis on backpacking and hiking.

Moore, Terris. *Mount McKinley: The Pioneer Climbs*. Seattle: University of Alaska Press, 1967.
> An interesting chronology of North America's highest mountain and successful expeditioning under primitive conditions.

Mountaineering: The Freedom of the Hills. Seattle: Mountaineers, 1960.
> Probably the most complete book on mountaineering; almost exhaustive in what it covers.

Off Belay (Ray Smutek, ed.). 12416-169 Ave., S.E., Renton, Wash. 98055. Published 6 times yearly.
> A periodical put out by the Seattle Mountaineers; good informative articles on equipment, medicine, and natural sciences related to mountaineering.

Pallister, Nancy, ed. *NOLS Cookery*. Emporia, Kans.: Kansas State Teachers College Press, 1974.
> Nutrition and cooking appropriate to extended wilderness backpacking trips.

Peterson, Roger T., and Margaret McKenny. *A Field Guide to Wildflowers of Northeastern and North-Central North America.* Boston: Houghton Mifflin, 1968.
> Standard reference guide; includes both edible and non-edible plants.

Petzoldt, Patricia. *On Top of the World.* New York: Crowell, 1953.
> An early biography of Paul Petzoldt.

Rébuffat, Gaston. *On Ice and Snow and Rock.* New York: Oxford University Press, 1971.
> A beautiful and interesting book on mountaineering techniques.

Robbins, Royal. *Basic Rockcraft.* Glendale, Calif.: La Siesta Press, 1971.
> A good beginning book on rock techniques.

Sayle, Murray. "Defeat on Everest," *Life,* July 2, 1971.
> A horrendous example of poor expedition behavior.

Shackleton, Ernest H. *South.* New York: Macmillan, 1962.
> An abortive expedition to the Antarctic, showing outstanding leadership.

Smith, Phil D. *Knots for Mountaineering.* 10th printing. Redlands, Calif.: Citrograph Printing Co., 1971.
> Good for mountaineering knots.

Steck, Allen, and Lito Tejada-Flores. *Wilderness Skiing.* San Francisco: Sierra Club, 1972.
> Good on modern ski mountaineering techniques and equipment.

Summit (Jene M. Crenshaw and H. V. J. Kilness, eds.). P.O. Box 1889, Big Bear Lake, Calif. 92315. Published monthly.
> Periodical articles of general interest to backpackers and mountaineers.

Ullman, James R. *Americans on Everest.* Philadelphia: Lippincott, 1964.
> Interesting data on a large expedition; appendices helpful for food and equipment.

Washburn, Bradford. *Frostbite.* Boston: Museum of Science, 1963.
> Describes the physiology related to frostbite.

Wilkerson, James A., ed. *Medicine for Mountaineering.* Seattle: Mountaineers, 1967.
> A fairly complete book on mountain maladies; the only such book available.

Index